SPLIT FOCUS

An Involvement in Two Decades

by

Peter Hopkinson

Rupert Hart-Davis
1969

© *Peter Hopkinson 1969*
First published 1969
Rupert Hart-Davis Limited, 3 Upper James Street, Golden Square, London W.1.
Produced by Design Yearbook Limited, 21 Ivor Place, London N.W.1.
Printed in Great Britain by Compton Printing Limited, Pembroke Road, Stocklake,
Aylesbury, Bucks.

SBN: 246 64468 0

ACKNOWLEDGEMENTS
The photographs on pages 20, 38–44 and 47–81 are reproduced by kind permission of
the Imperial War Museum. The quotation from Name and Address *by T. S. Mathews,*
is reproduced by kind permission of Anthony Blond Limited.

TO MY FATHER AND MY MOTHER

CONTENTS

INTRODUCTION: *The Cinema of Childhood*   **9**

PART ONE: *Frontiers of the Russian War*
Of Commissars and Caviar   19
Of War in the Desert—And a Victorious Combination of Cameras   37
Adriatic Adventures   50
Conquerors on Borrowed Bicycles   63
The Russians At Home—What There Was Left of it   79

PART TWO: *Indian Equinox*
In London Recognition—And in New Delhi Freedom   97
Twelve Million on the Move—And an Army of Twelve-year-olds   107
A Lonely Man in Karachi—And War in Shangri-La   116
Sidetracked to China   127
Six Men of India   135

PART THREE: *Borders of the American World*
A Conflict of Principle—And the Promise of Pakistan   153
On an Island in the Pacific—Time Marches Off   160
On a Smaller Screen—A Greater Opportunity   174
A Retreat into the Greatest Screen of all—-And a Flight to Egypt   181
The Atom is Neutral   199
The Nature of Reality   202

All eras in a state of decline
and dissolution are subjective;
on the other hand,
all progressive eras
have an objective tendency . . .
Our present time is retrograde;
for it is subjective;
Every healthy effort, on the contrary,
is directed from the inward
to the outward world . . .

GOETHE

INTRODUCTION: The Cinema of Childhood

I believe that faith is an extension of the mind. It is the key that negates the impossible.
Charles Chaplin

The Coliseum was one of the earliest super-cinemas to be built outside London. It had twin domes which surmounted a moorish facade. Uniformed acolytes accompanied one forward into a palace of mysteries. An organ boomed the overture, and then, cutting through the darkness, a beam of light materialised magic—the magic of the silent movies, in full stride at the height of the twenties.

The Harrow Coliseum, long since demolished, a supermarket in its place, was to me far more a temple of worship than the church on the hill nearby where I was taken by my mother to learn my catechism. Indulged though I was, my parents had to count the pennies. Cinema, however, was permitted.

At the Coliseum I saw *Metropolis*—that fantastic achievement of the German silent screen, *Metropolis*, the great city, in which the workers toiled like robots underground at vast inhuman machines to maintain in indolence and luxury an idle class above. Its settings, design, spectacle are still to this day unsurpassed. I crouched on the steps between the seats of the cinema's mezzanine, my eyes starting from my head in terror, at the climax of the film, when the elevators that could bring the workers out of their hell crashed in flames to the bottom of the shafts. These were my first visions of a world beyond suburban streets, my first intimations of the horrors of a world at war with itself. I was eight years old.

I saw the first films ever to be shown in Britain, produced twenty-four years before I was born, projected on the original equipment, in the same theatre. My father took me to an anniversary demonstration of the Lumière brothers' first programme at London's Regent Street Polytechnic.

I remember being incarcerated at home with measles, and pleading in vain to be allowed out to see Douglas Fairbanks as "The Black Pirate". I remember visit after visit to that same great showman's fabulous *Thief of Baghdad*. I remember seeing Buster Keaton, Harold Lloyd—and Charlie Chaplin for the first time. There was a tinkling upright piano beside the screen as the tramp adopted "The Kid". They used a full scale orchestra "fortissimo" below the screen for the *Entry of the Gladiators*, in *The Circus;* they used it "piano" to underscore the pathos of Chaplin's immortal *Gold Rush*.

I was an only child, but never a lonely one. I had many cousins. We spent our holidays together, terrorising the farmers and fishermen of the Norfolk coast. I press-ganged everyone to play a part in the "dramas" we staged in home-made theatres. An uncle had a film projector. From the moment I found out he always loomed larger than life in my eyes. Clickety-click he would crank his Pathéscope 9.5 millimetre original "Home Movie". Howling with delight, as flickering for a few minutes on a screen he had erected in the midst of the furniture of his living room, we would watch the early cartoon antics of Felix the Cat—who always kept on walking. Another favourite was the adventures of Charlie's brother Sidney

9

Chaplin in *The Submarine Pirate*.

A film projector of my own was beyond attainment. My mother was devoted to the "get-rich-quick" competitions of the newspapers. Another uncle tried the Irish sweepstake. Solemnly I drew up documents in which they pledged themselves to buy me a film projector if ever they won. Just as seriously they signed. I cut slots in the sides of a cardboard box, drew a series of pictures of scenes from the Coliseum's current film, stuck them together in a roll, and pulled it, scene by scene through the little frame set up on a table. The girl next door helped me with colour when necessary. Although films were still silent, *The Black Pirate* had already blazed in early Technicoloured splendour.

On the slopes of the hill I continued my formal education. At fourteen I was no longer obliged to chase foot or cricket balls. I could use Wednesday as well as Saturday afternoons for film-going. Sound had now arrived. In the streets former cinema musicians played and begged for pennies—"ruined by the Talkies". The Coliseum had converted gradually. In the afternoons, for a time, it showed one of the silents still in the pipeline. In the evenings it showed a film with "synchronised sound". Fascinated I watched—and heard—the shadows of Laura la Plante and Joseph Schildkraut sing the songs of Jerome Kern in a *Show Boat* of 1929; I heard Richard Dix successfully, if somewhat nasally, speak "Nothing but the Truth". The upright piano had been banished from the smaller Harrow "Cinema", the fleapit, as we knew it. We used to smoke the surreptitious cigarette in there. I saw it move into the era of sound with the crash of gunfire at Gallipoli—in Anthony Asquith's *Tell England*.

A cousin of my mother's came to the rescue. When his own local cinema was converted to sound, he had acquired one of its old projectors—and with it a quantity of real, full size silent film. It was too big for his workshop. Would I like it?

Erected, in my bedroom, it dominated everything. It was higher than I was, and left little room for any movement other than the cranking of itself. Its original arc lamp had been replaced by a modest incandescent bulb. It was, none the less, a highly dangerous machine to have in the home. Those old films were all highly combustible. The merest spark would set them off like a bomb. The uncle who owned the original Pathéscope "Home Movie" was in the insurance business. He took one look at my pride and joy, and fled the house. But my parents took a chance—bless them; and we all survived.

With the projector had come four cans of highly inflammable nitrate film. There was a two reel "drama", which at silent speed meant a half-hour of screen time, a one-reel comedy of vintage silent slapstick, and a collection of what the trade described as "interest films": short three or four minute looks at far away places and distant ways of life—miniature forerunners of the documentary film. It was the highlight of my month to lug these cans of film across London to a place where I discovered I could exchange them for fresh ones of equal length, for half a crown a thousand feet. Acquiring the ten shillings, and the fare, every four weeks was the problem to which all else was subordinated. My regular pocket money was devoured in twice, or more likely now, thrice weekly visits to the current cinema.

A local ambulance unit wanted a body on which to practise. I became a body. Once a week I was bandaged, splinted, trussed up, left for dead, revived, treated, and dismissed—but richer by half a crown as a reward. In a shed, in the garden of a house in a side street of Leytonstone, I had located treasure trove. Stacked to the roof were can after can of the silent films now rejected by the cinema. The choice of my exchange had been carefully made from the catalogue that 'Filmeries' now mailed to me every month.

Their titles and arrangement meant far far more to me than the Latin 'prep' that I had to catch up with in the train. Who cared about Caesar and his Gallic War when he held in his hands tinted and sometimes even coloured motion picture film of:

In Roman Africa	200 feet
Ancient and Modern Artillery	250 feet
Elephants of India	175 feet
Fishing in the Arctic	275 feet
Hair fashions through the ages	250 feet

Joining these fragments of old travelogues into an order all my own was pure heaven; the smell of the amyl-acetate which stuck that ancient nitrate film together intoxicating.

The day of reckoning came at last. I failed my school examinations. The day before had been set aside, free, for final study and revision. I had rushed to London to see *The Tunnel*—a mighty British spectacular not of the building of a tunnel underneath the English Channel, joining Britain and France, but a tunnel under the Atlantic, linking Britain with the United States. Fighting fire and flood, Richard Dix dug his way from the American side; against financial failure and sabotage, Leslie Banks drove forward from the British end. The two broke through to each other, the nations were one. Solemnly the President of the United States shook hands with the Prime Minister of Great Britain: Walter Huston and George Arliss.

For me a stern lecture from father followed. Film-going was restricted to the weekends of three further terms of study; but in the summer of 1936 I was free of school at last.

To England in 1931, via Hollywood and France, had come a Hungarian film producer and impresario—Alexander Korda. Two years later, with *The Private Life of Henry VIII*, he had made the first British film to achieve a truly international success. Money was his for the asking. He poured it into the building of Europe's largest film studios, at Denham, nineteen miles out of London on the Oxford road. From Harrow I had bicycled to its site, gazing entranced as the great sound stages rose high above the surrounding countryside. I had to get into this new British Hollywood.

Korda also sank his borrowed millions into films, the most spectacular being an epic production of H. G. Wells' *Whither Mankind*. For me *Things to Come* was *Metropolis* all over again: the fantastic power and magic of film technique deployed on a vast scale in the service of the same essential theme—the betterment of man's condition.

Things to Come opens on Christmas Eve at Everytown. The streets are filled with shoppers and carol singers. To a menacing counterpoint, without a word of dialogue or commentary, newspaper placards proclaim the imminence of war; unemployed miners beg for bread. For full five minutes sound and picture build up an overwhelming impression of this Europe of the'thirties; it was a Europe in which my generation were the teenage children of those who had survived the First World War. We were well aware that the world into which we had been born was one of slump, mass unemployment, starvation. Unless a miracle occurred war was inevitable, war on an even more ghastly scale than its predecessor.

That Christmas, on the screen, war did come to Everytown. The bombers of *Things to Come* rained death from the skies, armies clashed and counter-clashed, civilization collapsed. In the second part of this extraordinary film, somewhere in the nineteen-seventies, the nucleus of an extra-territorial force took over from the warlords, and remade the world.

With the aid of his special effects department—and the magnificent music of Arthur Bliss—Korda rebuilt the world in the image of H. G. Wells' scientific control. It was the year 2055. War, pain, hunger, disease—all were banished. But man was, as ever, restless. He demanded the conquest of further frontiers. He reached out into space. In the film's fabulous climax, a rocket shot towards the moon, bearing with it the son and daughter of the two archetypal figures that had spanned the generations of its story. On a huge projection of the heavens, they traced the progress of the rocket:

"There! There they go! That faint gleam of light".

"Will they return?"

"Yes. And go again. And again—until the moon is conquered. This is only a beginning."

"Is there never to be an age of happiness? Is there never to be rest?"

"Rest enough for the individual man. Too much of it and too soon, and we call it death. But for MAN no rest and no ending. He must go on. It is all the universe—or nothingness. Which shall it be?"

Overwhelmed, as years before I had been by *Metropolis*, I wrote to Korda—with all the hope and anguish of my sixteen years.

"Mr. Korda has asked me to thank you for your letter of the 28th August, and to say how sorry he is that there is no possibility of offering you anything in these studios".

An aunt lived near other studios at Ealing. An acquaintance told her the name of their studio manager. I wrote again, able, thanks to my father's admonitions, to list educational qualifications as well as unlimited enthusiasm. A reply came. Would I present myself? Like a shot I was at the gates.

"What do you want to do?"

"Be a film director."

"There's no future in that! You would have to start as a third assistant director, and spend all your time knocking on doors, getting the actors on the set. There's a vacancy in the camera department, loading film. Can't pay you any money though."

I leaped at the job. I would have swept the studio floor if he'd asked me.

And so I entered the film industry: the British film industry of the thirties. Ealing may have lacked the glamour of Denham, but it made films. Two Lancashire comics were its mainstay, both products of the old British Music Hall at its best—Gracie Fields and George Formby. After a month I was officially engaged, at the princely salary of one pound a week, as a film loader and clapper boy on a new Formby film.

Before every take of every scene, I would leap in front of the camera with a

Enlargement from frame of original film clip of author's first day's work. Oct 6 1936

board on which I had numbered that particular scene and take—photographic
identification to the laboratory and editors. As sound and picture cameras came
up to speed, to the cry of 'Mark It' I would slam the levered slat flush with the
top of the board: creating an audible 'clap' on the separate sound film, and a
visible 'clap' on the picture, without which the two strips of picture and sound
could not be brought together into synchronisation. Then, jumping out of the way,
and hoping that I would not collide with any of the lamps or equipment that
ringed the set, I would watch the camera follow the antics of the actors. Whenever
he was satisfied or displeased with the goings-on the director—awesome figure—
called 'Cut'.

Musicals followed Formby. Musicals in which I had to clap my board right on
the third blip of the 'Playback' of the already recorded song to which the actors
mimed the words. Musicals in which Frances Day sang of dogs lost in the fog,
and herself all alone; Gracie Fields that The Show Must Go On; and Formby of
Leaning on a Lampost At The Corner of the Street.

Of the war now raging in Spain, of the army of unemployed beyond the studio
gates, of the Welsh miners marching to London demanding food and work, there
was no reflection in these synthetic carryings-on. The ultimate of ingenuity seemed
to be always the construction of a mammoth night club set. But the studio was not
all that remote from the economic facts of life. Ten months after I had walked on
air through its portals, it shut down. Money had run out. My father shook his head.

"It's a completely unsafe, insecure business. You had much better get a job in a bank, with a pension at the end. You can always make films as a hobby."

"I bet you five shillings", I rashly countered, "that within a week I will get another job at another studio."

Armed with a letter of introduction from Ealing's studio manager to the chief of its camera department, I crossed the threshold of Denham. I was in luck. The clapper boy of a picture just commenced had been suddenly switched to a unit filming the North West Frontier of India in Wales. (Korda had now discovered the British Empire). I got the job of his replacement.

David Niven was the star of my first film at Denham, a typical frolic of the 'thirties in which gamblers and gunmen chased each other on and off yachts and in and out of casinos. But I had won my bet. I was now in the big time. This was an American produced film, the third of Twentieth Century Fox's major British productions. The greatest of them all, Metro-Goldwyn-Mayer, was about to descend on Denham. Firstly they were to make *A Yank at Oxford*, in which Robert Taylor set that ancient seat of learning about its ears— and then it was to be *The Citadel*.

A best-seller of 1937, A. J. Cronin's *The Citadel* tells the story of an idealistic young doctor who, first practising amongst the poor and down-trodden of the Welsh coal pits, is forced by prejudice and ambition to move to London. Here he falls in with the smart and the smooth of a medical profession in which practices were sold like vested estates, and patients exploited like peasants. The death of a friend under the incompetent hands of a corrupt surgeon brings our hero face to face with himself. He leaves the shallow world of the fashionable and the fake, and organizes a cooperative clinic in which he can genuinely practise his Hippocratic oath to:

> "... Look upon him who shall have taught me this Art even as one of
> my parents ... I will impart this Art by precept, by lecture and by
> every mode of teachings, not only to my own sons but to the sons
> of him who has taught me ..."

Here, at last, was a film about to be made in a British studio, of a great and noble theme, and one which really reflected the reality of the struggle outside. I had to get on to this picture. I had to work with its director—King Vidor.

One of the really great figures of the American cinema, Vidor had first come to Hollywood in 1915, at the age of twenty. He had driven up from his native state of Texas on the strength of eighty-five dollars earned from making a film about the manufacture and marketing of sugar. He had written—and failed to sell—more than fifty scripts, before he found nine backers each prepared to put up a thousand dollars to finance a film of his own. It was a success, and he had gone on to make eleven more. In 1923 he had been signed up by Metro-Goldwyn-Mayer. Two years later he made one of the greatest successes of the silent screen: *The Big Parade*—the first major film to take a cool and clinical look at the reality of life in the trenches of the first world war. It had broken box office records everywhere. Next Vidor had made, by way of complete contrast, *The Crowd*—a simple and moving study of a young couple, fighting for survival in the jungle of a great city. In 1929 came a masterpiece, the first film to present the negro on the screen in terms of simple human dignity—*Hallelujah*. It was an early sound film. He not only broke fresh ground in theme and subject, but just as daringly used his sound track to counterpoint, and sometimes even to conflict with, the actual image on the screen. Then he had brought out *Billy the Kid*, the first big-screen western; he had made *Street Scene*, from the Elmer Rice play; and in 1934 a breakaway from mighty M.G.M. to make, once again, a film all his own—*Our Daily Bread*.

By then the depression was at its height. In the United States millions were out of work and on relief. The human material of Steinbeck's *Grapes of Wrath* were already trekking from the dustbowls to the elusive eldorado of California. Vidor put all his money into a film that would reflect this social catastrophe, and point a way to its solution. By now the young couple of *The Crowd* had long ago lost both identity and employment in the city. With others they set out to found a cooperative community on the land: using their bare hands to dig a way for the water for their daily bread. (Not, as did Bonnie and Clyde in a latter-day re-creation of the period, to stick up banks).

Our Daily Bread had been a commercial disaster. The major distributors and theatre circuits refused to touch it. Vidor returned to M.G.M., and here he was, in England, forgiven his aberration by the Hollywood moguls, assigned to film *The Citadel*.

I had to work with this man. No, I did not want to go with the unit to the Sudan for a recreation of Kitchener's conquest and the battle of Omdurman. Korda, discovering that the golden age of British Imperialism was good box office, was about to launch *The Four Feathers*. The cameraman of *The Citadel* was to be Harry Stradling. He had come to Denham with Jacques Feyder, when Korda brought that French director over to guide Marlene Dietrich and Robert Donat through the intricacies of the Russian Revolution in *Knight Without Armour*. Stradling wanted only a crew on his camera with whom had worked before. But with my work on *A Yank at Oxford* M.G.M. had taken kindly to me. Production executive Harold Boxall stood by me. Stradling, and his camera operator, conceded; but for the first week I was very much on sufferance.

On *The Citadel* I was determined to be the best clapper boy—or second camera assistant as I was by now more flatteringly described—that had ever been. My acceptance came when, from my experience at Ealing, I was able to adjust the tension of the camera's sound proof blimp, which had hitherto baffled an operator more used to French equipment. From then on I was in the clouds, and lived that film just as intensely, I am certain, as did its director.

Never have I seen anyone so quietly in command of his medium than Vidor. He knew it all. He could light the set, re-write the dialogue, position the camera, direct the actors with the minimum of fuss—and talk to me.

He talked of his early days in Hollywood, of a boarding house where he wrote his first rejected scripts; just around the corner had been built the most enormous set in Hollywood's history—the great processional street, temples, and battlements of ancient Babylon. Young Vidor had hung about, watching David Wark Griffith direct *Intolerance*. This, he assured me, was the greatest movie ever made. It was the bible in which the full potential of film was, for the first time, fully revealed—and Griffith was its master.

I saw the film. It was shown by the London Film Institute Society: a special screening of an original print, in which each sequence was tinted its appropriate colour, projected at the correct speed, with complete musical accompaniment. Even then, in 1938, *Intolerance* was already more than twenty years old. It burst on me like a bomb. *Metropolis* had made me drunk with film, *Things to Come* had

The Citadel 1938. *Author on camera*

confirmed me in my addiction, but this, this was a revelation.

With *The Birth of a Nation* Griffith had been accused of preaching the very intolerance that he chose as the title for the film he followed it up with. He took a contemporary tale from the slums of an American city. Capital fought with labour, an innocent man was sentenced to death. To this he added three other stories of hypocrisy and intolerance: the massacre of the Huguenots in Renaissance France, the betrayal and fall of Balshazzar's Babylon, and the Crucifixion. In combination all four would speak of man's inhumanity to man in the name of virtue. With an initially interlinking image of Lillian Gish rocking a cradle, coupled with the lines of Walt Whitman, "Out of the cradle, endlessly rocking, Uniter of here and hereafter", Griffith developed all four stories simultaneously. In his own words: "The stories begin like four currents looked at from a hilltop. At first the four currents flow apart, slowly and quietly. But as they flow, they grow nearer and nearer together, and faster and faster, until in the end, in the last act, they mingle in one mighty river of expressed emotion".

In the climax of what has been called the only film fugue, he cut and counter-pointed scene by scene, shot by shot, across the centuries. Never has the crucible of cinema boiled with such passion, such reckless resource of technique. However equivocal, inconclusive, and naive its attitudes might seem to be, *Intolerance*, still to this day, represents the furthest advance in the art of the film. And if anyone still doubts that the film is an art, let him take a look at this fifty year old movie.

After *Intolerance*, after *The Citadel*, everything was anticlimax. With my number board I nipped in and out of the opening few feet of scene after scene, in film after film, for which I had naught but contempt. Gangster films, song and dance films, spy films—even an early religious essay on the part of J. Arthur Rank, who was just beginning to nibble at the British Film Industry.

Korda's London Film Productions went broke. He lost control of his wonderful studios. He formed a new company, Alexander Korda Productions, and rented space from the new owners to produce an even more spectacular version of *The Thief of Baghdad* than Fairbanks' own original. This was in Technicolor. Held aloft on wires, I was borne along on a pseudo flying carpet, with a light meter, measuring for the cameraman the intensity of his arc lamps, as I progressed against the background of a painted sky.

But the real skies above Britain were about to black out. On the great open-air 'lot' down the road from the studios, the original set of Everytown's City Hall still stood—a reminder of *Things to Come*. Alongside, Vincent Korda had constructed old Baghdad, and we had been filming pink elephants in procession. From the sky above, rain: the light too drab for the Technicolor cameras. In a tent we sat, and played cards, and listened to the radio. Hitler had invaded Poland. Within two days I was in uniform, and Britain was at war. I said goodbye to Denham, and to all my dreams. Or so it seemed.

But destruction did not immediately rain from the air. Hardly a shot was fired in those first winter months of 1939's Phoney War. After a couple of weeks, despite the black-out, the cinemas re-opened. I realised that I might survive the war, and that maybe all would not end in chaos, as it had done in *Things to Come*. I would have to work out my own plan of campaign, of survival.

And so, as I was shunted around England, my unit posted from one strategic backwater to another, as Dunkirk came and went, and the Blitz began in earnest, nowhere near a camera or a strip of film, I set myself a course of intellectual cinema.

I read every book on the subject I could lay my hands on. I received permission to carry about with me a portable 16 millimetre projector, with which to entertain the troops—but on it I ran for myself copies of all the classics I had never had a chance to see before. I wrote scripts. On paper I experimented with what I believed to be radical techniques. I heard that a unit was being formed to film the war. I pestered the War Office for further details. Two years passed in aimless military futility. I read more and more, all the books I thought I should. I discovered the Russian silent film: its technique a masterly derivation of Griffith, its content a revolutionary challenge to anyone who, like myself, searched for a solution to a world gone mad. I read Marx—maybe he could tell me what it was all about.

I discovered a new idol. Eisenstein. The Russian who, at the age of twenty-seven, entrusted with the production of a film of the first, abortive revolution of 1905, had created in *The Battleship Potemkin* a revolution all his own.

At the time of Russia's defeat by the Japanese in the war of 1905, the *Potemkin* had been patrolling the Black Sea. Mutiny broke out. The crew tossed their officers overboard. The cruiser put in to Odessa for supplies. The townspeople hailed their action and lined the great flight of steps that led down to the harbour, waving on and cheering the fleet of little boats carrying food and fuel to the mutineers. Suddenly, at the top of the crowded and densely packed steps, appears a line of Cossack troops. Step by step, shot by shot, they march down, discharging volley after volley into the helpless mass of people. In an inspired synthesis of art and action, Eisenstein struck lightning from the screen.

Greatly daring, I showed *Potemkin* to the troops. But there was no mutiny in the ranks of 'B' Company. They preferred my other films of Tom Mix and Hoot Gibson: early cowboy heroes of the American silent cinema. Our officers slept securely in their beds.

To myself I showed other classics of the Soviet silent screen: a dramatization of Maxim Gorki's *Mother*—Pudovkin's reconstruction of the dress rehearsal of 1905; *Earth*—an elegaic poem of the land and its people by the Ukrainian Dovshenko. These films were like nothing I had ever seen before. This was indeed a vision of a new world.

Hitler invaded Russia. I fumed with frustration. I volunteered for active service overseas, was accepted, and went on leave. I telephoned the War Office. If they were ever going to form a film unit they would have to move fast to catch me.

"But weren't you at the Board last week?"

"What Board?"

"The Selection Board for cameramen."

"Never heard of it."

"But your name was on the list!"

"Nobody told me—and now I'm going overseas."

"We'll fix that. Report here tomorrow."

And so, at the very last possible minute, I was whisked into the Army Film Unit which had just—at last—been formed.

The enemy had appreciated the enormous power of the film as a weapon long before their invasion of Poland. With every German unit which had crossed that frontier, and launched the Second World War, had gone a cameraman. Their assembled and edited film, *Baptism of Fire*, had been followed by *Victory in the West*, a brutally effective treatment of the invasion and conquest of France. Copies of these films had been widely shown in such countries as Portugal, Spain, Rumania Turkey, and the United States, overwhelming their audiences with their impression of invincible German might—and confirming them in their neutrality.

Britain had hitherto employed only a handful of newsreel cameramen and Public Relations Officers to film and photograph her war. Only with a large scale and fully organised Army Film and Photographic Unit could she ever hope to beat the Germans at this game. The War Office had now combed through its files and records. Every soldier who had ever had any acquaintance with a camera was being pulled out of his unit, promoted sergeant, and prepared for action. One of the first draft of thirty-five, I clambered up the gangplank of a troopship. I had never been out of England before. Of film making I had an experience more theoretical than practical. Of the great big world I knew nothing beyond the covers of books and the screens of cinemas. Now I was about to learn a great deal of both – the hard way.

It was December 1941 and I was twenty-one.

PART ONE: Frontiers of the Russian War

Of Commissars and Caviar

The Russian danger is therefore our danger, and the danger of the United States, just as the cause of any Russian fighting for his hearth and home is the cause of free men and free peoples in every quarter of the globe.   Winston Churchill

It was on the troopship that I first heard of a new British offensive in the Middle East, and the Pacific explosion of December 7th 1941 that at one stroke committed the United States to British and Russian survival. The *Highland Princess* was one of a huge convoy in Mid-Atlantic recently sailed from the Scots port of Greenock, whose snow covered hills were to be my last sight of Britain for four years. With a small group of fellow sergeants of the newly formed Army Film and Photographic Unit, I was on my way to film the war.

We were a very miscellaneous collection. Mustered in our ranks were a military policeman whose pre-war days had been spent behind the counter of a photographic shop; a fashion photographer straight off an anti-aircraft gun site; some Fleet Street professionals; an assistant director with some time in Hollywood; one or two cameramen from Wardour Street; and a few young camera assistants from the film studios such as myself. Four youthful lieutenants with similarly assorted backgrounds commanded and chaperoned this motley group of individualists. Immediately before our departure we paraded in a strange style of battle-order which had probably taken some back-room brass-hat some weeks to devise. Festooned like Christmas trees with steel helmet, gasmask, revolver and ammunition, equipment and film-packs, we had a still camera hanging from our necks and— just for that once— a motion picture camera, held in the hand. The impossibility of working both at the same time did not occur to officialdom for quite a while to come, and what seemed an equally unrealistic attitude had been brought to bear on the question of rank. Actual camera work, although in the un-coordinated past it had been performed by a few officers, was now to carry only the rank of sergeant. To be commissioned in the AFPU was to become little more than a chaperone, collecting and delivering film from and to non-commissioned cameramen, with the sometimes stimulus of shifting them around the battle field.

After photographs had been taken of one of our number thus apparelled— presumably to frighten Dr. Goebbels—we stripped off all this equipment, and adjourned to the basement film theatre. The Director of the British Army's Public Relations, Walter Elliot, then addressed us. Outlining the problem of licking the Germans in our own private war of propaganda, he screened for us some enemy film just obtained from the Russian front via Portugal. The lights went out, and onto the screen came the by now all too familiar picture of the invincible Wehrmacht carrying all before it in those early months of 'Operation Barbarossa'. The seemingly

Supplies to Russia

invincible panzers smashed their way through burning village and blazing wheat-field: to be followed by some of the most unexpected and eye-opening film that any of us had ever expected to see. The German army was seen to enter Kiev, capital city of the Ukraine, and the streets were filled with deliriously happy Ukrainians, cheering and kissing the invading troops, smothering them with flowers, and quite obviously hailing them as liberators. Giant pictures of Stalin were torn down from the walls of buildings, and danced on and trampled under foot.

In Britain at that time the heroic resistance of the Soviet people was a source of inspiration—with which it was hard to reconcile these quite obviously genuine and unfaked scenes. None of us were then aware of the Ukrainian separatist movement, or could know that more than three quarters of a million Russian prisoners were to volunteer to fight with the Germans in a 'Russian Liberation Army'. All of this, and a great deal more besides, I was to learn at first hand myself, in Kiev, five years later.

After the parade at the War Office, we naturally had not walked off with our equipment.

We had handed it back.

The War Office had placed a large order for the American built Bell and Howell Eyemos. It was unfortunate the order had not been placed earlier, because Pearl Harbour had since intervened and all these cameras were now needed for the United States Armed Forces. A number of substitute DeVrys were said to be on their way, but none had arrived. It was not until June 1944—nearly three whole years after its formation—that the AFPU was able to go into action using a British camera designed for the purpose. The still photographers were luckier. They had all been issued with Zeiss Super Ikontas before leaving Britain. For us movie men, it was a case of scrounge as scrounge can.

In charge of this newly formed Army Film and Photographic Unit in the Middle East—at that time Britain's major theatre of military operations—was David Macdonald. For the task of combating Dr. Geobbels' hitherto victorious propaganda machine he needed a great victory with which to confront his cameras. His previous life fitted him well for the task.

He had started out as a rubber planter in Malaya. The slump of the thirties had knocked the bottom out of that market, and he had found his way to Hollywood.

Cecil B. DeMille was just starting to make a film about "Four Frightened People" lost in the Malayan jungle. Macdonald got a job as technical adviser. He stayed on as one of DeMille's assistants, and in 1936 came to England as first assistant to the American director Raoul Walsh, signed by Gaumont-British to make an epic of the British Army. This officially inspired recruiting poster—for it was little more—was typical of the hybrid nature of pre-war British films.

O.H.M.S.—'On His Majesty's Service'—starred an American, Wallace Ford, as a small-time gangster on the run, who sought anonymity and refuge in the British Army. (This was supposed to guarantee an American release.) He sailed to China with his regiment, and after many a deed of derring-do, gave his life for his comrades attacked by Chinese bandits.

Macdonald now became a director in his own right, and made several successful, fast-moving, low-budget entertainment films. *This Man is News* attempted a British version of M.G.M.'s most popular *Thin Man* series, in which William Powell and Myrna Loy 'sent-up' the detective tales of Dashiell Hammett. A sequel, *This Man in Paris*, had been made at Denham, and there our paths first crossed. With the outbreak of war he moved into documentary—and made the first wartime film to blend successfully a situation of fact with dialogue, spoken by non-professionals, which did not grate on the ear. This was *Men of the Lightship*— a reconstruction of the attack by German aircraft on an unarmed British lightship. In the early months of the 'Phoney War', when nothing seemed to be happening on any battle front, audiences had lapped this up—and loved to hear one of the seamen describe the enemy as 'bastards'. British films were beginning to move out of middle class living rooms.

David Macdonald's theatre of operations was now the entire British Middle East Command. This stretched from the battle front in Libya to the west, to Persia's borders with India to the east. He had recently toured his parish, and was now positioning his cameramen around its perimeter.

"I am sending you to Persia", he said to me one electrifying afternoon in Cairo.

The Japanese were in control of the Pacific. There were only two channels through which Britain and the United States could send help to their desperately hard pressed Russian allies, now fighting for their lives in the suburbs of Moscow and Leningrad. The first route was in the north, by sea through the Arctic to Murmansk, where the British navy and allied merchant marine wrote a page of imperishable glory as they fought their way again and again through freezing seas. Now, here in the Middle East, Britain and Russia had joined hands in Persia; and this second, overland supply route had become possible.

Supplies to Russia! What a subject for me to film! I was being asked—commanded

A crate worth guarding at Pahlevi

—to make a film of the one subject nearest to my young heart and hopes: the aid the allies were sending to save the country which, in my innocence and inexperience, reading and film-going had convinced me was the hope of the world.

But there was only one snag. I still had to wait, and old soldiers will not need to be told what I had to wait for.

There was no camera with which to make the film.

On his way back through Baghdad Dave Macdonald had found an old and only single-lensed Newman Sinclair in a local photographer's shop. He assured me that arrangements were in hand for its purchase, and that it would be awaiting my own arrival in Baghdad.

Walking on air a few days later, I loaded my film and accessories on to the Palestine train, and set off to meet the Russians.

Most of the AFPU were now in the desert with the 8th Army; of those left, however, several boarded the Palestine train with me, but their destination was Jerusalem and the 9th Army.

The Army Film and Photographic Unit had been organized on the basis of a corps of cameramen, with the rank of sergeants, a movie and a still photographer paired together with a jeep, assigned to brigades or divisions—from which they attached themselves to whatever regiment looked like producing the most spectacular action—with an officer in charge of some half dozen or so of such, at a Corps Headquarters.

My still-photographer companion was Bill Smith, and we were under the control of a so-called Conducting Officer. With a third sergeant to handle either still or movie photography as the occasion arose, we were the only ones proceeding to what was called 'Paiforce': the 10th Army holding Persia and Iraq. We left the train at Mount Carmel and transferring to a staff-car drove along the coast-line of the Crusaders, Acre, Tyre, Sidon. We camped in a forest of cedars and then drove over the mountains of the Lebanon into Damascus. We found Syria full of bitter and all too recent memories, where Vichy and Gaullist France had clashed and French had fought French.

The last lap of our journey was to be by desert bus, and we had little time to explore what is claimed to be the oldest inhabited city in the world, or to look for the tombs of John the Baptist and Saladin.

The First World War had drawn attention to a need for a reliable and fast means of communication between these two capitals of Damascus and Baghdad, a need which had led British private enterprise to form a company with a fleet of large air-conditioned buses. Ten years later I was to do the journey by plane in under two hours; but we were fortunate to be able to enjoy the romance of the long overland trip before developing air transport made it historical curiosity, and travelling in a convoy of two of these pullman type motor coaches one of which pulled a trailer its own size and length packed with luggage and freight, by nightfall we were eating eggs and bacon at a Syrian customs post deep in the desert.

We were wakened next day by the enormous red globe of the sun rising out of the rim of the desert straight ahead of us. We had already covered over four hundred

Meeting at Andimeshk—Author with Soviet Supply Officer

miles of this almost invisible highway: a journey which could only be likened to a voyage at sea, there being virtually no more distinguishing features in the landscape than a sailor could steer a ship by. The Armenian and Arab drivers had travelled this route hundreds of times, and were almost able to tell one piece of camel scrub from another, but a sandstorm could still make this crossing a hazardous enterprise. Breakfast was served in the cool garden of the Iraqi customs post at Ramadi where, from its walls, a picture of the ten year old Feisal looked down upon the latest visitors to his twenty-one year old kingdom. A few hours later the dust-covered buses were pulled up outside the offices of the Nairn Transport Company in Baghdad, and we were unpacking our kit and looking for somewhere to sleep in the large Turkish style house that was now the headquarters of Public Relations, 10th Army.

Here was the first of the fabled names. Alas, Baghdad scarcely lived up to it. No carpets flew, no houris beckoned. The city of Haroun al-Rashid—and more recently Prime Minister Rashid Ali, who had allied the country with the Germans—was a sprawl of dirty, tumbledown buildings, and the Tigris ran filth. Baghdad came as a shock. But there was worse to come. The camera was still in the shop.

Ever-obliging, its Armenian owner was pleased to permit me to set it up in his back room. But remove it from the premises, that I could not.

The Army had not bought it. Furious, I ragèd my way into the presence of my Conducting Officer. The question of its purchase, so I was indifferently informed, was still in channels. Meantime, while this personage luxuriated in the comfort of

The rail route through the Zagros

On the side of a locomotive north of Qum—A truly mobile hand-held camera
The road route through the Elburz

the Sinbad Hotel (Officers Only), I was ordered to take still pictures of British soldiers sharing cigarettes with the citizens of Baghdad—just to show how happy our hosts were with what was, after all, now a new British occupation.

Week after week went by. Desperate, I offered to give the army the purchase price of the camera out of my own sergeant's pay. A hopeless flight of fancy. Only the enemy has ever been able to force the British Army to move faster than the momentum of its own inertia. But somewhere, from the mountain of forms in the Adjutant-General's Department of Paiforce, someone finally got the correct signature on the right piece of paper—and the camera was at last in my hands. Not even Rashid Ali, when he fled the country, left Baghdad in more of a hurry than I did.

I caught the train for Basra, breathing again.

Sinbad the Sailor must have been better adapted than I was to his native city and the stifling heat of the Persian Gulf. I went down with an attack of 'Gyppy tummy'. In the days before Entero-Vioform became the traveller's friend, this internal embarrassment could pursue the sufferer for hundreds of miles beyond the Egyptian frontier. I had it badly, but nothing mattered now that I had my Newman Sinclair. It was bought, paid for – and it worked.

Collecting transport proved easier than collecting cameras. A Ford sedan awaited our conducting officer. Smithy and I myself found a Morris truck. Our drivers, Rangaswami and Tana Pilai, were both from India, and they looked a little mournful at the prospect of exile from the Indian Army Transport Company in the wilds of Southern Persia. But their spirits kept up well enough for the five hour desert journey to Ahwaz, the Persian rail centre, and when we got there, mine soared. I was in business again.

Strolling up the line of parked transport I saw my first Russian, a lieutenant of Engineers. Number one on the long, long road north.

Allied Aid to Russia—never more vitally needed than at that critical moment, when the beleaguered Soviet Union seemed near to crumbling before German pressure—was soon to reach immense proportions. Britain was sending light tanks and military equipment; from the Commonwealth came the raw materials for Russia's evacuated factories—aluminium, tin, copper, jute, shellac, phosphorus and lead. The United States was a mighty watershed from which fighter-bombers by the hundred and six-wheeled trucks without number were beginning to flow. These crated tools of war had to make the journey all round South Africa. Now, from the shores of the Persian Gulf, they awaited transport across the entirety of Persia to the Russian border in the north, where the Azerbaidjan Soviet Socialist Republic marched with Persia's own province of Azerbaidjan.

The Russians serving on this long supply line were all convalescents. They were men who had already been wounded fighting the Germans. That did not make the discipline they were subjected to any the less harsh. Field punishment was on the dire side. The penalty for wrecking a truck was simply death. To be discovered drunk outside camp was similarly rewarded. I had listened to all this with something of the same awe as I had felt at tales of heroic Russian resistance at the front. Not unnaturally, I had expected my first Russian to be a superman. It came as a shock to me that he was quite a little fellow, with a mild expression and his vehicle, of Russian origin, was far inferior to the products of Detroit.

From a cameraman's point of view, the railway side of this supply-line story had still more possibilities than the road-haulage. The railway was the key to the whole vast enterprise. Ironically enough, it had been built by German engineers. It had been a magnificent achievement, but both locomotives and rolling stock were in pitifully short supply. The haul was growing to greater and greater tonnage, and it had to cross two great mountain ranges before it got anywhere near its goal.

It needed supplementing badly.

Russian rolling stock was not too far away, but it was too wide for the gauge. Indian was too narrow. Only Britain at this stage could fill the gap. The Railway Operating Companies of the Royal Engineers, our hosts, were therefore coping with British locomotives, which had come the long way round by sea, together with thousands of wagons. The marshalling yards of Ahwaz were a stirring sight, and one not without some wry humour. I found myself filming the very London-Midland-and-Scottish locomotive that might have taken me to the Lake District on a school vacation. Behind it, a brake-van bore the curious legend NOT TO RUN ON THE SOUTHERN RAILWAY BETWEEN TONBRIDGE AND WEST ST. LEONARDS AND ALSO THE WHITSTABLE HARBOUR BRANCH.

A strange scene for 'somewhere in Persia'. I thought it would make a great beginning for my film. To get the most dramatic results, I climbed up on the roof of Ahwaz station. Just as I was stepping off the ladder that took me up, I felt something give just beneath my shoulder, and the sudden easing of a weight.

The leather strap of my camera case had broken. The Newman Sinclair crashed down on to concrete thirty feet below.

I had known more elated moments.

For this one and only movie camera, Dave Macdonald had scoured the Middle East. It was my only weapon of war, and to use it I had been sent ten thousand miles. I had waited for it ten weeks in Cairo, three weeks in Baghdad. Now it lay thirty feet below me, smashed.

I very nearly followed it.

At the bottom of the ladder I picked up the battered leather case. Nothing rattled inside. I opened it. The camera was still in one piece, and its one and only lens unbroken. But not so the release-mechanism at the front. The trigger was badly bent. When I freed it, nothing happened.

But if the Royal Engineers could lift their seventy ton British locomotives on to Persian tracks, and re-route rolling stock from Tonbridge to Teheran, they ought to be able to mend my camera. They could. They did. In a mobile workshop a master-sergeant and I took it apart, like a watch. We put it back together again, and no gear or spring was overlooked. All were still intact. We wound up its clockwork springs. It ran. The sweetest music I have ever heard.

I lived again. The next day I filmed the marshalling yards of Ahwaz, and then went on to a railroad scene of still greater possibilities—Andimeshk.

Here, a little further still to the north, the railroad was largely relieved of its burden. The freight wagons were run into a siding and unloaded. There was a war on.

Directing the unloading of supplies at Bandar Shah

The process did not take very long. The crates were unshipped and split open, the contents were unpacked and grouped—and there and then, on the spot, trucks were constructed from the crated parts.

I filmed one as it took shape. My lens followed the wheels and axles lifted from one crate, the engine from another, the gear box from a third, and so on. Immediate assembly. Instant automobiles. An hour before, there had been nothing but a freight train in a siding. Now, under this improvised scheme of mass-reconstruction, thirty trucks had already taken on recognisable form. And the scene of this desperate urgency was six thousand miles from Detroit—and twelve hundred from Stalingrad.

Stage three in this massive inter-allied Operation Dodge and Chevrolet, was the six hundred and fifty mile journey of the trucks themselves, to the north. This was where the convalescent Red Army men took over, and a special portmanteau word had been coined for the phase of military activity they represented—'Iransovhans' —'the organizing of the supply-line from Iran into the USSR'. I filmed a Major from Rostov taking actual delivery of a line of vehicles, and joined his convoy, keeping up with it as far as the foothills of the Zagros Mountains. Through clouds of dust, I focused the trucks winding their way upwards, on the first lap of a journey that was to end three years later in Berlin.

My fellow-sergeant and I now transferred to the Trans-Iranian Railway, riding in the solid German comfort of a passenger-coach while our own motor transport followed on an open wagon hitched to the train. It was a relief to leave the flat, featureless desert, dotted here and there with a few miserable centres of habitation, which is Persia at Persian Gulf level. Soon we were climbing up, over, and through a vast range of mountains. Between them and the distant Elburz in the north, the real Persia lay as if in a huge saucer with these mightly curving ranges for its rim. It was not quite the desert again, but indescribably bleak. Vast outcrops of rocks and giant boulders sprawled over its desolation. We might have been travelling on the moon. With the following dawn, however, we saw our destination and the city which was to be our base for the next two months—Teheran.

Teheran, approached thus from the south, with the glittering white peaks of the Elburz behind it, looks a strange and striking place. The reality was stranger still. This mighty capital city of Persia, the grandiose dream of Reza Khan, the self-appointed Shah of Shahs, was a ghost town.

Everything was on a scale of magnificence—dead magnificence. There was an opera house, a monster opera house. But not an aria was ever sung there. The stock exchange spread its cavernous and echoing halls over an area as great as that of Grand Central Station. But within it, no stocks or shares ever changed hands. No proud feature of the cities of the west had been overlooked. Every avenue was broader than the one before it, every square more lordly. But there was no plumbing. The sewage coursed merrily down open drains, alongside the magnificent boulevards.

The pro-German Shah of Shahs, who had once been simply an officer in Persia's army, was now breathing purer air in South Africa. The British had interned him there, for the duration of the war. His young son had been somewhat summarily sworn in as Shah-in-charge, but it was to be another twenty-six years before he felt secure enough to have himself crowned upon the *Naderieh* Throne.

Daily I explored Teheran in a sort of 'droskie' drawn by a gaunt and sad looking horse. I liked the broad avenues, I liked the crowds, even more colourful than Cairo's, and I found the invigorating mountain air ample compensation for the

Author with Russian officer and interpreter

effluence of the drainage.

But we were not supposed to be in Teheran as tourists. Our job was to film and photograph allied supplies to Russia, and we were still only half way there. But all Persia north of Teheran was controlled by the Russians themselves. It seemed they did not want us in their area of occupation with our cameras. Our Conducting Officer had applied for permission for us to enter and accompany the convoys, but not a word came from the Soviet representative of 'Iransovhans'. To my dismay, I was ordered back on my tracks to, of all places, Baghdad once again; but I travelled in good company.

With the defeat of Poland at the beginning of the war, Hitler and Stalin had divided the spoils. Over a million Poles had been interned in Russia. Now that Stalin had been turned into Hitler's deadliest enemy, the Polish Government in exile had pressed him for the release of these men. The machinery had worked very slowly but at last, under General Anders, the million Poles, or what was left of them, were beginning to trickle through to Britain—who had undertaken to re-equip them with the arms Russia could ill afford to spare—via Persia.

We had already photographed them in their reception camps outside Teheran. Now I drove in convoy with them and my camera, at the start of their new odyssey —which was to be climaxed in their storming of Cassino two years later.

In Baghdad, at the end of this dramatic drive by way of Kermanshah, Hamadan, and the Paitak Pass, there was still no word of any permit from the Russians. But back once again in Teheran, there was Dave Macdonald.

He was very pleased with what I had shot—all of which he had screened after

Filming from the platform on a train south of Teheran
Shot made from the train platform

its processing in a Cairo laboratory—and had a suggestion to make.

"What the film lacks so far", said he, "is movement".

"Get your camera on the supply trains. Let it be the eyes of the audience, as if it were they themselves actually travelling across Persia".

We could not go north, so back I went south. To Qum; where, in the shadow of the great golden-domed mosque which is the burial place of Fatima, the daughter of Islam's seventh Iman, the ever-resourceful Royal Engineers built me a camera platform to mount on their trains. They provided me with a brake-van to mount it on, and a locomotive all my own to push as well as pull. This was playing trains on the grand scale. I had the time of my life going up and down one of the world's most exciting railroads—nine hundred mostly mountainous miles with eight hundred bridges and two hundred tunnels. I shot moving pictures of moving trains seven thousand feet up the sheer side of a mountain, winding round curves beneath deluges of water from the melting snows, emerging from darkness into dazzling sun and scenery that was sheer spectacle.

Sometimes I got soaked and once ran into a worse fate: an episode bordering on the comic which at first I thought far from funny.

On this occasion we had loaded our own basic transport—our fifteen hundred-weight truck—on to an open flat-topped wagon, and were returning to Teheran in the comfort of a passenger coach on the same train. All went well till I began to feel those all too familiar qualms of 'Gyppy tummy.'

I had to lie flat. The passenger coach gave me no chance of doing so. It was full of upright sitting fellow travellers. I climbed out through the rear door, across the couplings, and lurched my way back along the train till I came to the wagon carrying our truck. I climbed up into it and stretched out on one of its long seats. Alas for the flimsy and precarious protection of its flapping canvas sides. It was not enough for a journey of nine hours and a hundred tunnels behind a locomotive's soot and smoke. I reached Teheran not only feeling like death, but blacker than any chimney sweep.

This attack lasted some days. I owed my recovery to the Russians, but not to their medical service.

We had at last received our permit to enter the Russian-occupied zone.

My first glimpse of the Caspian endures still as one of the unforgettable moments of my life. For hours we had been driving through the Elburz—the mightiest mountains I had ever seen. Eight thousand feet up we plunged into the darkness of a tunnel—a road tunnel this time. Far ahead of our own head-lamps was a pin-point of light. Slowly it became an arch. Then it grew bigger and bigger till through it, gleamed a new world.

Below us, in a zone not so close to the snow-line, we saw huge forests that seemed to float like cloud upon cloud of green dark, and gorges two thousand feet deep, from whose sides sprang a vegetation almost tropical in its luxuriance. We looked down, down, and still down, till at last we made out the dwarfed coastline of a wrinkled sea. Its sparkling blue stretched away to limitless horizons.

I was swimming in it next morning and our truck-camp was pitched on its shore.

Till now we had encountered but one Russian soldier—manning the frontier check-point. With his automatic rifle at the ready, he was a grim reminder of war. But the permit worked wonders. He smiled and his barrier lifted at once. The next Russian we met was a little more difficult, just at first.

We were now at our first port of call, Bandar Shah, the terminus of the railroad. Here the trains were finally unloaded. The crates and bales, manhandled by Persian labour, were stacked ready for shipment by sea to the Soviet Union itself. The marshalling yards were a hive of activity. I set up my camera.

At once, a whistle blew and everything stopped.

All the workers had vanished, to a man. Gone to earth. Disappeared. Before me lay nothing but an empty spectacle, as dead as the stage of the Teheran opera house.

I approached the Russian official who not half an hour before had fully endorsed my permit to film the scene. Through the ever present and ever necessary interpreter, I asked the reason for this curious transformation.

"Your permit clearly states", I was informed, "that you may photograph the supplies in transit. Go ahead. What are you waiting for?"

"But I can't film still life", I protested. "I am taking moving pictures. I must show movement and action. I must show the men actually unloading the supplies or my film will make no sense."

"It says nothing about that on your permit", argued the Russian. "It says you may photograph the supplies".

Stalemate lasted for forty minutes, during which I grew more and more eloquent and the interpreter more and more harassed. At last, however, the magic whistle blew. All hands were back again on deck in no time, and my camera was soon turning. I left Bandar Shah with a full coverage of the marshalling yards, and I also had been lucky enough to find a small ship loading at the jetty. But I felt somewhat chastened. Russian bureaucracy could be as unyielding as the Russian front.

My most memorable meal (for me Persia was a land of superlatives) came the next day. We were working our way along the coast to the other Caspian port, Pahlevi. Lunch time drew on. We began to look for a suitable spot in which to brew up some tea and open up yet one more supremely uninspiring can of corned beef. Before we had quite got to it, however, I found myself gazing at a strange and extraordinary edifice.

Before us loomed a hotel. But this dwarfed any hostelry that I had ever seen before. Only the Hollywood of the roaring twenties could have constructed anything else like it. Before he succeeded in almost bankrupting his employers, Eric von Stroheim might have flung up such a set for *Foolish Wives*. It was a simply colossal rococo building, fronted by more than a mile of ornamental garden leading down to the sea. (Resnais would have loved it for *Marienbad*.)

Feeling somewhat alienated ourselves, we drove up to its enormous portals, past row upon row of formal statues. We entered through vast revolving doors—and walked into total emptiness. Our boots echoed on acres of polished floor louder than the clip-clop of the 'droskies' in the streets of Teheran, as we explored yet another of the Shah of Shah's flights of fancy—the pearl of his inland sea, Ramsar, his attempt at a Caspian Monte Carlo. Suddenly an immaculately dressed head waiter appeared.

"Lunch Gentlemen?"

The Ramsar Hotel

Tabriz—The Universal Chaplin

His English was as correct as the cut of his tail coat. He led us through a gargantaun and ghostly dining room to a corner table overlooking the terrace. It was pathetically obvious that in this gilded opulence, we were to eat alone. We ate for absent guests too. Between the Caspian caviar our meal began with and the tiny wild strawberries which marked its eventual close, stretched a luncheon on the same pattern as every other extravagance. We feared the bill would be even bigger. But one more Persian miracle awaited us. We found we could pay it, quite easily, and on our sergeants' pay too.

Our hotel in Pahlevi was on a more modest scale. But it provided a very comfortable place in which to stay while we waited for the chance of aiming our cameras at a Russian ship.

Persia was beginning to teach me the virtues of patience, and it does seem that everything does finally come to him who waits. One evening after we had been there about a week I saw a steamer with a hammer and sickle on the smoke-stack and by next day, through the good offices of the Russian Liaison Officer, I was filming it as it took on supplies. These now included crated aircraft parts.

We went on board. The only severe faces were those of Stalin, Lenin and Marx in the ward-room. Everyone else was smiling—especially the one woman among an all-male crew. This cheerful, buxom, round-faced lady was not a stowaway, but the cook. We made friends with her over lunch and when the little ship sailed for Baku, loaded down with the products of Detroit, her smiling face beamed goodbye to us from the porthole of her steamy and fragrant galley.

From Pahlevi we returned to Teheran, and after giving our truck a quick check-up, we shipped our exposed film off to Cairo, and prepared for our next sortie into Soviet-Occupied Iran. This time our goal was Tabriz, the home of some of Persia's most fabulous carpets, and an ancient provincial capital. We drove through the bandit country of Kazvin without encountering anything more formidable than the Russian soldiers at the check-point, and began the hair-pin descent into Azerbaijan.

It was here in Tabriz, to our delighted surprise, that we discovered that we were not after all the only representatives of an allied army isolated in the mysteries of the Russian zone. A quartet of American technical sergeants had arrived in Tabriz the month before, in order to supervise the maintenance and repair of the hundreds of thousands of Dodge and Chevrolet trucks on the last lap of their gruelling seven hundred mile drive up from Andimeshk.

At a large open air workshop established outside the town for this purpose, the accents of New England mingled with those of the Russian republics, as Edward Schaeberle from Pennsylvania (whom the Russians affectionately called 'Fat Boy'), Kenneth Smith from New Hampshire, Roy Eldridge from Massachusetts, and Joseph Cudo from Connecticut checked over each and every one of the trucks before they finally left for the Soviet Union seventy miles to the north.

The Russian in charge of this Tabriz maintenance base was a twenty-nine-year-old Captain, Boris Ivanovitch Pirgoff. Like the rest of his unit he was always ready to be filmed. His interpreter was also from Moscow. Julia did her best to uphold the party line, but her perseverance was no match for the constant good humour and leg-pulling to which she was subjected, as much by her fellow Russians as the Americans.

It was however impossible to convince her that the King of England had a ration book identical to that of the lowliest of his subjects.

"I know all about London," Miss Chembareve retorted, "it is a city of monstrous social privilege. Why, I have read that in England children toil in the mines and factories, and the aristocracy have hundreds of servants."

Duly rebuked, by an obvious devotee of Dickens, and my filming of the maintenance base completed, I went off for a look at the Blue Mosque and other reminders of a Persian city's spacious past.

In Tabriz we lived in a large and otherwise unoccupied guest-house, mysteriously placed at our disposal by the manager of a British bank. We made ourselves as comfortable as possible to sit out one more wait for one more permit. For I did not see my film-story as complete without a shot or two of those Dodges and Chevrolets actually entering the Soviet Union itself. However, as time wore on, and I read my way deeper and deeper into the bank manager's library, I began to wonder if we had not in fact reached the end of the line. We were up against a bureaucratic wall higher than the hundred-foot ramparts which still surrounded Tabriz' ancient Citadel. Despite almost daily pleas to General Melnik, commanding the South Caucasian Red Army which garrisoned this northern part of Persia, this could be a permit which might never arrive.

More of a genuinely Persian city than cosmopolitan Teheran, Tabriz possessed not only a variety of carpet factories, but also many cinemas showing a diverse assortment of films. I made my way from a battered collection of early Chaplins to Pudovkin's recently completed biography of Suvarov, Catherine the Great's favourite general and the greatest Russian soldier of his day. Sitting in almost

The Tabriz Maintenance Depot

solitary darkness, still wondering at the back of my mind whether I would ever receive that final permit, I watched this grandiose re-enactment of his famous crossing of the Alps, when directed to drive Napoleon's forces from Switzerland: an impressive sequence staged on an epic scale only two years before in the nearby mountains of the Caucasus, where now the heirs to Suvarov's example were locked in real and bloody combat with the invaders of their country.

Apart from my one day's filming, more than two weeks were to elapse before the arrival of the next convoy up from Andimeshk brought my camera once again into the streets of Tabriz and the approaches to Captain Pirgoff's maintenance depot. With the realisation that we had reached the limits of Russian accessibility, we decided to return to Teheran.

It was now July 1942, and the climacteric of the war in the Middle East was now at hand. Defeated in the western desert the British 8th Army had retreated to within sixty miles of Alexandria. On the Russian front the Germans were making fresh assaults against Stalingrad and driving down towards us through the Caucasus. It looked very much as if these two great pincers would meet in the Middle East: from where India—threatened on her eastern frontier by the Japanese—could then be assaulted. In the face of this crisis my now completed work in Persia seemed to be of small consequence and, back in Teheran, I sent urgent pleas to David Macdonald for my recall to Cairo. Eventually these bore fruit and, passing through Baghdad, I heard of the holding of the Alamein position and the arrival of reinforcements in the Middle East.

Behind me I left the subject of this my first film: the opening up of the southern supply route to the Russians which, with the virtual destruction of Arctic Convoy PQ-17 this same month, was now about to go into very high gear indeed. Of the thirty-five mostly American merchant ships which set sail laden with supplies in that ill-fated convoy, only eleven survived the repeated German attacks to dock in Murmansk. In the face of such catastrophic losses there was simply no alternative but to concentrate on the Persian route, and agreement was reached between Churchill and Roosevelt that the United States Army should take over the entire operation. Heavy American locomotives more suited to the gradients of the Trans-Iranian railway than the lighter British engines that I had filmed soon made their appearance; the ports and harbours on the Gulf were extended and enlarged; aircraft were assembled at Basra and flown direct to Russian airfields; and the roads developed to speed the thousands of trucks soon assembling monthly at the Andimeshk railhead.

By the summer of 1944, the Russians were receiving well over a quarter of a million tons a month—through a country whose only railroad had been hard put to shift the cargo of a single shipload during the October of three years before. In all some 427,000 trucks and 13,000 combat vehicles were despatched; railroad equipment included nearly 2,000 locomotives and 11,000 wagons, all especially manufactured for the wide Russian gauge; a billion dollars worth of machinery was sent, and more than four million tons of foodstuffs. The total value of Lend-Lease to the Soviet Union was eleven thousand million dollars.

My film showed the beginnings of this great allied supply operation. It got to London safely and, edited by Roy Boulting, was shown throughout the world by the British Ministry of Information under the title of *Via Persia*.

But this was still in the future. For me it was now farewell to that battered old Baghdad camera, whose springs had finally given out. Ahead lay Britain's last great solo feat of arms – and American-built Lend-Lease DeVrys with which to film it.

Of War in the Desert –
And a Victorious Combination of Cameras

The Western Desert is a place fit only for war. James Lansdale Hodson

Returned from Persia, I spent a week's leave in a still far from confident Cairo. Wished the best of luck by David Macdonald, I drove off into the Egyptian desert with a fellow sergeant in one of our newly arrived jeeps. These mechanical marvels might have been specifically designed for our own purpose, so well suited were they to the Army Film Unit's now proven tactic of working with two-men teams of sergeant photographers in this manner—one equipped with a motion picture camera and the other taking photographs for press release.

Pitched in tents, trucks and caravans on the seashore only half an hour's drive along the coast road from Alexandria, for the Army Film Unit, 8th Army Headquarters was synonymous with Geoffrey Keating. A former newspaper photographer this restless perfectionist had been commissioned into the Rifle Brigade in the early days of the war, and had seen a great deal of service in the desert, where he had become one of the most widely known characters. That evening he told us that we were to be attached to one of four fresh divisions newly arrived from England, and, after a sound night's sleep on the sand, he led us the next morning to the headquarters of the 44th Infantry. This amounted to a furious drive across what, to me, might well have been the other side of the moon. Introducing us to the Divisional Intelligence Officer, who lived with his maps, like a mole below ground, he then departed on further lightning visitations to his teams of cameramen spread out along the front, leaving me feeling completely disorientated and utterly lost.

In this desert there were no points of reference to previous ways of thought or habit. Life had been stripped clean. Everything was superfluous except survival. My world suddenly shrank to a hole in the ground six feet long, two feet wide, and three feet deep.

During the next four days I endeavoured to get my bearings. We visited the brigades and, from their Intelligence Officers, built up a picture of the entire division's role and commitment, deciding which battalions would probably provide the best opportunities for photography and filming. The 8th Army was now once again building up its strength after the long retreat of the summer, but was not yet ready to undertake an offensive; in the meantime Rommel was expected to make a further effort to break through the line, capture Cairo and Alexandria, seize the Suez Canal, and occupy the oilfields to the east.

Six days after my arrival in the desert the German attack began. The assault was pressed home in the south: where the Germans pushed through the British mine-fields and swung north in an attempt to envelope the 8th Army position. 44th Division were holding a ridge directly in the line of this advance, and we had a grandstand view of the Afrika Corps attempting to break through the screen of British armour that separated us from the enemy. From time to time we were attacked by enemy aircraft, but this discomfort was more than mitigated by the spectacle of wave after wave of British planes passing overhead as they bombed the German armour and supply columns; but the action was too far away from our position for us to be able to photograph it in any detail.

I was beginning to feel too much a spectator of these events for the satisfaction of my conscience when Geoffrey Keating unexpectedly appeared. We were whisked off to one of our brigades which had now suddenly been moved alongside the 2nd New Zealand Division. We were positioned north of the point where the German 90th Light had originally broken through on the left flank of the Afrika Corps.

Rommel had been out-manoeuvred. He was attempting to withdraw. For the first time in the fluid fortunes of this desert warfare the British armour had not rushed forward into the fray, easy targets for the Germans' hitherto vastly superior

'The Desert is a place fit only for war'.

eighty-eight millimetre anti-tank guns. Every attempt of the Afrika Corps to break through to the north had been blocked. Bombed from the air, and bombarded from the ground, the Germans—almost paralysed by lack of fuel—were attempting to disengage.

The task of the New Zealanders, with the British troops to which we were now attached, was to cut across their escape route. This would close the gap in the belt of the defensive minefields through which the assault had first come. The Germans were now retracing their route in full retreat. The attack was mounted on the night of September 3rd, the anniversary of Britain's declaration of war against Germany. Enemy reaction was desperate. The 'Panzerarmee Afrika' was in danger of being trapped. The war in Africa could be over at one stroke.

That night was for me an incoherent and terrifying shambles. Shells crashed down all around us. The brigade control vehicle was hit and went up in flames. An ammunition truck disintegrated in a blaze of exploding light, revealing our nakedness on the exposed desert all the more.

In the face of this devastating German defence, everyone dug in; and I scraped as best I could a shallow trough out of the unyielding ground in which to press down what seemed to be my far too conspicuous self.

Nothing in life has ever surprised me more than the realisation that, having done so, I actually feel asleep for more than an hour in the midst of this inferno. To have something immediate to do, and on which to concentrate, gives the soldier something to hold on to. For a cameraman, who can only work in daylight, such a baptism of fire was at the very least something of an ordeal. All I could do was hope to survive until the rising sun lit up some sort of scene of action that could be filmed in the morning.

Dawn did indeed reveal the hangover of battle in all its confusion. Knocked-out trucks still smouldered, to a chorus of mortars still firing from trenches all around us. Both sides seemed to be momentarily spent, and as immobile infantry, hard down in scattered foxholes, presented a picture very much at variance with the War Office's conception of tightly bunched soldiers rushing headlong against the skyline to victory, we decided to pull back with the first evacuation of wounded, and see if we could get some idea of what might be happening.

Rommel had been decisively defeated. He had swung north in the direction expected, into ground already prepared and ready for his reception. To every move the German made the counter-move was already in being. He found himself the impotent dancer to another man's tune, forced to retire ignominiously, and passively await his opponent's assault.

This was the first action fought in the desert by the 8th Army's new commander, arrived from England to take over only twenty days before. Hearing that he was visiting the neighbouring Greek Brigade, we rushed across to film and photograph his meeting with these survivors of Argyrokastron. He had not yet adopted the beret, but his British Army General's red-banded cap had already been traded in for a bush hat presented by the Australian division holding the coastal flank. With MacArthur in the Pacific his only rival in self-designed headgear and military flamboyance, Montgomery was about to give the British the victory and the hero that they craved.

Successful propaganda can only be based on achievement. All the cameramen in the world could have made nothing more of Britain's previous military endeavour than a chronicle of failure. In their somewhat perverse way, and with no successful candidate of their own, the British had built up an enemy general into a far greater and more glamorous figure than he ever was in his own country. Their own military inadequacy contributed more to the Rommel legend than anything else.

Montgomery saw this. Vain perhaps, but his was no more than the vanity of the true professional at the top of his form. He was the first British General to give the camera as great a priority as the cannon. In this he was assiduously assisted by Geoffrey Keating, who made certain that his new master never took a step without one or other of us being in attendance with a camera.

But film records or none, Montgomery had made his date with destiny.

The 44th Division was now moved up to the Deir el Munassib—the escarpment

Greeks prepare for battle.

which our ill-fated Brigade had failed to reach during the previous battle. Montgomery needed the New Zealanders for the attack he was now in the process of forming. Once again I carved a resting place for myself out of the shale of this inhospitable desert. To our left General Koenig commanded a unit of the Free French. To the south of these heroic survivors of Bir Hachim lay the impassable Qattara Depression, the lynchpin of this natural defensive position. Between ourselves and the enemy at the southern extremity of the Alamein line was a large expanse of open country. Both British and German were busy with patrols in this 'no man's land', probing each other's intentions. As this was the only activity anywhere along the front at this time, I decided to film a story of one such patrol under the title of *Message Received*, in order to illustrate the reality behind what had now become laconically brief daily communiqués.

In Bren-gun carriers these sorties drove out through the screen of defensive minefields and often bumped into the enemy engaged on a similar purpose and errand. Shots were frequently exchanged and prisoners taken. Most filming in the desert had been of necessity smash and grab attempts to capture whatever violent action might explode within the vicinity of the cameraman's viewfinder. I felt that for myself a greater satisfaction lay in the development of such sustained incidents which, with a beginning, a middle—and one hoped a happy ending—could provide a clearer picture of what life was like in this lull before the storm. I built up my story with scenes of the Intelligence Officer planning a patrol with its Commander. I showed the loading of ammunition and weapons; then the departure into the waste land beyond. Unfortunately my carefully planned filming was denied its climax. Once again everything that happened after these carefully filmed preparations took place at night. The darkness inhibited my camera even more than it protected my cast. A few days later I was surprised to receive a report from Cairo congratulating me on these prepared sequences. David Macdonald was in a position to take a longer view. He needed such developed sequences for the feature film that he had already begun to conceive.

The Greeks were the latest recruits to the 8th Army club, whose membership now comprised Australians, New Zealanders, South Africans, Indians and French, as well as the six divisions from various parts of Great Britain. I returned to Army Headquarters, one evening after my camera had seized up at the moment of filming a great explosion of captured Italian ammunition set off by the Royal Engineers, to be assigned the task of filming in detail the preparation and build-up of one brigade of the two armoured divisions that had recently received the new Sherman tank.

When four months before Rommel had rushed towards Egypt, seemingly invincible, President Roosevelt had at once ordered the despatch to Suez of three hundred of these powerful new American tanks. They were only just coming off the assembly line, and had only just been issued to the United States' own armoured divisions. Now, in this autumn of German defeat, I filmed the British tankmen's growing mastery of their heavy guns—at long last a match for the Panzerarmee's Mark IVs.

During the final days of our filming and photographing this story of 2nd Armoured Brigade's preparations for battle, we found it had begun to melt away into thin air. We drove up from the desert training area on to the coastal road to find out what was happening, and found ourselves engulfed by both 1st and 10th Armoured Divisions moving up towards the front. Mile upon mile of Sherman tanks on their new transporters, packed tightly nose to tail, slipped behind us as we drove on. Making straight for 8th Army Headquarters, we found David Macdonald and the entire unit foregathered.

The attack was to go in the following night. Pencilled arrows on the plastic-

Tank men prepare to eat.

covered maps indicated the direction of the twin thrusts the 8th Army was to make. Dave Macdonald and Geoffrey Keating explained the details of its intention to us, the cameramen.

After a tremendous artillery barrage, and while a diversionary attack was being mounted in the south, the infantry were going to tear apart the enemy defences in the northern sector. On their heels and through the gap, was to burst the armoured corps that I now realised I had been filming in preparation for this vital role. This was going to be the final show-down, and Montgomery's battle order, read out to us as to every other one of the two hundred and twenty thousand of the 8th Army that day, radiated confidence. In the phraseology of the cricket field he was "Going to hit Rommel for six right out of Africa."

The second of the two infantry divisions which had been rushed out to Egypt four months before was the 51st from Scotland; and we found ourselves attached to these Highlanders. With the Australians, they had been chosen to blast one path for the tanks a few miles below the coast road. The New Zealanders and South Africans were to force the second. The 23rd of October 1942 was a night of the full moon, and had been selected for this very reason. The thin light from this neutral satellite would illuminate the struggle through the five miles of heavily mined enemy defences which had to be breached by morning. In the afternoon we established ourselves beside a concentration of artillery, and awaited the beginning of what the Army Commander had claimed would be "one of the most decisive battles of history."

The sun at last went down, the evening chill descended on the desert. Then the moon slowly rose to the muffled chorus of the squealings of tank tracks. The massed armour of 10 Corps moved up six lanes to its start line behind the infantry, now poised for assault. At precisely twenty minutes to ten, a few feet away, the artillery captain yelled "Fire"—and his guns crashed into action in

Battle of Alam Halfa

common with another nine hundred opening up at this simultaneous second all along the thirty mile front.

The uninterrupted flashes of gunfire lit the scene with stark clarity. My camera had been already lined up in daylight, so I filmed both at close quarters and from a distance the virtually unbroken line of flashing light set up by the greatest concentration of shell fire that the British army had set down in the war.

At normal speed the motion picture camera takes separate exposures for approximately a forty-eighth part of every second that it is running. It had dawned neither on myself or on many of my colleagues that it only needed a gun flash to occur in any one of the other forty-seven parts of the second for nothing to appear on the film at all; and this is in fact what happened both to myself and to many others filming this great barrage! A few more experienced at such filming knew the answer: they either ran their cameras very slow, or let the gunflash itself make the exposure by leaving the camera shutter open throughout the gun's firing, and only moving the film on frame by frame manually after each such momentary explosion of light. From the work of these wiser ones that night was built up the record of this tremendous bombardment.

The next morning—that should have seen the British armour bursting through the enemy minefields—everything seemed confusion. By now I realised a battle always seemed so to an isolated individual unable to see the whole perspective. It was clear that an immediate breakthrough had not been achieved. The tanks were held up. A blood-bespattered turret of a shattered Sherman near me was witness to the tenacity of the German defence.

Between shell bursts I filmed the first prisoners that were brought in. They were mostly Italian. Rommel always used them to hold his fixed defences, while he kept the Afrika Corps uncommitted until he was certain of the direction of the main attack. After bombing had interrupted what little sleep we were able to catch the second night, we again came under heavy fire the following day. We crouched on, filming and photographing our own guns delivering and receiving the explosive metal. One enemy burst sent jagged fragments whistling past my ear into the side of our jeep with startling effect. Receiving a stream of machine gun bullets through the radiator of their truck twenty-four hours later, another Army Film Unit team with this same division were completely immobilised. All around the Highlanders remained stuck in the narrow defile which they had driven barely half-way to Kidney Ridge, the immediate objective of their first assault.

At 30 Corps Headquarters, delivering film of the German prisoners that were now beginning to come through in increasing numbers by the 31st of October, an urgent telephone call summoned us to Geoffrey Keating at Montgomery's Tactical Command Post. The General's caravans were parked on an isolated spit of sand at the end of a narrow causeway on the sea shore, well in advance of the army's main centre of operations at Burg el 'Arab. Here our own commanding officer gave us the news that the Australians had succeeded in breaking through and that, code-named 'Supercharge', a new assault was about to be mounted by the re-grouped armour of 10 Corps along the axis of their success. We were to be attached to our old friends of the 2nd Armoured Brigade for what was to be the climax of this historic battle.

A tank battle in the desert was like nothing so much as an action at sea. The opponents operate across the sand just like the manoeuvring of two fleets over water.

Sidi El Rahman—after Alamein

Their wide separation makes it virtually impossible for cameramen ever to get really satisfactory pictures of armoured conflict. The cinema-going public had been brought up to visualize masses of tanks bunched together, hitting out in all directions, and continually charging about as they did so. After two dispiriting days in which the reality was brought home to me with uncomfortable effect, we chanced upon a small station on the coastal railway from which the front had now moved forward. This was, as a result, in a position to receive its first train for many days. Filming the unloading of supplies at this previously unknown and least significant of wayside halts—in the past at most a whistle stop for commuting bedouin—the name above the platform on which I focused my camera was now about to ring throughout the world: Alamein.

At last the armour had succeeded in getting through. Rommel was in full retreat. But his ever formidable anti-tank defences denied Montgomery the total triumph he had hoped for. Most of what was left of the 'Panzerarmee Afrika' got away in whatever transport it could grab—leaving its abandoned Italian allies only their own feet with which to walk into captivity.

Beyond El Alamein we drove, through a landscape stinking with the oil and blood of knocked out tanks. We passed the Hill of Jesus whose capture by the Australians had turned this tide. We left behind us another tiny station on the coastal railway, Sidi Abd el Rahman, south of which had been fought this last great armoured battle of the desert war. Back on to the road beside the sea, a few miles further on we came across a jubilant Dave Macdonald at a hastily improvised headquarters.

After three years of defeat and withdrawal Britain had at last won a great victory. Of the thirty thousand prisoners taken, no less than nine were enemy generals. A dozen Italian and German divisions had been virtually destroyed, and the threat to Egypt and the Allied position in the Middle East removed for ever. Over captured chianti that night we talked long of the feature length film that David Macdonald now planned to produce from the great volume of film which we had all been making in the desert. We also had another film to discuss.

Many of us had recently seen the Soviet *One Day of War*, a feature length documentary which vividly illustrates a cross-section of twenty four-hours in the Russians' fight for survival. From besieged Leningrad to the agony of Stalingrad; from the incongruous spectacle of Shostakovich playing the piano at an air force fighter base to the roar of evacuated machinery in the factories of the distant Urals; everywhere, every one of two hundred and forty cameramen had been simultaneously directed by Mikhail Slutsky to film whatever might be happening within his own particular territory during the course of a single day and night. The magnificent editing confirmed this film as a tremendous panorama of national faith and power. The concept was originally suggested by Maxim Gorki. Moscow's Central Newsreel Studio had already used it in pursuit of peace in *A Day in a New World*. Ian Dalrymple and the British Crown Film Unit had been so impressed that it was hoped to make a similarly fashioned epic of the British Commonwealth under the far from inspiring title of *Morning, Noon, and Night*. They were asking us for ideas and sequences from the Middle East.

Believing that such a film could easily become no more than a diffuse assembly of martial scenes from all over the place, I realised that here in the Middle East we had a location and situation which could provide both a moment of tranquillity and a reminder that this war was being fought for more than national survival. It was claimed also that it was being fought for certain spiritual standards, particularly values deeply rooted in a Christian heritage.

A day's drive from Cairo, and a favourite leave centre for the 8th Army, was Palestine and the Holy Land. There, in any twenty-four hours I could find Commonwealth soldiers, either on furlough or convalescing from their wounds.

Through the good and holy offices of a chaplain in Jerusalem, my camera was granted access to the cradle of the nativity in Bethlehem. I filmed the evening shadows of Gethsemane, and followed a pilgrimage on the Via Dolorosa and its Stations of the Cross. Despite Montgomery's adoption of a crusader's shield as the emblem of his army, my carefully composed sequence met with raised eyebrows when screened in Cairo. As a counterweight to these scenes of convalescent soldiers in the setting of an earlier crucifixion, we went on to film a round the clock episode of a machine gun post holding a position in the desert—but even so the entire project of *Morning, Noon, and Night* faded away into oblivion. I never heard of it again.

But in any case we had now at last a film ourselves in every way the equal of anything produced either by our ally or our enemy: David Macdonald's *Desert Victory*, brilliantly edited by Roy Boulting. It was shown to sensational effect both in Britain and the United States. Its appearance was eagerly awaited in the Middle East, where it was given in Cairo a full scale première. At the Egyptian State Broadcasting Studios, I was asked to relate some of my own experiences during its production. Confronted for the first time by the terrifying presence of a

Author films Commander-in-Chief giving awards to 4th Indian Division

live microphone, I had at least some experience to fall back on in the recording of a commentary to my filming of a huge ordnance depot at Tel-el-Kebir. The hub of a vast supply operation making possible the army's inexorable advance.

Desert Victory fittingly closes with units of the 8th Army marching past a triumphant Winston Churchill in Tripoli. Tripoli was the goal of all the hard fighting over the years. It had been entered by Highlanders riding on tanks at the end of the third week of January. Now, by the first week of April, Montgomery was well into Tunisia itself. The North African campaign was about to reach its climax. The British and American armies landed in Algeria five months before in Rommel's rear had never made the progress expected of them. But, with the desert veterans closing in on the right flank of a united and unbroken front, the end was now in sight.

With my partner of the broadcast, I was flown over to the Anglo-American Headquarters in Algiers so that we could reinforce the British 1st Army's Film Unit in this great and imminent victory.

From this unmistakably French city, still looking hard over its shoulder at the recent Vichy past, we drove on into Tunisia. We passed the packed transports of the 7th Armoured and 4th Indian Divisions that General Alexander was moving over to the 1st Army sector for his final *coup de grace*. The sight of the desert veterans cheered our spirits. The younger army, fresh from England, had none of the cynical sophistication which characterised the 8th. In their battle dress and steel helmets, these text-book soldiers looked askance at the tatterdemalion tramps from the Desert Units, sitting any old how in their dusty and battered sand-painted trucks. The veterans were now almost at the end of their eighteen hundred mile advance from Alamein—clothed for the most part in no more than shorts and shirt, a pair of socks and boots, and their pride.

We reported to Hugh Stewart, in charge of the 1st Army's Film Unit at his headquarters near Medjez-el-Bab. He, with Sidney Bernstein, a visitor from the Ministry of Information, was planning the film and photographic coverage of this fast approaching culmination. Persistently refusing to yield an inch of conquered territory Hitler had committed more than a quarter of a million men to his doomed position in North Africa, and it was inconceivable that attempts would not be made to get as many away by sea as possible, rather as a similarly trapped British army had escaped from Dunkirk three years before.

Traditionally the silent service, the Royal Navy had never developed a film and photographic unit to the same degree as the Army and the Air Force. In order to rectify its inability to do justice to the spectacular engagements and destruction which would now ensue at sea, we were despatched to Anthony Kimmins at Bône, and placed aboard one of the destroyers about to commence a constant patrol off the waters of Cape Bon. It was here that the Germans were expected to embark upon their evacuation to Sicily and Italy.

The Allied Air Forces had instructions to attack any vessel, of whatever shape or size, within five miles of the coast. Our bridge structure was painted a vivid red in order that they might tell friend from foe. We set sail to discharge our share of Admiral Cunningham's order to the fleet to "Sink, burn and destroy. Let nothing pass."

Not one single German in even a canoe came our way, and less than a thousand ever put to sea in any form. Day by day we steamed up and down, while night by night we could hear the drone overhead, as Von Arnim, whom Rommel had left behind him to his fate, flew his key personnel out by air.

I returned ashore just in time to embark in the leading landing-craft of the first convoy to sail to Bizerta. I had no sooner made my bed on the floor of the wheel-house when all hell suddenly broke loose outside. As every anti-aircraft gun in Bône opened up, I scrambled with my camera into the flickering light of the fires

Filming Churchill—Cairo 1943

of an air raid. I hung perched above the stacked cases of ammunition with which we were loaded, surrounded by streams of tracer tearing into the heavens. This last night of the North African campaign was, for a few minutes, at least so far as I was concerned, as spectacular as any. Still intact we sailed on time and, preceded by minesweepers, cautiously crept through the tangled trap of sunken shipping in the entrance to this great Tunisian naval base, just captured by the United States II Corps supported by units of the rapidly recovering French Army. Leaping ashore, we filmed and photographed the rapid replacement of the cargo that we had brought with some of the two hundred and fifty thousand prisoners just surrendered.

It was all over, and Africa was purged of Italian and German imperialism. Now her peoples were free to ponder the principles of Roosevelt and Churchill's

Desert Victory

'Atlantic Charter', the right of everyone, everywhere, to "choose the forms of government under which they will live".

This first combined venture of British and American arms had resulted in a victory as total and complete as that of the Russians at Stalingrad fourteen weeks before. Now the tide of German conquest was at last being rolled back upon itself; in Churchill's words this Tunisian triumph marked "The End of the Beginning".

This was the title of the film that Hugh Stewart now set about producing, proposing to Colonel Darryl Zanuck and the United States Army Signal Corps— our opposite numbers—that we pool resources and material. But Zanuck planned to beat the British with his own film of the American contribution to the campaign. The British production was finished first, much to Zanuck's embarrassment.

Washington stepped in. The cause of allied unity demanded its suppression. The film of the end of the war in Africa had to be as allied in its making as it had been in theme and execution. Hugh Stewart started all over again, with veteran Hollywood director Frank Capra his partner, for the production of *Tunisian Victory*.

From then on the official films of the Mediterranean and European campaigns were combined Anglo-American operations. *The Road to Rome* drew upon film from each country's corps of cameramen. *The True Glory*—the Normandy invasion and the final defeat of Germany—was master-minded by Britain's Carol Reed and America's Garson Kanin.

In the Far East, we parted company. David Macdonald went on to produce *Burma Victory*—the film of the campaign in which the Japanese suffered their greatest defeat of the war, at the hands of British, Indian, and West African troops. Island-hopping with MacArthur in the Pacific, American combat cameramen shot the most striking action film of all. The landing of marines on Tarawa was to be shown to us as an example of the blood and thunder that the War Office was always screaming for. No cameraman put ashore with an entire division, landed on a tiny beach only a few yards deep, in broad daylight, could miss. We had had to cope with the fluid dispersal of troops and tanks scattered over the vast distances of the desert—and so much always took place in the dark, at night.

Even so, *Desert Victory* still puts them all to shame. Writing in *The Nation*, James Agee paid us this tribute:

> "In the camera work, the cutting, the music and sound, the commentary, it is a clean simple demonstration that creative imagination is the only possible substitute for the plainest sort of good sense—and is, after all, merely an intensification of good sense to the point of incandescence . . . There is hardly a shot which by any sort of dramatizing, prearrangement, or sentimentalization gets in the way of the high honest average chance for magnificence which any face or machine or light or terrain possesses, left to its own devices . . . 'Desert Victory' is a stunning textbook on how to make a nonfiction war film."

Well, that's 'how I won the war'. Writing now more than a quarter of a century after these events and attitudes, what can I add as postscript?

We provided the raw material for today's TV compilations and cinema send-ups. We were soldiers, and our job was to film the war, real war. But we derived no pleasure from its violence, no kicks from its cruelty. No soldier that I have ever met enjoys killing people.

After the breakout from Alamein, we ran into a German rearguard at Mersa Matruh. A shellburst only yards ahead of the speeding jeep sent it sharply off the road. I found myself among the foremost tanks of the advance, hull down behind some dunes. One had been hit. Towards me was being helped a wounded man. He caught sight of the camera in my hand, and let out a stream of shell-shocked abuse:

> "Take a picture of my mate, go on.
> He's been blown to bits. Go on. Go on.
> Take his bleeding picture. Bastards. Bastards."

Sobbing, he was led away.

But in those days not even that poor man doubted that the war had to be fought —and filmed.

Adriatic Adventures

In Jugoslavia, man means everything . . . our revolution had a different basis from that of the Russian revolution, and our party had different partners, for our revolution developed under its own particular conditions in the course of the war of liberation.

Josip Broz-Tito

I spent the next two years of the war in Italy. I landed with Montgomery from the Messina Straits, taking cover as a lone German Messerschmidt dropped a welcoming bomb or two on the first great Allied landing on the mainland of Europe. I waded through mud and mine fields. I lived in a large drain near Cassino and in a princely villa—familiarly known as the 'Villa Roughit'—on the outskirts of Naples. I saw the Poles I had first filmed in Persia storm the monastery of Cassino. I filmed a Jewish wedding in a concentration camp whose fascist guards had fled. I saw one of my fellow cameramen killed. I came to love Italy, and some time in the middle of it all I became an officer, if not a gentleman.

With the promise that I could still operate as a cameraman, even though commissioned, I exchanged the stripes on my sleeves for 'pips' on my shoulders, the hashed corned beef and bare wooden table tops of the sergeants' mess for asparagus and mahogany in the officers'—and, a fledging second lieutenant, set out for Anzio.

In charge of the AFPU's teams of cameramen on that beleagured beach head was Alan Whicker. Whicker had landed in Tunisia with the British 1st Army's Film Unit, with which we of the old Desert 8th were now combined. I found him ensconced in a shell-battered villa on the beach at Nettuno. From the tantalisingly close Alban Hills, heavy German artillery methodically dropped shells outside the back door. Command Headquarters was in a system of caves deep below the ground. For a while I became a 'Section Leader': driving by night delivering mail, liquor and film to cameramen crouched in fox holes, returning through mortar and machine gun fire from both sides.

Whicker liked his creature comforts, and craved company. Despite the monotonous crump of shells bursting in our backyard, we wined and dined well.

We hid in ditches from German fire—as we waited to enter Rome—and looked up to marvel at an Italian wedding-procession, proceeding along the Via Appia in the direction of the enemy as if the only sound that existed in the world was wedding-bells.

A month of jubilation, in the Eternal City, and I followed Whicker to the front; and found him, as ever, well entrenched—dwelling in medieval splendour in a monastery near Siena. Now we dined, on army rations, beneath frescoes of the saints. I went to bed in the spartan simplicity of a monk's cell overlooking the hills of Tuscany.

In July 1944 my presence was demanded in Bari. This was my second great solo opportunity since I had joined the Army Film Unit. My instructions were "to stay with Land Forces Adriatic for up to a month and to accompany them on any suitable expedition". I had barely discovered so much as the whereabouts of H.Q., L.F.A. when a "suitable expedition" materialized, and I got the chance of accompanying and filming a commando raid on Albania.

This raid was a lone venture for me, and I was determined to make a success of it. I carried a still as well as a movie-camera and—for once a facsimile of the War Office's conception of a combat cameraman—had actually worked out a technique for using both on the same occasion. I was still practising it in the landing-craft as we made the forty-mile sea trip across the Adriatic. We landed at one o'clock in the morning, three miles from the small port of Himara—which was also the nearest German outpost. Our objective was the village of Spilje.

Author in ruined church after the Battle of the Garigliano, Italy 1944

Dawn found the Commandos in position for attack, and myself on the top of a hill overlooking the German outpost. My camera started turning as the destroyers lying off shore began to fire, as Hurricanes of the Balkan Air Force screamed over-head—and a few Albanian shepherds stirred from their humble homes, seemingly indifferent to the hell that was breaking loose all round them. Even when the tiles began to fly off their roofs they took it with a shrug of their shoulders. The only thing they appeared to resent was the loss of their doors when, later on in the operation, we had to turn them into rough and ready stretchers for the wounded. Apart from that, they continued their daily ritual in the fields with sublime disregard for the battle raging all round. The sole exception among them was a little girl who brought us water.

When the Commandos went in to the attack, I scrambled down to join one of their companies. The ground was heavily defended, with German troops emplaced on ridge after ridge. A Scots piper played us on with his bagpipes. Resistance was sharper than we had reckoned for, but from prisoners we took, we soon learned why: we had been mistaken for Partisans, and Partisans took no prisoners. Among the Germans, there was undisguised relief when they realised that their captors were British.

Author in sunny Italy February 1944

The attack was a complete success. The German garrison near this tiny village of Spilje was wiped out, and we withdrew to the coast. In company with two other young officers, I reached the heights above the embarkation beach and with our packs propped up against a stone wall, we watched the Commandos trudge their way down the valley as we talked over the raid.

After a while, the three of us seemed to be alone in a quiet and entirely peaceful landscape. But it was only noon. There was still an hour to go till departure time —1300 hours. We went on talking and lazing in the sun.

"Don't you think", I suggested, a little diffidently, when it came to half past twelve, "that we ought to be making a move towards the beach?"

"Not a bad idea at all if you want to go back to Italy", smiled one of my companions, still showing no signs of activity. 'But we're staying'.

At that, I moved my aching legs very fast indeed.

I had met my first British Liaison Officers, parachuted to Resistance Groups throughout the Occupied Balkans: not to be confused with hit and run Commandos!

I managed to clamber aboard just ten minutes before the landing craft up-anchored and sailed away.

It was in Jugoslavia that the really stirring Balkan story was taking shape, and one of the war's great men beginning to emerge.

Yet no one seemed to know what was really happening.

Jugoslavia seemed a shadow-land of rumour, which reporter and photographer had seemed unable to penetrate. But at least they had tried. An Anglo-American party of war-correspondents and cameramen had already been despatched to Bosnia, to tell the world about Tito, the ferocious Resistance Movement he was

Commandos in Albania

leading, and the few British Liaison Officers who had been dropped to him to organise supplies.

They had reached him, and his German wolf-hound, Tigar, in his H.Q.—a cave. It so happened, however, that the Germans had planned an exactly simultaneous operation.

The Partisans were a continual thorn in their sides. They had mounted combined operations of their own to capture Tito in person. Their airborne troops started landing at the cave's very entrance. My predecessor was captured just as he had taken his first few feet of film. Tito and his closest followers climbed the dried-up channel of a waterfall at the back of the cave into safety. Tigar was hauled up after them. Randolph Churchill, one of the British Liaison Officers, was still wearing his pyjamas.

The Partisans had made things hot for the Germans. The Germans retaliated.

Albanian raid—waiting for final assault

They made the mainland too hot to hold Tito's Headquarters. Partisan attacks were now being made on a bigger scale than ever. Tito, however, found it more prudent to establish a new H.Q. twelve miles off the Jugoslav coast—on the island of Vis.

TOP SECRET letter of the 8th of July 1944, from Chief of Staff Land Forces Adriatic to Commanding Officer No. 2 Army Film and Photographic Section:

> "We are not directly connected with Force 399, but are a perfectly ordinary formation commanding British soldiers in the field. We are directly under Allied Force Headquarters and our mission is to intensify the war in the Balkans".

Letter of the 11th of August 1944 from Chief of Staff Land Forces Adriatic to Commander, H.Q. No. 1 Forward Base:

> "Lieutenant P. Hopkinson of the Army Film and Photographic Unit has come to your island to take cinematograph and still pictures . .
> I would be very grateful if you would give him all the assistance and welcome you can and let him take both the work on the island and operations from it."

With this letter in my hands, I sailed to Vis. It gave me full permission to film the Royal Marine Commando and the Battalion of Highland Light Infantry that had been added to its defence. These units had been established to add fire-power to the sorties made on the mainland, and to train the Partisans in the use of new weapons which were reaching them in ever-increasing numbers. I had not been told in so many words that I could also film the guerillas of the Jugoslav National Army of Liberation—as Tito's partisans were now known. But the Jugoslavs were not the Russians. Indeed the Russians had a very small finger in this pie. Their mission had only landed comfortably by plane months after the first British had parachuted in. The Jugoslavs right up to Tito himself—now a figure of the highest respectability in a new uniform and a Russian style cap—never raised the slightest objection to being filmed.

Here was a picture postcard island, a natural home for heroes, whom I found in plenty, along with heroines too. We approached the rugged coast-line through a misty dawn, shrouded from the German E-boats which were for ever on the prowl in these waters. The towering cliffs before us appeared to have some signs painted on them. At last we were near enough to be able to read, in lettering that was ten feet high:

Smrt Fascismu—Sloboda Narodu

Death to Fascism—Freedom to the People.

It was the first successful descent into the Balkans by an Army Film Unit. I was with two others: Dave Johnson, a Fleet Street press photographer, and Harry Wicken, the cockney driver of our jeep. We were soon driving up from the quay-side of Komisa, over the hills that cradled its small harbour, to the tented head-quarters of the British Commando Brigade.

Summer 1944 had seen an intensification of British Commando activity in support of resistance movements in the occupied Balkans, and Vis was now the forward base for such strikes into the enemy's long and vulnerable coastline.

To the Jugoslav National Army of Liberation, as the Partisans were now officially known, was accredited a British Military Mission engaged in training them in the use of new weapons with which they were now being supplied. At the apex of this tight little island in the Adriatic was the remote headquarters of Tito himself, established once again in a cave. With him was the British Mission to the movement itself, led by Brigadier Fitzroy Maclean, commanding all the many similar missions now attached to Partisan formations all over the occupied mainland of Jugoslavia, with whom contact was maintained by radio.

The interior of Vis certainly lived up to the *cri de guerre* on its cliffs. From our

German prisoner in Albania

tent above Komisa, we set forth daily to film and photograph an enthusiasm, a dauntless hope, and a grim sense of purpose which we had never come across anywhere before. These Partisans, readying themselves in camps all over Vis for the moment of attack, were not just young men of military age. There were women too, and even boys. Their weapons were still largely those seized from the surrendered Italians, but British made and supplied arms were also now beginning to arrive. Schools of Instruction in their use had been set up by the British Military Mission. On one range the Jugs—as their British tutors called them—were being trained in the use of the American 75 mm pack-howitzer, which my Commando friends had already put to good use in Albania.

It was the same story in the schools of radio, mine detection and other techniques of war, which till now these eager pupils had had little chance to learn—except the hard way. Their enthusiasm was deadly. In the School of Sabotage it was deadlier.

I went through the Field Hospital. More serious cases—of which there were already some ten thousand—had been evacuated by air to Egypt and Italy. But here on Vis, in a primitive operating theatre, a British surgical team was at work too.

From an office almost barren of furniture, except for a trestle table and a chair, the young English surgeon led me over to a rough shed.

"Eleventh bed down", he said. "This side".

I saw a girl with a head almost shaven of hair, uneasily asleep. She looked very young. At the same time, her very eye-lids were eloquent of the pain, sweat and anxiety of half a lifetime and more. As we watched, she woke. She tried to change her position. She could not. It was as if she lay paralysed. Then for a moment the eyes opened. Even at that distance, in that dim ward, I was aware of the black intensity of their gaze. She had an exotic, half-slav beauty. Mercifully her face was uninjured.

Her name was Neda. Her unit the 3rd Proletarian Brigade. She was one of many

Albanian partisan with British commandos

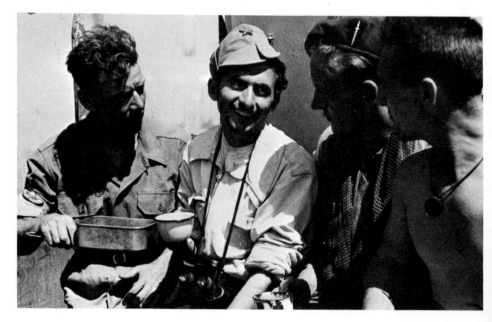

16 year old Jugoslav girl partisan

'Partizankas'—girl Partisans who were Tito's proof that the female could indeed be more deadly than the male. I was told that a boat had brought her over from the mainland, where it had taken her three weeks to reach the coast, crawling her way through the German lines. Her legs were full of shell splinters. My companion held out little hope of saving them from amputation. She was nineteen, and had already accounted for forty-one of the enemy.

There was just enough light in the rough and ready operating theatre for me to film the carrying to and fro of these Partisan wounded. It seemed to me then, and it seems to me now, that there could never be enough light shed on the sublime faith of these people in the future they were fighting and dying for.

Today those Jugoslav beaches are the playground of the international jet set. Casinos cater for the avarice of other people's affluence. Nightclubs stage the Mediterranean's most swinging strip shows. In 1944 Neda Mestrovitch lost a leg. Has she, I sometimes wonder, still kept her faith?

The Partisans often risked their lives to save American airmen. Crashed in the forests of Jugoslavia, after a raid on the Ploesti oil-fields or the marshalling yards of Moravska Ostrava, or some target deep within Hungary, they would be cared for and evacuated through the same undercover channels.

Sometimes, too, they were rescued by the Cetniks. These were the original resistance fighters under Mihailovitch, the man whom "the gale of the world blew away". Britain had sent her first Military Mission to Mihailovitch, but when it became apparent that the real impetus had ceased to come from him, and that the task of killing Germans had passed out of his inactive hands into those of his rival Tito, that Mission was recalled. The United States, however, continued to maintain contact with the Cetniks' H.Q. in Serbia, largely in order that their stranded airmen should be able to take advantage of Cetnik escape-routes.

But it was Tito's Partisans that were the real fighting force: and the girls, living and fighting as rough as any of the men, their girdles of chastity a belt of ammunition dangling with hand-grenades, had superhuman powers of endurance. But they could relax, as we soon discovered when, thinking it would make excellent film-material, we persuaded the Commanding Officer of the Battalion of Highland Light Infantry to give a concert and dance, inviting a Jugoslav unit. I had shot three thousand feet of grim splendour, and could do with a few hundred of light relief.

The setting was a drab and roofless building and at first everything was very formal. But the dry Dalmatian wine did its work well and it wasn't very long before a Scots sergeant was leading out the first girl-warrior—on to a rough stone floor at that—for a highland reel. There seemed to be a natural affinity between Scot and Jugoslav—as between their music, and their dancing. The Jugoslavs had a very similar reel of their own, the kolo.

Before I left Vis, I managed to take part in a raid on the mainland. Our objective was the German defences of Korcula.

We stepped off the landing-craft ramp at two o'clock in the morning, on to a stony and hostile shore. We had beached at a deserted fishing village. The little stone houses, gutted in the course of German reprisals, were eerie shapes of darkness against darkness. But before sunrise at six, we could clearly make out the outline of a hill overlooking the village. Here, there was an observation post. Our movements must have been noted, for German shells began to burst uncomfortably close. Our own early morning salvoes therefore failed to achieve quite the surprise we had intended, but for hour upon hour, our guns fired, loaded and reloaded, till the German battery was well aware that what had attacked them was British twenty-five pounders, supported by a screen of Jugoslav infantry. Nine hours after the landing, a tired body of men faced the thankless task of getting the guns back to the beach and re-embarkation.

The task continued through the blazing heat of noon, with German shells still bursting in our midst.

While I was filming the gunners splashing and falling into the water as they man-handled their begrimed artillery aboard, I slipped, and grabbed a gun-barrel for support. I very soon realised my mistake, and my hand came away as if struck by lightning. Hours of firing had made the guns too hot to touch.

We had lost very few of our own party. The Germans had deeper wounds to lick. For them, this was only a foretaste of things to come. The pace of the future was to be stepped up indeed. Preparations were by now under way for a landing in Greece, as well as another operation in Albania, and I had to get back to 'Land Forces Adriatic' in Bari, in order to co-ordinate the film and photographic coverage of this fast expanding Balkan war.

The success of the first Albanian raid, with its destruction of the German garrison at Spilje, had been further exploited; and a patrol of 40 Commando, already landed in southern Albania, with the object of disrupting the German lines of communication through the port of Sarande to their garrison on the island of Corfu, had discovered that across the border, Greek guerillas had cut the only other escape route from this important Greek island. 'Land Forces Adriatic' had decided to reinforce the original Commandos and capture Sarande, thus isolating and cutting off the enemy garrison on Corfu, which would have no alternative but to surrender.

Jugoslav partisan

Joined now by Denis Fox—seconded to us with his camera from the 8th Army stalemated in Tuscany—Johnson and I embarked with 'Hound Force'—as the substantial reinforcements of 2nd Special Service Brigade had been code-named—and the Commander of L.F.A., Brigadier-General G. M. O. Davy, who had led the 3rd and 7th Armoured Brigades in the desert fighting of 1941, and who had come to this new appointment after two years as Director of Military Operations, Middle East.

Jugoslav partisans sail from Vis to resume the fight on the mainland

In total darkness the landing craft crept into a little cove, held in secure readiness for our arrival by the original patrol and Albanian partisans. Unable to cover with our cameras the silent disembarkation moving up from the beach before daylight, we stretched out on the sand and went to sleep. At dawn we woke to German gunfire from Corfu, which was looming out of the sea in the half light behind us. The shells burst just short of our position. After a hurried breakfast we started to film and photograph the infantry and supplies still moving up from the beach, and, leaving Dave Johnson to concentrate further on this, Fox and I accompanied the Brigadier on what was for me another only too familiar back-breaking climb into the Albanian coastal hills. On the summit we were rewarded with a magnificent view of the country's wild and rugged interior, the Adriatic sparkling far below and behind us under a cloudless sky, while, in the distance, lay the port of Sarande, the objective.

On the heights of this magnificent vantage point we filmed the Brigadier and his Force Commander planning the attack. Then we turned our cameras on 'Hound Force' digging in and mounting its weapons for assault. With this duly recorded we made our way back to the beach. The first stage of the operation, the build up and preparations for battle, was now complete. Dave Johnson and I had to be back in Italy for the landing in Greece now scheduled to take place in less than seventy-two hours. We had therefore arranged to return on a landing-craft due later that evening; Denis Fox remaining behind to cover the assault on Sarande, and—we hoped—the ensuing capture of Corfu. Feeling very pleased with our day's labours we plunged into the sea, and in the ominous shadow of Corfu enjoyed a lazy swim followed by a very welcome hot meal. Fox then retired to bed in a deserted enemy gun emplacement, while Johnson and I settled down to await the arrival of the landing-craft.

We waited a long time.

It's overdue, said Johnson, at nine o'clock.

There was no sign of it whatever.

An hour later I awoke with gentle drops of rain falling on my face, and in a matter of minutes a tremendous thunderstorm was raging. Those of us still on the beach rushed for the only shelter, the Signals Office, established in a cave where we had previously stored our cameras and unexposed film. Outside the rain came down in torrents and suddenly, with a burst of thunder directly overhead, the roof collapsed. Momentarily stunned by a piece of falling rock, I joined Dave Johnson as, guided only by the lightning flashing through the wall of falling water, we groped our way to the refuge established earlier by Denis Fox in his pill box.

Soaked to the skin we now attempted once again to settle down, but the level of the water pouring in steadily rose, and when it had reached a height of six inches we were forced to climb on to baskets of carrier pigeons—all chirping away like mad. They had been landed earlier for some communicative role of their own. But the water still continued to rise, higher and higher, in our shelter only four feet from floor to ceiling, as relentlessly as at a climax of one of the silent film serials of the ever embattled Pearl White—and when it had reached a depth of more than two feet and the whole structure had started to creak and display signs of

Partisans relax after the Korcula raid

imminent collapse, we judged it time to beat yet another retreat—back outside into the deluge once more. There was by now literally nowhere else to take cover. All we could do was stand, miserable and helpless, as gallon after gallon fell on us for the next five hours, in what could only seem to us the greatest natural deluge since the Flood.

With the first thin glimmer of daylight the downpour slowly eased, revealing a very bedraggled scene of waterlogged Commandos attempting to review the extent of the night's havoc.

Shedding water at every step, Fox and Johnson collected some strips of wood from broken ammunition boxes. I acquired some temporarily unattended cans of gasoline. By the simple expedient of pouring four gallons of this most volatile fluid on to the sodden timber we got a fire going, our clothes moderately dry, and some tea boiled and inside us. Thus fortified we reviewed our position. The wrecked Signals Office was two feet deep in water, and from it I fished out our unexposed film and equipment. Opening my own camera I poured out from it a good half pint; Denis Fox had the same dismal experience. All our precious exposed films had been stored in my pack and left on the beach throughout the deluge—covered only by a groundsheet. To our amazed and delighted surprise we found it to be bone dry. Our efforts had not been in vain. We had defeated this counter-attack from the elements and our film and photographs of the Albanian landing were saved.

It was, of course, this same great storm that had kept our landing–craft away. A motor torpedo boat of the now co-belligerent Italian navy appeared in the bay at last, and we lost no time in scrambling abroad with Brigadier Davy and his staff. Through still mountainous seas we hurtled back to Italy. This final act of the drama was for me a crowning misery: never a good sailor at the best of times, I was soon very ill indeed as the powerful craft leapt from the top of one great wave to another, crashing its way across the Adriatic. Taking pity on my condition, the Captain offered me the comfort of his bunk on which to lie down, a courtesy which I promptly repaid by being sick on the floor. After what seemed an age, the crazy convulsions of the boat came to an end, and, tottering up on deck, I gazed at the so very welcome sight of Brindisi harbour. Meanwhile Dave Johnson, Denis Fox, the Brigadier and all his staff were once again soaked through to the skin, the open deck providing no shelter from the great seas which had broken over them during the crossing. As we wearily but thankfully clambered onto the quayside, a crowd of curious spectators began to gather, wondering from what maritime disaster this obviously shipwrecked group of survivors had been rescued, and what type of people had been voyaging in the greatest storm that the Adriatic had known for years.

Once more the waiting Harry Wicken rushed the exposed films to Rome, where, despite vicissitudes, they arrived and were processed. The still photographs were in the London newspapers the very day they were announcing the raid, and the film was in the newsreels later that same week. An achievement that brought us some acclaim from a War Office more often inclined to blame than praise.

At nine o'clock the next morning I was in the secret operations room of 'Land Forces Adriatic', an attentive listener to the final intelligence report and briefing on the landing about to be launched in Greece.

Conquerors on Borrowed Bicycles

Irregular war is far more intellectual than a bayonet charge.   T. E. Lawrence

The first British move into Greece in 1944 was a truly 'combined' operation—in the end it even took to bicycles. 'Operation Towanbucket' was led by George Jellicoe, whose father had fought the battle of Jutland twenty-eight years before. Major Jellicoe commanded a Force of the Special Boat Service, an offshoot of the Special Air Service and one more element in the order of battle of 'Land Forces Adriatic'. S.B.S. was composed of a number of rugged individualists trained in attack on Aégean islands from any and every sort of craft from a Greek fishing caique to an inflatable dinghy. This time, just for a change, they were to drop by parachute.

They were adaptable.

Dave Johnson and myself asked Jellicoe if we could drop with them. However, we were smilingly discouraged. The objective of Jellicoe's small force was to capture an airfield on the edge of the Peloponnesian peninsula of Western Greece. We were to land by sea with the R.A.F. Regiment. The airfield of Araxos thus secured would then provide a forward base for the fighters of the Balkan Air Force.

Such were the humble beginnings of the liberation of Greece.

We travelled in a small tank-landing craft into which we had somehow inserted not only ourselves and our equipment, but our jeep, and Harry Wicken too. For two days we wallowed our way through the rough waters of the Adriatic and the slightly calmer stretch of the Ionian Sea. To keep my thoughts above my stomach I read *Greenmantle;* involved in adventures as exciting and fantastic as any of John Buchan's flights of cloak-and-dagger fancy. Soon after Zanthe, Ulysses' island, our small convoy of landing craft reached the mainland. On the deserted beach of Katakolon I filmed the R.A.F. armoured cars as they came ashore.

The airfield of Araxos was already in the Paratroop's hands. We drove straight to it.

'The glory that was Greece', commented Johnson, as we passed through one more wretched village.

There was no sign or gesture of welcome. There was no sign of anything. Years of German occupation had left a pall of numb apathy. Glum, dazed, remote, these villagers seemed past all care, all interest in what was, after all, the spearhead of their liberation.

Once arrived at the captured airfield, the R.A.F. Regiment took up positions on its perimeter. And that was that. Mission accomplished. All we had to do now was stay put.

But such a passive situation, in a situation that offered exciting possibilities by the score, was not to the liking of Jellicoe and his airborne boatmen of the Special Boat Service. That evening he held a conference, and announced his intention of capturing Patras, the third largest town in Greece.

Patras was fifty miles off, to the east. It was known to be garrisoned by some 1500 Germans. We numbered fifty. We had nine open jeeps, a handful of armoured

Liberated Greece—Author centre, flanked by Dave Johnson and Harry Wicken in Patras

cars and our heaviest weapons were machine-guns.

Jellicoe, undeterred by statistics, split his laughably meagre forces into several groups whose members could almost have been counted on the fingers of one hand. He created the impression of an attack in mass from several different directions—and the age-old trick worked yet once again. The Germans suffered heavy casualties and withdrew—into the safety of the Zygos mountains on the other side of the Gulf of Patras.

After the dazed apathy I had seen in the villages I could scarcely believe my eyes when we entered Patras. I found myself filming fifty thousand inhabitants, mad with joy. We had to crawl through crowds of deliriously happy people, showering us with scent, fruit, flowers, rose petals and kisses. We were slapped on the back so many times that we could hardly stand. The Mayor, returning from the hills with the Partisans, made a ceremonial entry to the rolling of drums and the blare of trumpets. Where the swastika had been torn down, he hoisted once more the flag of Greece.

Established in a local hotel, vacated by the Germans only an hour or so before, we prepared to relax and enjoy this great Greek welcome. But I was speedily disillusioned by George Jellicoe, who announced his immediate intention of pushing a patrol on to Corinth, which the Germans were rumoured to be evacuating a hundred and fifty miles further east. And barely fifty miles on from Corinth was—Athens.

"Yes", said Jellicoe, "I am going to try and get there".

Athens was the objective for Operation Manna, a fittingly large-scale affair under the command of General Ronald Scobie. But with the Germans leaving the Peloponnese very much faster than anyone had thought, our own Operation Gatecrash, as it might well have been called, received official permission to go ahead.

We joined forces with the S.B.S. in this fighting patrol, lashing on to our jeep —one of a highly impressive force of four—as many cans of gasoline and ration cases as it would carry, to set off on the journey of a life-time. And in two days the whole twenty of us drove straight through to the outskirts of Corinth. All the bridges had been blown up by the departing Germans, and finding detours for them was a time-consuming business. But the only really serious obstacle in our way was the Greeks themselves, so fantastic was their welcome.

This time, carpets and cushions were laid out in the streets for us to drive over. The potent Greek wine, retsina, was forced down our throats. The villagers lay down in the road, forcing us to stop so that they could kiss and embrace us. We were a carnival procession. But at Xilokastron we found ourselves driving through the usual delirious crowd under something more grim than banners. A gallows rose overhead. From it swung no longer the body of a patriot, but a board on which the Greeks had written a crude but telling slogan.

At Corinth, which had been entered by the Resistance one day before our arrival, there was yet another ceremonial entry. The S.B.S. were joined by the Greek Partisans as they flocked back to the city from the hills—for yet another flower and rose petal carnival on a still grander scale. But tragedy lay in wait. The Germans had not evacuated without leaving mines behind them. A Swedish Red Cross truck

Xilokastron

was blown to pieces as it drove into the city.

No one had yet been up to the Corinth canal. Along the road to it we drove with more than our fair share of due care and attention. It stank of mines. Following our track the next day, two sappers from a newly arrived engineer unit were blasted into eternity. Where the bridge had been, the road broke off. We looked down two hundred and fifty feet. In the depths of the gorge lay a twisted mass of steel. For our further advance our tiny force had to be ferried across the Isthmus. Little was left of the highway on the other side. The demolition squads had been busy. But a secondary road, built quite recently by the Germans, still appeared to be intact. Going forward with caution, we reached Megara that evening. Only twenty-eight miles now lay between us and Athens; but a German rear-guard force was reported only five miles ahead.

'Why worry?' said Dave Johnson. 'We're a whole army now'.

He was referring to the massive reinforcements we had received: three R.A.F. Armoured cars, two six-pounder guns and one German 75 mm captured at Patras. Our strength was doubled.

From Megara onwards every corner held ugly possibilities of enemy ambush— and a fire-power vastly superior to our own. Then, round one of them, came the strangest and most incongruous sight I had yet seen in a war sometimes bloody, always bizarre. Even more incongruous than the Italian wedding procession that had walked into the German road block outside Rome four months before.

Mounted on a pony, and accompanied by a young Greek boy, it was an apparition and nothing less that rode towards us. We gazed upon an air of disdainful

Approaching Corinth

indifference, on a uniform of impeccable cut, impeccably pressed, and buttons and riding-boots that gleamed in the sun.

'Good afternoon', it said.

It was a British Liaison Officer.

And after that, I was ready to believe anything.

How this officer had got into, and out of Athens I never knew, but there he was, and he had come to tell us that thousands of Germans were still in the Greek capital. They were evacuating fast, but it would still be forty-eight hours before the last had gone.

At this Jellicoe decided to send a small patrol inland to watch the German withdrawal along the Elevsis road, while he himself made a lightning dash back to Patras. In view of the increasing difficulties of his lines of communication, and his vastly swollen responsibilities, his journey was highly necessary. The Major of ten days before, the conqueror of Araxos, was now a full Colonel with twenty thousand miles of liberated Greece to answer for. We sent our film back with him.

But before they finally left Athens, the Germans decided to test the strength of the force that kept harrying them so relentlessly. They sent a fifteen man patrol along the road to Megara. The S.B.S. captured it. The German reaction to this impertinence was to mount a full-scale counter-attack. Now advancing towards us was the rear-guard of nothing less than the entire German Army Group in the Balkans.

I was ordered down to the beach to report any signs of simultaneous German landings on the coast. Barely had I reported that there was nothing to worry about when the sky began to fill with four-engined bombers and transports. They were ours: the airborne fore-runners of the operation so fortuitously code-named Manna.

A ground-wind was blowing at thirty miles an hour—enough to call off any drop. But reinforcements had seldom been more urgently needed. The Squadron Commander rushed to the air-strip to fire a green smoke signal, letting the paratroops know that it was safely in our hands. And then the drop began—from five hundred feet.

Reaching the air-strip myself, breathless and almost too excited to use my camera, I was soon surrounded by chaos. The Paratroops' chutes had scarcely opened before they were being blown and dragged over the ground, without a chance of slipping their harness. I soon abandoned my camera. I had a more urgent task—to catch what few I could, turn them straight into the wind at the moment of impact and help them, often bleeding and injured, to their feet. The men were followed by sticks of supplies. These had a similarly rough passage.

Then came the first German shell.

There were not many paratroops who escaped injury: but the lucky ones took up position on the perimeter of the air-field. The rest of us, quickly joined by two S.B.S. men with a jeep and a handful of Greeks with some ancient trucks, drove round and round amidst the shell bursts collecting the ammunition and supply canisters dropped and scattered all over the area. One paratrooper was marooned in a tree with a broken leg. Dave Johnson brought him down. Like the men, the parachuted supplies had been blown all over the place. Harry Wicken and I fished the battalion radio set out of the sea. Then we went to the aid of a man who had suffered the same fate.

Chaos was at long last reduced to order, but the German counter-attack never

Megara

came. This aerial avalanche had evidently made the enemy think twice and when, next day, still more planes flew in with gliders behind them, they clearly thought a third time—and pulled out and away.

Jellicoe and the Squadron Commander entered Athens the following evening on borrowed bicycles. We followed using two modes of transport almost as unorthodox.

Leaving Harry Wicken to follow with the jeep as soon as the road was clear, we boarded a caique, with the now tired but jubilant 'L' Squadron of the S.B.S. that had blazed the trail all the way from Araxos, to land at an obscure fishing village eight miles north of the Greek capital. Welcomed by Partisans, and to the sound of small arms fire blazing away in celebration all around, we stumbled ashore in total darkness. In an old peasant's house we drank toast after toast to victory, while some of the Greeks slipped away to try and hunt down some form of transport to take us on into Athens.

Long before the retsina was finished, two very old and decrepit motor buses materialized. In these we set off on the last lap. The start was rough—straight across ploughed fields where the road had been blown, and with no lights either: we did not care to show any. Soon enough, however, we got into what seemed to be a main highway; we came upon a glimmer that stood for the Gulf of Aegina, and against it, a deeper, massed dark. Athens. Through streets that were silent, darkened and deserted, and up to the Grande Bretagne—the main hotel, and three long years before, British Headquarters.

It was close on midnight. The S.B.S. prepared to get what rest they could before one more tumultuous day began, and spread their sleeping bags on the floor of the candle-lit ball-room. I myself felt anything but tired, and welcomed the hotel manager's suggestion of a drink in the kitchen. He produced a bottle of magnificent pre-war Scotch.

'I have saved it for this day', he told me reverently.

In the midst of our private celebration, the hotel porter approached us, timidly.

'Excuse me, sir', he began, 'excuse me, please—but there are some people outside who ask to see you'.

'To see me?'

'Yes. Or anyone else British'.

A party of working people were outside the hotel, having walked all the five miles from the Piraeus on hearing a rumour that the British were back. Was it true, and if it was, could one go out to them? As no-one else was still awake, I did so.

Half a dozen poor and ragged people were standing in the darkness of the pavement outside. Striking matches, they held them up to my face, convincing themselves that I was Flesh, not Fantasy.

I was real.

To make quite sure, a hand touched my grimy and unshaven face.

Among the Greeks, however, the Germans had found some friends. There were still Greeks who looked upon the Germans as the lesser evil and the Communist-led guerillas as the greater. These formed the personnel of the so-called Security Battalions, and next day, as soon as it was light and long before any thought of any further celebrations, the S.B.S. had moved off to disarm one of them.

Celebrations were however the order of the day. The streets were soon packed with the same deliriously happy people we had seen in Patras—and indeed, in every other place where they were not too numbed, starved and blunted to care. Hanging on to the roof of our ancient bus, I filmed one more moment of history.

Outside the Piraeus we could see the great fleet that represented the second phase of Operation Manna. Aboard it was the 23rd Armoured Brigade from Egypt—and all the correspondents and photographers accredited to this liberation of Greece. They were thirsting to land and get to work. But the harbour was too heavily mined, and until its approaches had been swept, there they were, stuck outside.

Thanks to Jellicoe's unorthodox pugnacity, we had the scoop of a lifetime. The two of us had full and exclusive coverage of the liberation of Athens. But the arrival of a naval photographer landed from a seaplane reminded us that unless we got our negative away fast, we might yet be beaten at the post.

The S.B.S. had taken the buses over for themselves. We were marooned among wildly happy crowds far from the hotel. A motor-cyclist whose mount had a side-car came to our rescue. After a crazy journey we reached the square beside the Grande Bretagne—only to find ourselves still separated from its entrance by a crowd impenetrable in its joy. Before either of us realised what was happening, Johnson and I were lifted bodily from our transport and passed from hand to hand for a good two hundred yards, over the heads of a vast concourse, to be deposited breathless, but intact, at the hotel's very door.

My friend the manager produced for us a dilapidated Ford. It got us to the fishing village where we had landed from the caique. Another was just about to sail. We jumped on board. At last we made the air-strip at Megara and got the film on to a plane.

Three days later the Greek Government returned to the capital of the country from which it had been exiled for three and a half years. We filmed and photographed the Prime Minister, George Papandreou, as he drove through wildly cheering streets to hoist the blue and white pennant of Greece over the Acropolis once again. Then we surrendered ourselves to the delights of the greatest welcome British troops have ever known. For twelve days we languished, like Ulysses with Circe; while our friends of the S.B.S., not so fortunate, but more diligent, chased the Germans north. From Italy the 4th Indian Division set sail for Salonika where, in northern Greece, contact might conceivably have been made with the Russian army across the border in Bulgaria.

Having no desire to miss such a possibility we joined forces with the R.A.F. Film Unit and flew up with them in their own plane. We were the first to land on the deserted airfield at Salonika, which for all we knew at the time might have been mined. Making our way into the town we found a small British Naval detachment already established, the forerunner to the large landing that followed us in a few days' time. We filmed and photographed the Indian troops of this veteran 8th Army Division coming ashore, and were as ever delighted to see Harry Wicken at the wheel of the indefatigable jeep, driving up towards us from the landing craft in which he had sailed from the Piraeus.

An unpleasant air of decay hung over Salonika. The Germans had turned the occupation of this north eastern area of Greece over to the Bulgarians, who had long wished to incorporate it into their own domain. Towards their northern neighbours the Greeks entertained feelings of an abiding and contemptuous hatred, constantly enjoining us to drink with them a toast calling for "Death to the Bulgarians!"

On one of these convivial occasions we had been joined by a newly arrived major, immediately recognisable as a British Liaison Officer from the parachute wings on his jacket. He had spent the last eighteen months with the Resistance in eastern Macedonia. He was now established in Drama, a hundred miles to the north east, and close to the Bulgarian border. "There's nothing to stop you driving right across as far as Sofia if you want to," he said; "why don't you come and stay with us for a while?" Determined to see as much of Greece as we could, we had no objections to meeting up with the Russians if the chance presented itself. We accordingly drove north from Salonika, over the mountains dominating the Strydom plain, through Seres and across the melancholy landscape of Macedonia, long the cockpit of conflicting Balkan nationalism.

In Drama, enjoying the Mission's hospitality, discretion overcame enthusiasm. I reluctantly decided not to cross into Bulgaria. We were, after all, under the command of Allied Force Headquarters in Italy. We were attached to British troops. Such a move into a purely Russian area might have led to international complications of no mean order, even if we had got away with it. Greece was now completely free of the Germans. Winter was upon us. It rained unceasingly. The already ruined roads were a quagmire. I judged it time for our return to Athens.

Meanwhile Churchill had met with Stalin in Moscow. Our second day in Corinth they had sat together in a room in the Kremlin. "How would it be", Churchill asked his host, "for you to have ninety per cent predominance in Rumania, for us to have ninety per cent of the say in Greece, and go fifty-fifty about Jugoslavia?" Winston was now about to put this bargain to the test.

The drive to Corinth

At no point between Salonika and Athens did we meet a single British soldier. The British were still concentrated on the three principal cities. Effective administration throughout the country as a whole was almost entirely in the hands of Partisans. Following the example of the Jugoslavs such dominion had been established during the occupation wherever the communist-led resistance had been able to maintain control. During all the recent celebrations, loud had been the shouts for EAM, their National Liberation Front: the 'Ethnikon Apeleftherotikon Metopon'. By the middle of 1943 a complete EAM state had already been set up in the Pindus mountains of northern Greece. Seven months before the end of the German occupation, this had formed the basis of a provisional government, with Alexander Svolos, formerly Professor of Constitutional Law at the University of Athens, as its second president. Svolos had been leader of a delegation to a conference held in the Lebanon during the early summer of 1944, at which the Greek Government had been reorganized under Papandreou to include representatives of EAM. At that point a satisfactory merger of the de jure government with the de facto administration of the resistance had seemed possible. By the time we arrived back in Athens, we found matters had moved fast towards disaster.

The crucial issue was the position of the Greek King. After the king had fled to Cairo three and a half years before, representatives of virtually every political persuasion had declared that he should not attempt to return to Greece before a plebiscite had been held to decide whether or not the people wanted him back. Now, to increase the fears of a possible royalist coup d'etat, the Greek Brigade had just landed from Italy. These were the same Greek troops that I had first filmed with Montgomery in the Western Desert before Alamein. They flaunted the royal crown uncompromisingly on the crests of their caps. Their ranks had been purged of all but the most extreme royalists after a succession of mutinies eighteen months before. Their arrival in Athens was going to lead inevitably to a clash with the left wing republicans of the resistance.

Saddened and depressed by the collapse of all the high hopes of liberation, and the prospect of a civil war in which British troops might well be forced to take sides, I prepared to leave Greece, with no reluctance whatsoever. I was in pursuit of further operations planned by 'Land Forces Adriatic' elsewhere.

The German garrison on Crete was now so isolated it could be ignored. Plans were now far advanced for the most ambitious operation yet envisaged by the British troops in the Balkans. It was nothing less than a permanent landing in Jugoslavia below Trieste. From there the force was to drive forward in conjunction with the Jugoslav Army of National Liberation to the borders of Hungary. This would cut off the remainder of the German troops still in Jugoslavia. It would also open up another front on this flank of the British 8th Army, which was once again halted in Italy by the strong German defences of the Po valley.

Arrived back in Bari I found 'Land Forces Adriatic' concentrating every unit under its command. It was receiving tanks, heavy armour and reinforcements, having been placed on a higher priority than even the two main Allied armies in Italy. In his Chief of Staff's office, Colonel Macnamara explained to me the strategic background and tactical purpose of this 'Operation Fairfax.'

Churchill and the British Chiefs of Staff had consistently maintained that the

L Squadron on the last lap to Athens

L Squadron reach the Acropolis

strength of the Anglo-American position in the Mediterranean should be utilised for a drive through the Balkans into the heart of Europe. Just as tenaciously Roosevelt and his advisers had refused to divert a single soldier from the armies destined for France. From Italy Field-Marshal Alexander had been forced to yield seven of his original divisions to the landings in Normandy, four American and three British. After the fall of Rome, and much bitter argument—in which he was supported by the American generals under his command—he had lost another five on what he considered to be the "strategically useless" invasion of southern France. This had been demanded by Stalin at Teheran. The British had maintained that these troops would have been better employed in crossing the Adriatic. They could land on the Istrian peninsula, drive up through the Llubljana gap onto the plains of Hungary. Here such a threat to the upper Danube would force Hitler to withdraw substantial forces from western Europe. Not only would the allies achieve the same purpose as a landing in southern France but, by taking British and American troops to the gates of Vienna, they would improve the Allied strategic and political situation in central Europe. Despite the fact that Britain had nearly three times as many troops in Italy and the Mediterranean as the United States, the American leaders had turned a deaf ear to these arguments. Now, with a fraction of the resources considered necessary for such an operation a few months before, 'Land Forces Adriatic' looked as though they were going to make the attempt.

Infantry would be provided by the now well equipped and thoroughly proven Jugoslav Partisan Army. The port of Zadar would serve as a supply base. Specialised

British troops with artillery and tanks would back them up. They would be given constant air support by the fighters of the Balkan Air Force. Such smaller scale operations as the Peljesac landing and bombardment of Korcula had already proved that the combined British-Jugoslav operations of 'Land Forces Adriatic' could yield successful results. 'Fairfax' promised to be one of the great stories of the war. Its climax would be a meeting of British and Russian troops somewhere near the borders of Hungary.

During this last week of November 1944 I arranged for Harry Wicken and the faithful jeep to follow Dave Johnson and myself into Zadar on the first available landing craft. We were to accompany Macnamara on his initial reconnaisance of the area before the arrival of the main force. Meantime I resumed the co-ordination of the army's film and photographic coverage in Jugoslavia and Albania, which had been interrupted by my recent absorption in Greek affairs.

Returning to 'Hound Force' in Albania, and another landing further down the coast, Denis Fox had been wounded by an exploding mine and evacuated to Italy. Alan Wilson had carried on as best he could both still and film coverage. The capture of Sarande had led as anticipated to the surrender of Corfu. He had recorded similar scenes of welcome on this Greek island to those we were experiencing simultaneously on the mainland. None the worse for his fortunate escape, the redoubtable Fox had just been flown to Tirana, where he was recording the entry of the Partisans into the Albanian capital. Their leader Enver Hoxha, then emerging for the first time from the obscurity of the Resistance, was soon to come to be an isolated opponent of the Russian and Jugoslav desire for peaceful co-existence.

The Partisan's 'First Proletarian Division' had entered Belgrade a month before,

Athens—14th October 1944

Author top right—filming the liberation of Athens

after a week's savage fighting backed up by Russian armour, artillery and air support. After protracted negotiation with Brigadier Fitzroy Maclean's Mission to Tito, another Army Film Unit cameraman, Ken Rodwell, had been accepted in the Jugoslav capital. Based on Dubrovnik Alan Wilson, now joined by Geoffrey Loughlin, was attached to a force of British artillery sent across by 'Land Forces Adriatic' to assist further the Jugoslav Partisans in their encirclement of a strong German force on the Dalmatian coast. I planned to withdraw the whole of the latter team in order that they could join us on 'Operation Fairfax'.

Meanwhile, as a sombre and dispiriting background to the preparations for the major landing in Zadar, events in Athens moved inexorably forward towards catastrophe.

Since the Germans had left Greece it was maintained that the communist-led Partisans should be disarmed. To this their leaders agreed, on condition that the newly arrived Royalist Brigade also followed suit. Indecisive negotiations having failed to resolve the impasse, General Scobie ordered the resistance to disband its forces unconditionally, and EAM's reaction to this edict by the British General had been swift. Their Ministers promptly resigned from the Government and organized an immense demonstration in the centre of Athens for the following day. As thousands of people converged on Constitution Square—that same open space where Dave Johnson and I had been borne aloft in triumph seven weeks before—the police opened fire. They were the same police that had been the instrument of what passed for law and order under the German occupation. Seven demonstrators lay dead, just such a seven as had walked this same route one midnight to greet me on the steps of the hotel nearby. I had felt then a very unworthy representative of the country to which they had looked for deliverance.

Now thoroughly alarmed, Papandreou offered to resign as Prime Minister. Themistocles Sofoulis, the octogenarian leader of the Liberal Party, prepared to form a government in which EAM would agree to serve. Churchill thereupon intervened directly. He ordered General Scobie "to act as if you were in a conquered city where a local rebellion is in progress". Through the British Ambassador, he instructed Papandreou to remain. Civil war was now inevitable. Attacks on police stations shifted towards the main government buildings. British soldiers posted to guard them with the hated police were soon firing on the Greek guerillas hoping to occupy these centres of civic power. Within a week, supported by the R.A.F., all General Scobie's troops were engaged in bitter fighting. The ultimate purpose of 'Operation Manna' had been put into effect.

In London's Claridges Hotel King George of the Hellenes awaited the outcome. In Bari I followed the debacle in despair. A depression which was as nothing to the effect which this development had upon 'Fairfax'. It killed that operation stone dead. Tito would now have none of it, and no British soldier on his soil.

This was the moment of my loss of innocence. Starry-eyed I had gone forth into battle: the camera I held in my hand the instrument with which I would help in the making of a better world. I believed that our side was right, theirs wrong. Our cause good, theirs evil. The war had conveniently divided the world into these two extremes of black and white. The heroes of those silent Russian films, which had so persuaded me that they were the heirs to the future, wore red stars in their caps. So had the Partisans—our allies—whom I had been so recently and happily filming. But now my side was shooting them down. There were no longer to be any absolutes in my world.

Six months after this start of the Cold War in Athens, the Big War ended in Europe. Everyone's thoughts turned to home. For some of the 8th Army it was now four years or more since they had last seen their families in Britain. Transport and shipping were being rapidly re-allocated for the intensification of the other war against Japan, still at its height on the other side of the world. Always a law

The British bring Prime Minister Papandreou back to Greece October 1944

unto itself, the 8th Army came up with a leave plan all its own. Collecting together a fleet of heavy supply trucks, it established a chain of camps across Europe and proposed to drive itself home by instalments. The first of these leave convoys to drive overland from Austria to Calais was a story not to be missed. Great was the speculation as to who would be the lucky team selected to film its progress. Most of the original group with whom I had first sailed to the Middle East in 1941 had returned to England for the Normandy landings. I was now a veteran with the longest overseas service in the whole unit. There was therefore no ill feeling when I was presented with this final movement order—and the reminder that Calais was as far as I could legitimately go.

Lots were drawn for the few who were to go on this first convoy. With Geoffrey Loughlin handling still photography, I centred my story on two Alamein veterans of the Rifle Brigade. Harry Wicken put his foot down on the jeep's long suffering accelerator, and we were off on our longest, last, and happiest wartime journey together.

For five days we filmed our way through the heart of a ruined continent. Our nights were made merry by the competitive hospitality of the different rest camps. Through the Brenner Pass we came into Germany. We passed the beer cellar in Munich where Hitler's early ravings had first inflamed the German sickness. We passed Dachau, the shrine of Nazi infamy. We passed along the autobahn, feverishly converted in the final days of fighting to improvised and secret air-strips. We passed revolutionary fighter planes hidden from the air in clearings all along the edge of the forest—burnt out shells on the wings indicating where had been mounted the jet engines which German ingenuity had been allowed to develop too late. We crossed the Danube. We passed Mannheim and over the Rhine; into Luxembourg and the tree-lined avenues of northern France. The sign posts began to recall the ghosts of our fathers' battles, Mons, Cambrai, Arras. There was a great celebration in the rest camp at Calais. The generosity of his nature persuaded the 8th Army Colonel in charge to give me ten day leave passes in England for all three of us. We crossed the English Channel, and, with our two riflemen, got into the train at Shorncliffe. Over a final river, the Thames, and into Charing Cross.

Older, and perhaps wiser by four years of wartime wandering and experience, I was home.

But not for long. My war was still not over. David Macdonald talked me into joining the Army Film Unit in South East Asia. At that time I faced the not unattractive prospect of returning to Austria for the final year of military service which still lay before me. Freshly returned from the completion of *Burma Victory*, he poured scorn on such a prospect, and enthused over the exciting possibilities that were about to open up in the continuing war against Japan. After four years of intensive overseas service I required some convincing, but in the face of his enthusiasm, amply fortified by the conviviality of the bar at Pinewood Studios, which had served as the headquarters of the Army, the R.A.F., and the Crown Film Units, I gave way. The immediate result was a further month in England. In the last week of this the first atomic bomb burst over Hiroshima.

What a send off that was! The Japanese surrender was announced my last day in England. I barely made the plane for India the following morning, but by the time I finally reached Headquarters South East Asia Command those heady fumes had subsided somewhat. In Siam I filmed the survivors of the "River Kwai's" death railway coming out of their jungle prison camps; in Saigon the first exchange of fire with which the local inhabitants greeted the returning French; in Singapore a visiting Indian fresh out of gaol: Nehru, riding in state beside the Supreme Commander, Lord Louis Mountbatten – a partnership and a portent of which I was to see and film a great deal more.

The Russians At Home –
What There Was Left of it

The territory on which one day our German peasants will be able to bring forth and nourish their sturdy sons will justify the blood of the sons of the peasants that has to be shed today.
Adolf Hitler

With the Film Unit disbanded in England, and my allotted spell of overseas service more than fulfilled, I found myself at the beginning of 1946 awaiting my discharge from the army in one of England's oldest film studios at Elstree. Requisitioned as an ordnance depot it provided the storehouse for all the army's now idle cameras. I had taken over responsibility for their care and disposal, counting every day that passed of the four months which remained of my military career as impatiently as any schoolboy longing for the end of term. Soon after my arrival I was called one evening to the telephone, to find David Macdonald on the other end of the line, telling me of a job that he thought to be right up my street. UNRRA were looking for someone to take over the filming of all their relief and rehabilitation operations in Europe. He gave me the name of an Information Officer to contact in the agency's London office and wished me the best of luck.

Very early the next morning I went to these offices in Portland Place opposite the B.B.C. I had in fact already been active with a camera throughout many of the territories in which the agency was now working—including a return to Jugoslavia just before the end of the war, when I had filmed the beginnings of UNRRA aid to the ravaged province of Dalmatia. I travelled back to Elstree, a happy man, convinced that it was but a matter of days before the War Office would be asked to release me for this appointment with UNRRA. However absolutely nothing further developed whatsoever.

Two months later, after I had all but forgotten about the original interview, UNRRA suddenly burst into life and could not get hold of me fast enough. Back once more in the London offices I filled up forms and discreetly discovered the reason for the mysterious delay. They had been told that a cameraman from the army could not possibly be of any use to them, as he would only have been a sergeant working under the direction of an officer, without a camera of his own. No one had taken the trouble to verify the account that I had given of my background and experience. I had walked in on the personal recommendation of David Macdonald, wearing the uniform of a Captain in the Army Film Unit, personally responsible for all the army's cameras. Washington had been informed that they had failed to find anyone suitable. My application for the appointment had fortunately been noted by a member of the staff whom I had met in Split the year before. Instructions had been issued that I was to be engaged immediately: it was now remembered that my relief film in Jugoslavia was "one of the best UNRRA films yet made."

In one sense the report that no army camera, let alone cameraman, would be of any use to UNRRA's purposes was not altogether untrue. In order to overcome the shortage of satisfactory cameras that had first plagued us in the Middle East, a British camera had at last been designed and built especially for the army, incorporating advice from the air force and suggestions from the navy. The resulting photographic compromise had first gone into action during the landings in France, being appropriately known as the 'Normandy'. Nearly fifty of these unwanted pieces of apparatus, with their many shortcomings, comprised the bulk of the equipment for which I was responsible at Elstree. I had however discovered one isolated and magnificent portable American camera to which attachments had been designed and fitted, rendering it the equal of any studio model. This was the property of Britain's leading cameraman, Freddie Young. He assured me that he no longer had any use for the camera—which he had loaned to the army for the production of training films—and certainly he needed something far more elaborate when he shot *Lawrence of Arabia* fifteen years later. I rapidly routed the necessary pieces of paper through the correct military channels and it became the property of UNRRA.

I myself was sworn in as an international civil servant.

UNRRA—the United Nations' Relief and Rehabilitation Administration—had begun as little more than a gesture of faith in an Allied victory. On 9th November 1943 it was inaugurated at the White House. The United States and the British Commonwealth determined to come to the aid of less fortunate allies the moment they were free of German occupation. From an ill-omened start in Greece (where it was ordered out by a Britain sacrificing humanitarian principles to political expediency) it had now grown to mighty proportions and operated all over war-torn Europe.

Considerable criticism had been voiced in America that the people of the United States should be asked to donate money for the building of such a communist country as Tito was busily forging so aggressively in Jugoslavia. There, to make matters even worse, its spendings were the prerogative of a Russian, from whom American citizens were expected to take orders. Many attempts had been made to discredit UNRRA, particularly in the case of this Jugoslav mission, and allegations had been made that the distribution of relief had been denied on political grounds, and that clothing and transport had gone to the army. A three-man fact-finding team headed by a former adviser to the Government of Virginia, accompanied by a senior British army officer and a member of the French Department of Justice were to travel throughout Jugoslavia investigating these charges, only to find them totally groundless. Nevertheless the climate of opinion had moved away from acceptance of a situation in which Americans could serve happily under a Russian while assisting a third country, and from now on the possibility of another, even more destructive world war was never to be far from man's mind.

Like the League of Nations before it, UNRRA was given its death sentence in Geneva. There I listened to an only slightly premature post-morten on the first really effective international organization that the world has ever known. Then in its third and last year, delegates from forty-four member governments had gathered to evaluate its achievement. No less than three hundred thousand million dollars worth of aid had been allocated and distributed to fifteen countries. Seventy per cent of this enormous bounty had been provided by the United States; six hundred million dollars had come from Britain; and Canada, with one hundred and thirty million, was the third of the major contributing nations.

Tyler Wood spoke UNRRA's obsequies on behalf of the United States. Kenneth

Younger duly echoed them on behalf of Britain. But we were in business for a little while yet, and the head of UNRRA's Film Division, Bill Wells, was determined to make the most of the opportunities which still remained for the production of worthwhile films. First and foremost amongst these was the existence of UNRRA in two Soviet Republics. The Russians themselves were members of UNRRA—and the recipients of no less than two hundred and fifty million dollars worth of aid. At Geneva we met the American chiefs of the two Russian missions, both of whom agreed that it would be a wonderful idea for me to go in and film their work in Byelorussia and the Ukraine. They promised to do all in their power to get me and my camera into the Soviet Union.

I was not optimistic, or even by now all that enthusiastic. The letters U.N.R.R.A. now spelt no more than another lost opportunity; the letters U.S.S.R. had ceased

Young Port-Worker covered in U N R R A flour, Yugoslavia 1945

to represent the Promised Land. How wrong I was—so far as my own career was concerned. I went off to Poland, to film the return home of the Poles who, during the war, had been forced into slave labour in Germany; and, in Warsaw, two months later, visas for both Byelorussia and the Ukraine were stamped in my passport. My companion now was the veteran globe-trotter Julien Bryan, of New York's International Film Foundation. He was acquiring material for lecture tours based on 16 mm colour film.

We made the journey by air in a Soviet-built C-47 which the Russian pilot flew like a fighter, navigating by the few land-marks he could make out in an unending and almost featureless expanse of snow. We landed uneventfully at Minsk, though what there was to show we had got there it would have been hard to say. Andrew Steiger, Reports Officer to the UNRRA mission to Byelorussia, had come to meet us.

Inside the warm frontier-style log hut, Byelorussian customs officials waved us on, casting but the most perfunctory eyes over my camera and film, and feet squeaking on frozen Russian soil, we climbed into Steiger's heated automobile.

On the way we passed a few scattered log huts, half buried in the frozen snow. With some diffidence I asked when we would get to Minsk.

'We're going through it now', explained Steiger. 'There isn't a lot to see'.

For the fact was that Minsk had been to all intents and purposes totally destroyed.

The Russians had provided the UNRRA Mission with a house some four miles out in the country. Driving along we passed from time to time these log huts, amongst which figures moved slowly, their heavy clothing making them almost as anonymous as the rare buildings themselves, virtually hidden by the drifts of deep snow into which all life seemed to be crouching.

The UNRRA billet was a long, lonely wooden house and after Steiger had shown us into the end bedroom which he was already sharing with another member of the Mission at present in Moscow, we met the remainder of the group at dinner. It was an ample meal served by two plump and smiling Russian cooks in the dining-room next door, where a great stone stove the height of the intervening wall fought the sub-zero temperature outside.

With one exception, the Mission was wholly American. Its Chief, Robert Frase, had been formerly in government service, as had his executive officer, Theodore Waller. Both men had been in Minsk since the commencement of UNRRA's activities in Byelorussia seven months before. In charge of the Supply Department was Davis McEntire, with a similar background of civil service. Only Steiger had any previous experience of the Soviet Union, where he had lived before the war, teaching English and acting as a newspaper correspondent. Responsible for the Mission's administration was a New Zealander, who had served throughout the North African and Italian campaigns in the 8th Army. Handling the Mission's

Minsk

UNRRA feeds Russia 1946

reports and correspondence, two American girls served as secretaries.

The billet was the office, and the office was the billet. In that vast white nowhere, still marked on the map as a city, we lived cheek by jowl, we ate every meal together, we slept within a few feet of one another. We were a very closed and withdrawn circle in an alien wilderness of snow. In this claustrophobia there were neurotic undertones. The wife of a mission member had recently died and was buried in a Russian cemetery nearby.

The next day we were driven to the offices of the UNRRA Supplies Administration, the organization set up by the Byelorussian Council of Ministers to coordinate and handle the relief programme. Chief of the Administration was Ivan Semenonovitch Bylinsky, a pre-war chairman of the Byelorussian Council of Ministers and a delegate to the Supreme Soviet. His deputy was a former government official who had served during the war as a Red Army supply officer, Konstantin Lavrantievitch Lastovsky.

Lastovsky's office was on the fifth floor of a ramshackle building, the only solid structure of such a height and substance in the street on which it still precariously stood. Breathless from the first of many weary climbs up all those stairs, and with Andy Steiger acting as interpreter, I outlined my hopes and plans to put Russia on the screen.

'So you want permits for filming?' said Lastovsky. 'UNRRA supplies?'

I explained the position as I saw it. To film the supplies we should have to go into warehouses, stores, shops, homes, hospitals.

'That should be all right. We can provide you with lamps and electricians for such interiors from the Newsreel Studio'.

We were very pleased at this. We suggested that a Russian cameraman should come along with us. He would understand our problems, and explain them to all concerned.

'Certainly', said the Deputy Chief. 'And I will come along with you myself'.

I liked Lastovsky. He had a sense of humour. It was only later that I discovered that he had lost both wife and daughter in the war.

Alas, he was also blessed with a bureaucrat's due sense of all-in-good-time. Before I was allowed to start filming, I spent days cooped up in the UNRRA billet reading Osbert Sitwell's autobiography. This I had bought in Warsaw. Here certainly was escapism if one wanted escape. In my enforced isolation and inactivity this glittering chronicle of Edwardian eccentricity threatened to become more real than the life beyond the windows out there in the snow.

At last permission came. I was allowed to film the interior of the UNRRA warehouse.

This did not seem munificent, but there was worse to come. The weather had been glum and grey. Now came an unexpected break. It made me change my plans. This was evidently unthinkable.

'The sun's come out', I told Lastovsky. 'Can you delay my permit to film the warehouse?'

'Why?' he inquired, honestly puzzled.

'It's a perfect day for exterior filming, and once the sun's gone in again, there may not be many more for a long while. I can take interiors, with the necessary lighting, in any weather'.

'But what difference is there between exterior and interior photography?'

'Well, exterior photography . . . .'

And so it went on.

But when Lastovsky had seen my point, he agreed. He was a good-natured character. In my excitement at the possibilities offered by this unhoped for spell of sunlight, I had rushed into Minsk hatless.

'You should never do that', he warned me, proceeding to measure my head with his own hands, so that he could have a fur hat made for me.

Byelorussia provided a background of sparkling white desolation for my camera. Destruction on a similar scale stretched four hundred miles, from Minsk to Moscow. Here was the greatest devastation of Hitler's war.

On the outskirts of Minsk some new buildings were rising. They were office blocks. I could not see why I was forbidden to film them. I soon found out from Waller. More than a million German prisoners had been taken by the Russians in the war—yet Moscow continued to make no pronouncement on their fate whatever. The U.S.S.R. refused to acknowledge their presence—here were a few of them, laying bricks.

The sunny break continued and if anything it got colder. My clockwork-driven camera started to seize up before the end of every roll of film. Next day was a Sunday. The warehouse would be closed. I asked Lastovsky if I could film a service in the only place of Christian worship left in Minsk—a little wooden church, once more on the outskirts. In the city itself everything had gone.

Lastovsky agreed to this at once. I joined a congregation that consisted mainly of the old. Sometimes the lined and care-worn faces were scarcely distinguishable from those of the ikons that they worshipped. The intensity of their prayers and their prostrations was the sole source of warmth for these aged worshippers. The church was as cold as the grave.

A newer ikon, and a bigger one, adorned the walls of 'Grocery Store Number 35'.

This was the inevitable picture of Stalin, gazing benevolently down.

A store-keeper unpacking crates of butter, lard, biscuits, canned meat and cheese sounds a prosaic sight compared with a service of the Russian Orthodox Church. In these circumstances, it had more magic. Food was unbelievably scarce. The dark rye bread was strictly rationed and side by side with it, champagne—Russian champagne.

'Here', said Lastovsky suddenly. 'Film this'.

A bottle was actually being bought. I knew that its sale had been pre-arranged, for my companion added, 'This will show the high standard of life enjoyed by the people of the Soviet Union'.

The standard of life enjoyed by the people of the Soviet Union was something that seemed to haunt all Russians in contact with foreigners. It was the factor behind nearly all the vetoes. Later on, one more break in the grey clouds had set

Meeting in Minsk December 1946—Steiger, Waller, Bylinsky

me filming exteriors again. I had already made many interior sequences. I had filmed the food warehouse, 'Grocery Store Number 35', the clothing *artel* where UNRRA supplied the heavy, warm cloth, and the boot factory which owed its leather to UNRRA. Now I wanted the outside shots of these locations.

Patient, cheerful, at times even wryly humorous, Lastovsky went the rounds with me. At last we had everything but the 'Krasny Obuvnik'. This was the boot factory. Sounds of hammering rang out busily from inside. The building itself was no more than a wooden barn.

I lifted up my camera, switched to the right lens, brought it back to my eye once again—and received a tap on the shoulder. An indignant Lastovsky was at my elbow. He ordered me to stop. I asked him why. He replied that such a decrepit building reflected no credit on the *artel* at work inside, and that as it was in any case only temporary and they would soon be housed in a brand new building, there was no point in my filming it anyway. My answer was that we could not show the shoemakers at work in a vacuum as it were, without showing the surroundings and circumstances in which they had to do so. And that in any case, the fact that they were working away in such primitive and difficult conditions was in itself an effective illustration of the Russian people's determination to survive, whatever the obstacles. No, no pictures. The hell with it I thought, this really is unreasonable. I stepped to one side, lifted up my camera, and shot off twenty feet of film. Whereupon Lastovsky leapt into his car and shot off in a towering rage.

He bore me no ill-will over this incident which I thought afterwards might well wreck my chances of completing the film, but his attitude to the cinema was just as maddening. No-one went to the movies he assured me. It just wasn't cultured. I had no Russian money. I couldn't just buy a ticket and see a film. Beyond officially organized visits to the local opera—*Carmen* in the restored Red Army theatre—all I could do was go back to the billet and delve into the faraway world of Osbert Sitwell's youth.

I found the atmosphere in the mission at Minsk more than somewhat claustro-phobic. There was no escape. In the evenings we would all meet around the dinner table, to separate afterwards more often than not into mutually exclusive corners. Although living and sleeping but a few feet apart, two of our number had taken to writing long letters to each other.

However the filming proceeded apace. As soon as the first three thousand feet was ready it was taken to Moscow en route for London, where it would be developed under the control and auspices of UNRRA'S European Regional Office, to whom I was myself responsible, before shipment to Washington.

I continued to record the range and progress of UNRRA's activities in Byelo-russia. With no less than twelve million Russians killed in the war, the care of their surviving children had become one of the state's most urgent and pathetic legacies. More than 30,000 such Byelorussian orphans depended upon UNRRA for three quarters of the food prepared for them by the social workers substituting for the parents that had perished. An American child welfare organization had made a gift of half a million dollars, instructing UNRRA's Director-General Fiorello La Guardia to spend it as he saw fit in the alleviation of children's suffering in any of the countries receiving aid. During a brief visit to Minsk he had been so moved and impressed by 'Detski Dom No. 8', one of the 265 orphanages built as a matter of the highest priority from salvaged bricks, that he had decided to devote the greater part of this money to the care and welfare of its children.

The orphanage had been opened by its director, Vera Borisovna Botchersky, four months after the Germans had been driven from Minsk, and its one hundred and thirty little boys and girls between the ages of four and nine ate their main meal of the day at three o'clock in the afternoon: in which the only source of sugar was UNRRA jams, marmalade and surplus army rations.

With her hair tied in an outsize ribbon an eight year old shyly laid the tables in front of my camera, which was soon recording the hearty appetites of as healthy and happy a collection of children as anyone could have wished to see. Playtime and storytelling for the youngest followed, under the ubiquitously benevolent portrait of Stalin, beaming down upon the beloved teddy bears and dolls clutched to excitedly beating hearts; reminding one that of his oft-quoted sayings a favourite was that a country's greatest capital was its children.

That this dictum was fully appreciated in the Soviet Union there was no doubt whatsoever, the resident woman doctor in the orphanage constantly guarding the health of the rescued children in her care. One had been found as a baby, the only sign of life in a pile of three hundred bodies discovered in a liberated village three days after the massacre of its inhabitants. Laughing into the lens of my camera he was now the very picture of a healthy and happy little boy.

Music and dance were never far from the children's world, eager as they were to entertain themselves with concerts and pantomimes on the public holidays which seemed to fall at least once a month; and, with one such occasion falling due in a few days' time, we were able to film its dress rehearsal.

Running into the circle of light cast by our lamps, a tiny tot barely had time to announce the concert's commencement before fleeing bashfully from such un-accustomed notoriety; to be followed by a group of girls in Byelorussian national costume performing a harvest dance, their feet clad in long leather boots from the 'Krasny Obuvnik' beating out its rhythm. Enter four little girls dressed as kittens, singing and miming a nursery song, an item greatly appreciated by the youthful audience, whose excitement reached its heights as curtains were hung across the room to denote the start of the evening's highlight—a pantomime fairy story. Drawing them briefly apart one of the older girls appeared, describing the play that was about to be staged: a tale of a poor cook who, inadvertently spoiling the king's dinner, was driven from the palace in disgrace. At their next meal the hard and wicked king, his queen and all their courtiers were punished by the little cook's fairy godmother, who caused the noses of the assembled court to grow to extra-ordinary lengths as they ate the meal cooked by the banished hero's successor. With tremendous enthusiasm and no little talent, the children acted out this fable, rapidly turning their backs on the audience to don grotesquely long false noses at its climax, cheered by the wild applause that followed.

It was a more than usually happy group of children who went to bed that night in 'Detski Dom No. 8'; tucked up in UNRRA blankets to dream of wrongs righted and the wicked vanquished.

Every morning the older children walked from the orphanage with a teacher through the ruins of Minsk to another of the city's rare new buildings, School No. 23. The restoration and construction of new individual homes and housing projects was unquestionably accepted as being of lesser urgency than the provision of such essential amenities for the children—in whom the state set all its hopes for the future. As the line of orphans threaded its way across the snow, to be joined by other groups of children similarly muffled up against the piercing cold, my camera moved to include the words of a great banner stretched across the front of the new school building:

LONG LIVE STALIN, THE FRIEND OF SOVIET YOUTH.

It was a girls' school—co-education being at that time in no way a feature of the Soviet system. I filmed five different classes and age-groups. I started with five-year-olds learning their multiplication tables with the aid of an abacus—in Russia still an almost universal aid. I concluded with adults of eighteen studying the mysteries of trigonometry from intricate diagrams drawn on the blackboard. The thirteen-year-olds were instructed in what the syllabus described as 'Darwinism'— the creation of life and biological evolution illustrated by the skeletons of birds and animals. God was out. In their language classes, they studied the one foreign tongue obligatory throughout the entire Soviet Union, English.

The anniversary of the promulgation of the Soviet Constitution which had guaranteed citizens "the right to education . . ." was a public holiday. In the morning I took my camera to the frozen river behind the UNRRA house. Here schoolboys were skating, and some were fishing. They lay, flat over a hole they had hacked in the ice, with a pointed stick in their hands, in wait for any passing fish.

I enjoyed long and informal conversations with Semeon Dorsky, our bespectacled young interpreter who, in his final year of language study, had taught himself to understand English by listening to the B.B.C.

Dorsky was a key figure in a sequence that I filmed two days later, a routine conference between the UNRRA mission and the Supplies Administration of the Byelorussian Government. Acting as the interpreter of the needs and requirements expressed by Bylinsky and Lastovsky, Dorsky translated the replies while my camera recorded one of these periodically unique Soviet-American exchanges. This particular one on the evening of December 7th 1946 was largely taken up by the continually pressing problem of Byelorussia's shortage of fats.

The meeting was held in the 'Dom Pravitelstva', the House of Government, a magnificent and many storied modern building constructed in 1930. It was one of the earliest and most impressive architectural achievements of the famous first Five Year Plan that was to provide the basis for Russia's leap into the twentieth century and beyond. Its three great monolithic tiers soared high above an open courtyard dominated by a more than lifesize statue of Lenin, gazing sternly out into distant horizons and future achievements amidst the contemporary ruins.

Used as headquarters for their occupation of Byelorussia, the Germans had planted more than a hundred tons of explosives in its basement when they were forced to evacuate Minsk three years later; but advanced Russian patrols had managed to seize the building before the mines could be set off. The 'Dom Pravitelstva', together with the Red Army theatre, was thus one of the few large buildings still standing in Minsk at the end of the war. The Byelorussian Academy of Sciences served as a background of ruins for the scenes of children sliding and skating on its frozen approaches that I filmed at the beginning of the fourth week.

I found that the medical services of Byelorussia were appallingly handicapped. Ninety per cent of all hospitals, clinics and sanatoria had been destroyed— roughly the same proportion as with the schools. Members of the UNRRA Mission had been to hospitals where, for every thirty patients, the daily ration of food was no more than thirteen ounces of dried milk. They had been in maternity wards where soap had been unavailable for weeks.

We arranged to film the spacious and newly equipped operating theatre of Minsk hospital. We watched an operation for goitre performed by Professor Korchits. The Professor was a man of seventy-six. Less than two years previously he had been performing more than twenty operations each day in the service of the Red Army. One of the pioneers in Russian heart surgery, he had also made an extensive study of goitre in those wild regions of the Soviet Union where it is most prevalent: the Causasus and Kokand in Central Asia.

All the linen in the operating theatre and most of the blankets in the wards had been donated by UNRRA and the Red Cross. More than half the supplies of drugs and medicine came from the same sources. UNRRA not only supplied penicillin;

the organisation was providing two entire plants for its manufacture. Teams of medical engineers had been sent from Byelorussia and the Ukraine to Canada to master their assembly and operation. There was a great deal of tuberculosis. In one ward, as the result of years of privation and undernourishment, the patients were so weak that they were unable to stand either the lighting necessary for filming them or the strain of being photographed.

Arrangements were in hand for my move on to Kiev and the Ukraine. But before we finally left there remained one other sequence, the filming of which I believed to be essential to an understanding of what the German occupation had meant to the Byelorussian people. On the outskirts of Minsk, Lastovsky had led me to the edge of a great excavation, at the bottom of which a simple stone monument

The 'Red Partisan' Collective Farm

supported an inscription, carved in both Russian and Yiddish: "In Sacred Memory for Eternal Time to Five Thousand Jews who perished at the hands of Fascist-German enemies of mankind, March 2nd, 1942".

Now, with four survivors accompanying me into the bottom of the hell hole that had previously served as the city garbage dump, I filmed them as they stood before the memorial, silent witnesses to memories that defied the imagination. Afterwards Steiger translated for me the account of the massacre given to him by the eldest, seventy-two year old Andrei Antonovitch Samotya; and, in the old man's own words, this is the tale he told—

"The entire area for blocks around had been converted for some time past by the German occupation forces into a Ghetto, surrounded by barbed-wire. At eight o'clock in the morning with the Ghetto surrounded by Lithuanian and Byelorussian traitors, the Gestapo entered the Ghetto area, their swastika emblems displayed prominently on their coats. They entered one house after the other, smashing windows, doors, hurling furniture out into the street, and driving the people out before them. Women, children, old men, all were driven out together. If an old man was too weak to walk, he was bayoneted in the street and left to lie there. Others were killed likewise on the spot for resistance. Some Jews were ordered to pick up the corpses of the dead and carry them along the edge of the gully. People were lined up on the edge of the gully, and machine-gunners with the tommy-gun type of weapon, with a cylinder type of cartridge holder, trained their weapons on the people, who were shot down, falling into the gully. This kind of slaughter continued for some time. The gully became full of corpses, and some of the people who were shot and not killed were buried under the remainder. An occasional person would rise up through the dead bodies and covered with blood attempt to crawl up from the carnage. The movement of the dead and dying was like a molten mass, undulating like waves. The gully filled with blood. It was cold. The whole mass froze. To clear the gully for more victims, the Gestapo planted charges of dynamite and set them off, blowing the whole mass high into the air. More were brought up, this time of Jews killed outright. At times, some Jews were cast alive into the nearby stream of water, frozen to death, and then hurled into the gully. As many as ten or twelve corpses were tied together head to feet, and the whole long line of dead bodies pulled up to the gully by the feet of the foremost.

Kiev

Christmas Day in the Ukraine

This kind of slaughter continued for two days".

Samotya, his grand-daughters, and three thousand others owed their lives to a thirteen year old girl, who "managed to get unnoticed by the guards at night through the barbed-wire enclosure. She then went about to cellars and other hiding places where there still were some Jews living. These of us she led to safety through the barbed-wire out to the partisans in the forest".

Of the hundred thousand Jews who had lived in Minsk before the war, only 16,000 now remained; many of whom owed their survival to refuge with the partisan bands that controlled much of Byelorussia throughout the German occupation. Every second person that we met in Minsk had been in fact a former partisan: the saleswomen in the foodshop, the nurses in the hospital, the teachers in the school and orphanage all wore the enamel Partisan Medal alongside a second commemorating victory; and this great resistance story was the subject of the only film that I was ever able to see in Minsk, the feature length documentary record of this two and a half year partisan struggle behind the German lines.

Two further days of fortuitously fine weather saw the successful completion of our filming in Minsk.

We gave a farewell dinner at the Mission to all the Russians who had helped to make the filming the success that it undoubtedly had been in Byelorussia. We served the best American and Russian dishes that our excited cooks could create. As relays of vodka bottles were steadily emptied, even the dour Bylinsky was seen to smile. Toasts were exchanged and drunk. Recalling Lenin's saying that "of all the arts . . . the cinema is the most important", I proposed that we drink to the memory of all the allied cameramen who had died filming the war that had brought victory to the United States, Great Britain and the Soviet Union; expressing the sincere hope that we might continue to work together in the common purposes of peace.

The Priest reads the Christmas lesson

For New Year of 1947 we had moved to Kiev and the Ukraine. On the last day of filming at the 'Red Partisan' collective farm, the chairman invited us to feast at his house in the village. We were digesting a surfeit of food, drink and mutual goodwill when a call to look at the peculiar carryings-on of the superstitious peasantry had me running with my camera, before the others were even out of the door.

This day, January 7th, was Christmas Day in the calendar of the Orthodox Church, and issuing from the tiny village church opposite was the traditional procession of worshippers, led by their priest, bearing aloft the banners of the saints. They had spent three full hours encompassed with ritual in the church, and now, with snowflakes melting like tears on the faces of the processional ikons, the congregation moved three times round the crumbling walls of the church. Resting his great bible on the suppliant heads of the worshippers, the Ukrainian village priest once again retold the Christmas message that Saint Vladimir had first brought to Russia a thousand years before; and, with his blessing, this vision of another world vanished into the twilight.

More than half a million tons of UNRRA supplies should have been delivered to Byelorussia and the Ukraine by the end of 1946. The programme was to have been wound up with the international relief organisation itself. But, fortunately for my film, a wave of post-war shipping strikes in the United States had held up cargoes, and shipments were still due at Odessa well into the following June.

Taking a camera into a port and naval base anywhere in the world can be difficult at the best of times. Lastovsky's counterpart in Kiev, Vassily Vladimirovitch Khomyak, travelled down with me to Odessa to ensure that there was no hitch in the arrangements he had made for me to film the ships being unloaded.

The long train journey provided me with a chance to know this very senior Soviet official better. As the miles clattered away outside our first category compartment, the transparent sincerity of his convictions became more and more apparent. Totally selfless in himself, working sixteen hours or more every day at the desk from which this was but the briefest of escapes, Vassily Vladimirovitch had pledged his life to the service of his fellow men—an ideal which to him was synonymous with communism. His health had been permanently broken by years of hardship and suffering with the partisans behind the German lines. The thought of another war was something from which he recoiled with a horror which I encountered in every other Russian I met and talked with.

He expressed himself quite clearly, but the dogma of his Marxist dictionary defied translation.

'Yes', he said to me at one point in our discussions, 'in the Soviet Union we have abolished class'.

I made no comment. But it did occur to me that if class had been abolished in the Soviet Union it hadn't quite vanished from this particular train. Outside the very window of the comfortably heated two berth compartment in which he was speaking, old women were hanging on to the outside of the carriage. They were too poor and unimportant to travel in any other way than by clinging to its freezing door handles and ice-encrusted steps.

Odessa meant more to me than a chance to film the arrival of the crated penicillin plant for the Ukraine, or even the promised equipment for the manufacture of artificial limbs. It gave me the chance of an excursion into a legendary, and private world. Private, because there seemed to be nobody to share it. No-one appeared to have heard of Eisenstein and his epic motion picture—the story of mutiny at sea in 1905 and the adoption of the mutineers by the townspeople of Odessa.

Twenty years before, *The Battleship Potemkin* had burst like a bomb in the world of the cinema. Here was a New Realism, a new dimension, a new grandeur which had enthralled me when I saw it for the first time in the second winter of the war.

In a Ukrainian village, Christmas Day 1946

While Khomyak made arrangements for me to film in the port, I made my pilgrimage on foot, alone.

At the top of the great steps leading down to the harbour, the statue of the Duc de Richelieu still held an ineffectual laurel wreath over the dramatic perspective, unchanged from the day when it had first fired Eisenstein's imagination. But where, pursued by Cossack troops, a perambulator had once bumped its way into cinematic immortality, children now gaily tobogganed, chased by sweepers shovelling snow from the icy surface.

The ships in the port below were held fast by the coldest winter for fifty years. Around the rudder and the propellors of the *Winifred Smith* from Baltimore, the ice was piled high. The port's three ice-breakers had been destroyed in the war. To keep a path open to the imprisoned vessels, an old ferry was being tried instead. But it made a poor substitute. The ice was seven feet thick. A channel crashed through it froze up again at its beginning before it reached its goal. The precious supplies had arrived—and still could not be unloaded.

Two other UNRRA chartered ships were luckier: the *Marie Bakke* from Norway and the *American Victory* from Los Angeles, had docked before this phenomenal cold began. Both were unloading lengths of heavy piping for the industrial reconstruction of the Ukraine. The ill, the sick, and the maimed, still had to wait for the penicillin plant, the manufacturing equipment for synthetic limbs, and a milk pasteuriser destined for Byelorussia.

Rolling stock, to move the shipments on, had been destroyed. Even warehouses to take it into store had vanished. And once more, many of the dock workers, shovelling snow, clearing the rails, coupling the locomotives on to the trains, were women. So many men had vanished from Russia too.

In Odessa Bryan and I stayed at a hotel called the London. Like the rest of the city it had suffered little damage during the war. Every effort was being made to

The Odessa Steps—Twenty years after Potemkin

Author on the Odessa Steps

provide hospitality in the age-old traditions for sailors ashore. There was a five-piece band, and an assortment of rather tired charmers, who had obviously seen better days during the Rumanian occupation.

More elevated entertainment in the shape of a nightly movie was to be had at the International Club, in whose hospitable writing-rooms, where at least it was warm, I also wrote my reports. Here I saw Alexander Ptushko's fairy-tale of the Urals, *The Stone Flower*. It had been filmed, with great success, not in Russia at all but for the most part in Prague, and the captured German Agfacolour negative and processing equipment that went into it were to provide the basis for Russia's own colour films of the future. At the opera they were performing *Tosca*. I went with the chaperone in whose hands Khomyak had left me, once he was sure I should be given facilities to photograph the port: a most friendly and sympathetic ex-Colonel of an anti-tank regiment who had fought at Stalingrad. The cold at a concert, however, was too much even for him, and we committed the unforgiveable social sin of keeping our overcoats on.

I returned to Kiev with the entire film almost complete. The UNRRA Mission had failed to get the negative shot in Byelorussia out of the country. It had been brought back to me in Kiev. Frantic cables demanding my return to London were now routine. With the dissolution of UNRRA my job, strictly speaking, had ceased to exist. I had enough film to show that life had triumphed in Russia—in spite of four years of war and occupation. There remained just one sector of the Ukraine that was still tightly closed to me.

At the UNRRA council meeting in Geneva six months before, I had seen a brilliantly made Russian film about the work of reconstruction under way in the industrial Eastern Ukraine, where the coal-mines of the Donetz basin had been flooded by the retreating Germans. Yet again, for the last time in his office on Pushkin Street, I asked Khomyak if I could be issued with a permit to go there.

95

'But what is UNRRA doing in that district which you could film?' came the reply.

UNRRA was certainly supplying leather for the boots the miners wore in the mines. But my answer failed to impress.

So I made a final appeal from the heart.

'I want to show Americans how Russia has suffered', I said. 'At the same time I want to bring home to. the Russians the good-will that the United States have shown to them through UNRRA. Between the two countries, there's an increasing barrier of suspicion. My film may contribute towards a better understanding'.

Looking me straight in the eye, with a sadly resigned and tolerant smile, Khomyak brought me down from the clouds.

'Since when', he asked, 'has any film ever changed foreign policy?'

In a hotel room in Moscow I pondered on the truth of this reflection. I had a hundred and forty-seven separate rolls of exposed film—canned, boxed up and spread out over the floor. By diplomatic bag—or more literally speaking, by way of the three largest the British Embassy possessed—I sent back fifteen thousand feet of film.

And then, with three days to spare in Moscow before the next plane to Berlin and London, I did the town. I laughed at the satirical freedom enjoyed by Obraztsov's puppets, and rode on the famous Underground, whose great columns and lofty halls reminded me of the fantasies of some subterranean Cecil B. DeMille. I had dinner with a girl from the State Film School who was busily translating the script of *The Lost Weekend*. I watched Ulanova dance amidst the splendours of the Bolshoi, to the music of Prokoviev's *Cinderella*. But I found it all poor recompense for the silence represented for me by the telephone number Г1-77-56.

Just before my arrival in Moscow the American Embassy had screened the film *Anna and the King of Siam*.

A not infrequent visitor to the American and British Embassy's special showings of their countries' films had been Eisenstein himself, who had thus been able personally to witness the influence of his *Alexander Nevsky* on the battle of Agincourt in *Henry V*. After the screening of *Anna and the King of Siam* he wrote that: "we see a light ironical sometimes moving picture, often dramatic, always witty and apparently quite innocent. But it would be difficult to find more subtle propaganda of colonial politics"

I had also been invited to a dinner where I hoped to meet the other titan of Russian cinema, Pudovkin, whose most recent film *Admiral Nakhimov* I had seen in Kiev, a tedious and unimaginative production of the Crimean War that was far removed from his earlier great work. Unfortunately Pudovkin was out of town, lying low in his country villa.

Dovshenko had not been in his native Ukraine when I was there, but surely Eisenstein was still in Moscow. From the Embassy I got his phone number.

At the hotel were two attractive English-speaking young ladies whose function in life was to make arrangements for visitors such as myself. Again and again I begged them to try his number. It was always the same. There was no reply. A blizzard delayed my flight a further day. On the hour, every hour, I tried again. No reply.

And so I never met this great film maker. But I always kept his telephone number.

PART TWO: Indian Equinox

In London Recognition –
And in New Delhi Freedom

I decided that the only thing to do was to set a time limit and say: whatever happens our rule is ending on that date.   Prime Minister Clement Attlee

The Britain to which I returned from Russia was beset by a major fuel crisis in which fog, gales and snow added their assaults to an economy strained almost to breaking point by seven long years of sacrifice and struggle. It was the same appalling winter that had similarly paralysed Odessa.

Every motion picture laboratory was restricted by a shortage of power. The Foreign Office was lit by candles, and my precious negative lay there still undeveloped. Into this gloomy situation stepped an independent producer. Pulling a few fast strings he got the film accepted as a priority and, within forty-eight hours, in a small projection theatre not a mile from the screen on which I had seen the Ukrainians welcoming the Germans as liberators five years before, the legacy of this invasion now unfolded—crystal clear and perfect despite the three months' delay that had elapsed since its first sequences had been exposed in Byelorussia.

A month before, Washington had advised UNRRA's London office that they would negotiate American and Canadian rights to the material. We were free to arrange its release in the United Kingdom and Commonwealth through a British company. UNRRA's energetic Films Officer in London, Olwen Vaughan, despatched the original negative to Washington, and arranged a showing of our own copy to some selected luminaries of the British documentary cinema.

Their reaction was immediate. Paul Rotha at once offered me a job, and Edgar Anstey requested the film for release in the J. Arthur Rank series *This Modern Age*. My own desire was not to see the material edited down to the demands of a set pattern and formula, but released as the individual documentary feature that I had planned and devised in the first place. This would guarantee the maximum integrity of its subject which UNRRA's other partners in the enterprise—the Russians, had been led to expect.

Within the week, Washington had cabled us that *The March of Time* were definitely interested in the material. In view of the magnitude of theatrical screenings throughout the world—including Great Britain—that such a release would guarantee UNRRA, its Division of Public Information was obliged to agree to their demand for total and exclusive world rights for a period of six months.

Naturally no-one was interested in producing a film from material which *The March of Time* would already have released themselves. Claiming that this was international film, to which they had as much right as any competitive American company, the Rank Organisation had attempted to draw the British Foreign Office into the dispute. Agreement was nonetheless made with *The March of Time*, to whom all footage was delivered, with the sole proviso that UNRRA was to approve its final edited form and commentary.

In the confusion of UNRRA's own dissolution and the desperate desire to attain the saturation of showing that only *The March of Time* could achieve, something else was overlooked. This was the promise made to the Russians that they should be given copies of the film which, by virtue of their own membership of the international organization which had produced it, was as much their's as anyone else's.

I cabled anxiously to Washington: "All negative developed and is first class stop negative plus one rough cut print as guide leaving march second stop dope sheets leaving airpouch soonest stop both governments Ukraine Byelorussia expect documentary of material to be delivered to them stop this test case for future stop . . . this material . . . test case in international public relations with Soviet Union".

At first the Russian press had ignored the two hundred and fifty million dollars' worth of aid which UNRRA brought to the Ukraine and Byelorussia. On the request of the Missions in Minsk and Kiev, newspapers in both republics had soon carried adequate accounts of UNRRA's vital contribution to their economy. It had only been because the Ukraine and Byelorussia believed the film that I was making to be a combined undertaking in both our interests that the two governments turned over to its production so much of their own scarce lighting equipment and technicians. As they never received their own promised copies, all chances of the Ukrainian and Byelorussian peoples ever seeing any of the film disappeared, and with it the possibility of their ever becoming really aware of the extent and range of the predominantly American aid and generosity that they had received. Without fear of contradiction, Krushchev would be able to declare in East Berlin, March 7th 1959, that "Russia had been ravaged by war, and the allies should have helped towards its reconstruction. What did they do? They did not give a penny".

This was not the final chapter in the fortunes of the first uncensored film that the Russians had ever permitted anyone to make in their country. Although the original negative remained with the United Nations, *The March of Time* was generously allowed to keep the entire copy from which they had edited their own *The Russians Nobody Knows*. In time they were peddling it to any producer, whatever his aims and purposes, at so much a foot. This misplaced generosity offended me least when Nicole Vedrés used my old lady threading a needle in a Kiev Old Folks Home to illustrate the biological theories of Jean Rostand in *La Vie Commence Demain*. It offended me most when *The March of Time* itself brought out an issue devoted to the problems of American education three years later.

Surveying the parlous state of American schools, the editors then attempted to console their audience by illustrating the deficiencies of Soviet education. Selecting for their purpose my sequence of students in the Kiev Polytechnic, but substituting for a close-up of the innocuous·British motoring magazine that one had in fact been reading, a close-up of a Marxist textbook which they made in their own studios.

Great had been the raising of eyebrows and the shaking of heads when, after my return from Russia, I announced my intention of joining *The March of*

Time. Its parent magazines *Time* and *Life*, and their publisher, Henry Luce, were now hardly regarded as torch-bearers of liberalism by the British documentary film makers in whose company I then found myself something of a curiosity. But my reason was simple, and consistent. I was determined to keep my hands on my Russian film.

To anyone who, like myself, had been such a film fan in the 'thirties, *The March of Time* had often proved to be the most exciting and controversial item in the programme. In the days when I was bewailing the British cinema's indifference to the drama of the real world outside the studios, this American short film series was bringing to our screens, every month, a story of genuine purpose and immediacy—shot in its real surroundings, with the actual protagonists of its drama. Nothing like this had ever been seen before. The documentary films with which Britain was beginning to make a name for herself—and which were to achieve international acceptance and acclaim during the war—were seldom shown in commercial cinemas.

The March of Time had its origins in an American publishing revolution of the early 'twenties. Henry Robinson Luce had been only a twenty-four-year-old graduate of Yale—'most brilliant in the class of 1920'—when, with fellow alumnus Briton Hadden, he borrowed sufficient money to launch a new weekly news magazine. On hired typewriters, in an abandoned brewery, they had composed in 1923 the first dummy number of a magazine called *Time*. Until Hadden's early death at the age of thirty-two, the partners had taken turns in the editing of their phenomenally successful attempt to "get behind the story to tell what it means"; and Luce had gone on to found *Fortune*, which he followed with *Life*, the pictorial counterpart to *Time*. *Life* was to reach, and hold, the largest circulation and command the highest advertising revenue in the history of American journalism.

A year after Luce and Hadden set up their first issue of *Time*, a young Scot had arrived in the United States on a Rockefeller Research Fellowship. From an apprenticeship in American journalism, film study and criticism, John Grierson returned to Britain in 1927. On an April morning of the following year, he was summoned to a meeting with Leopold Amery, Sir Stephen Tallents and Walter Elliot, then chairman of an Empire Marketing Board considering the production of films. The Financial Secretary to the Treasury that would have to find the money was also the author of *The Herring: its effect on the History of Britain*. Grierson had thereupon boarded the *Maid of Thule* at Lerwick, cast off into the fishing grounds of the North Sea—and made *Drifters*. The documentary film was under way.

It was inevitable that such a spectacularly triumphant revolution in the field of 'pictorial journalism' as *Time* and *Life* would be applied to the newsreel, in the same manner as these weekly magazines now interpreted and amplified the background to the events reported in the daily newspapers. In 1934, Roy Larsen, then Circulation Manager of *Time*, accepted the challenge. Within four years *The March of Time* had become a regular feature on the screens of 12,000 cinemas throughout the world.

The March of Time was as much a child of the 'thirties as the New Deal and the Left Book Club, and for years' its title background of marching men bearing banners aloft was more reminiscent of *New Masses* than of the increasingly affluent and conservative parent company that had brought it into being. Born into a world of economic depression and slump, in the year of its first issue eleven million Americans were unemployed and on relief.

Attracted to the novel opportunity of *The March of Time*, many of the founding fathers of the British documentary film originally worked on its early stories of their own country and its problems, and Grierson himself was to write in 1938 that it:

"... does what the other news records have failed to do. It gets behind the news, observes the factors of influence, and gives a perspective to events. Not the parade of armies so much as the race in armaments; not the ceremonial opening of a dam but the full story of Roosevelt's experiment in the Tennessee Valley; not the launching of the *Queen Mary* but the post-1918 record of British shipping ... The world, our world, appears suddenly and brightly as an oyster for the opening: for film people—how strangely—worth living in, fighting in and making drama about. And more important still is the thought of a revitalised citizenship and of a democracy at last in contact with itself".

This seemed good enough to me.

Soon after my return from Russia the European Director of *The March of Time* had been instructed by his American superiors to place me under contract. Informed that if I accepted this offer their first requirement would be my presence in New York, in order that I might be filmed in a prologue to the film which they were making from the Byelorussian and Ukrainian material that UNRRA had assigned to them exclusively, and that such a visit would enable me to meet at first hand the producers of the famous film series for whom I would be working, the opportunity which this presented for me to be present at the actual editing of my Russian film became the deciding factor in my acceptance.

But once I had so committed myself the trip to New York was heard of no more; and the scenes incorporating myself for inclusion in *The Russians Nobody Knows* were made by their British unit in London.

Any disappointment and resentment that I may have felt had been resolved twelve weeks later by the receipt of a cable assigning me to the production of a film on the about-to-become-independent India; and forgotten in the excitement of preparing for what was to me the most challenging and worthwhile subject in the world.

The British position in India as alien masters of one fifth of humanity had long seemed to me morally wrong and, in Austria at the end of the European war, the first vote I had ever been entitled to in a British General Election had gone to the Labour Party; as much because of my belief that the Conservatives could never view sympathetically the cause of Indian freedom as anything else. With the massive service vote of so many like myself contributing in no small measure to the crushing defeat of the Tories, Indian independence had become an immediate and guaranteed certainty; and, in the summer of 1947, I set about to record on film this great historical achievement.

During the war *The March of Time* had made two releases on India: its unit finding itself in the sub-continent at the time of Pearl Harbour, when the threat of Japanese invasion had jolted the British Coalition Government into despatching Sir Stafford Cripps in an attempt to win the Indian leaders' support in the struggle now about to burst upon the borders of their own country. The Cripps mission had failed, and the Indian nationalist leaders had adopted a 'Quit India' resolution, calling for an immediate end of British rule, but offering to fight on the Allied side under a provisional national government; threatening to launch a mass civil disobedience campaign if their demand was rejected. Within a matter of hours Gandhi and his colleagues had been once again arrested. The Mahatma writing to the Viceroy that:

> "The declared cause is common between the Government of India and us. To put it in the most concrete terms, it is the protection of the freedom of China and Russia. The Government of India think that freedom of India is not necessary for winning the cause. I think exactly the opposite . . . Do not disregard this pleading of one who claims to be a sincere friend of the British people. Heaven guide you."

The March of Time's wartime filming had accumulated a mass of background material: the training of India's magnificent army; the government in Delhi; the release of some of the nationalist leaders from gaol. A comprehensive coverage of agriculture and industry—the latter engaged at the time principally in defence production—was still largely undated. This was of a very diffuse nature, and as the initial directive from New York now called for my concentration chiefly on political developments, a meeting was arranged with the about to be appointed first High Commissioner from a free India to Great Britain—Vengalil Krishna Menon.

For nearly a quarter of a century this austere figure had been the spearhead of the independence struggle in Britain. With little funds, and a handful of devoted workers, he had directed his campaign from the small and overcrowded offices of the India League above a shop in London's Strand, living as far as anyone could judge almost solely on a diet of innumerable cups of tea. It seemed only fitting that these years of sacrifice and faith should culminate in his becoming free India's first Ambassador to the country in which he had chosen to pass so much of his life, and against whose domination of his own land he had fought so long. This was the first diplomatic reward in a new career which was in due course to see him emerge in sartorial and dialectic splendour as a delegate to the United Nations—and become the controversial Minister of Defence of an Indian Union dumbfounded by Chinese aggression across her frontiers twelve years later.

Menon thoroughly approved of *The March of Time's* desire to produce a film on the subject of his country's independence. He promised to give me letters of introduction to the Prime Minister Jawaharlal Nehru, to his deputy Sardar Vallabbhai Patel, to the chief ministers of all the different Indian provinces and to various other influential people. These letters, fifteen in all, would not however be delivered until after August 15th, the date of India's freedom, as only after that historic date could he sign them in his capacity of High Commissioner. He was most interested in my plans and asked me point blank if I sympathised with the cause of a free India, and what my own politics were. Satisfying him on these issues, I arranged to film him as he presided over one of the last meetings of the India League's committee a few days later. After all the years of disappointment some of its members could still not quite believe that the goal of freedom was at last in their hands, suspecting in the British Government's plan a devious trick somewhere or other. "It is complete and absolute independence" he would continually reply to their doubts.

My next call was on Sudhir Ghosh, the Public Relations Officer at India House. This palatial building was in some contrast to the dingy offices of the India League. Ghosh was also very helpful, adding letters of his own to both Nehru and Patel. A conspicuous omission from Menon's introductions had been one to Gandhi, but Ghosh was one of his close disciples and he wrote another letter introducing me to people close to the Mahatma, who was then in Calcutta, where his presence and example had succeeded in halting the religious rioting which had broken out on the eve of freedom.

The British point of view in all this seemed not at all superfluous, so an appointment was also arranged with Arthur Henderson, Britain's Under-Secretary of State for India. The last of this illustrious line was sympathetic, but in the nature of things not in a position to offer much help for my future work, as his activities lay in the past of British rule. With the coming of Indian independence his ministry was going out of business, and its functions were being absorbed by the newly created Commonwealth Relations Office. But he did give me what proved to be most useful introductions to the British Information Services in the principal cities.

The Bombay to which the Skymaster of Trans World Airlines now brought me at the end of September 1947 was no longer the capital of a British administered province and, exchanging the rigours of the army transit camp of my previous visit for the luxuries of the Taj Mahal Hotel, I set about the task of chronicling and interpreting the fortunes of India and Pakistan's four hundred million people at this decisive moment in their history.

Twenty thousand feet of negative had been despatched ahead of me on the assumption that it would be cleared by an agent and stored on my behalf in Kodak's air-conditioned Bombay vaults. Discovering that it was still languishing in the customs shed, I was shunted to and fro from one office to another for two frustrating days before I was able to secure its release, and then only after a payment of substantial import duty. This imposition was the cause of no little concern, as apparently nowhere else, and never before, had *The March of Time* paid such a charge on film which was, in any case, re-exported after exposure for development in the United States. But the overworked and underpaid Indian civil servants were prisoners of a system which, on its lower levels at least, had inherited all the red tape and procrastination of its British progenitors without the latter's sometime capacity to treat the book of rules as something less than holy writ. For months to come, in the midst of strife and commotion, assassination and massacre, I was to be harassed by demands from London for the remission of this duty.

The British had decided to establish the centre of their Indian Empire in Delhi after the First World War. Excavations for the building of something worthy of this conquest revealed the remains of no less than five such previous capitals. Undeterred, Sir Edward Lutyens designed and built a seat of government monumental enough to enshrine forever his country's imperial power. A power which was in fact to last for only another twenty years.

In a waiting room in one of two vast and symmetrical office blocks, I sat awaiting a man who was more familiar with the less inspiring grandeur of India's gaols. There was a quick step in the passage outside and into the room walked Nehru. Sweeping me into his sparsely furnished office he rapidly read Krishna

Menon's letter, and I told him that Sardar Patel had instructed the Ministry of Information to give me all possible help in the carrying out of a programme which, apart from an immediate tour of the Punjab, was still very much in the planning stage. Nehru told me that the great refugee problem was absorbing everyone's attention and energy, and that until this had been brought under control the great schemes to combat Indian poverty that were close to his heart would have to mark time—but of their implementation there was no doubt. Before leaving for the Punjab I asked if I might film a meeting of his cabinet, coming to see him again on my return. To this he readily agreed and, not wishing to take up any more of his so courteously given time, I took leave of this great international personality until the following Sunday, when I had the pleasure of showing him, with Patel, *The Russians Nobody Knows*.

Nehru at cabinet meeting, October 16th 1947

In his letters Krishna Menon had mentioned the film that I had recently made in the Soviet Union, which he had seen before my departure from England. Both Nehru and Patel asked if they could see it, and a copy was flown up to me from Bombay by Twentieth Century Fox. Azim Husain, Patel's deputy in the Ministry of Information, arranged the screening in a small projection room used by the Indian Armed Services for the showing of their official films, inviting at the same time other senior government officials whom he considered it to be in my interest to meet.

Punctually at ten o'clock that Sunday morning in early October Nehru arrived, closely followed by Patel; and for twenty minutes India's leaders exchanged their preoccupation with the sufferings of their own people for this picture of post-war rehabilitation in the Ukraine and Byelorussia. Two republics in the Soviet Union of which Jawaharlal had written some years before that:

"despite all . . . possible distortions of the original passion for human betterment, I had no doubt that the Soviet Revolution had advanced human society by a great leap and had lit a bright flame which could not be smothered, and that it had laid the foundations for that new civilization towards which the world could advance".

Reminding me as he left that his next cabinet meeting was due to take place in three days' time, Nehru thanked me for showing him the film. But I felt that no thanks were due at all to me, and that a great deal were owed to him for finding time to see it during these desperately crowded days.

I also filmed Lord Louis Mountbatten—the last British Viceroy of an un-

Patel at same cabinet meeting, October 16th 1947

divided India and now the first Governor-General of the Indian Union—in his office, drafting and checking documents of independence; while the refugees from a Punjab which was now divided between India and Pakistan, and who were the pitiful pawns of this struggle, were the special concern of Lady Louis—for long an active director of the Red Cross. My camera followed them: from the work of the one at a clean and tidy desk, to the care of the other in the squalid world of the camps.

I was in close touch in Delhi with Azim Husain, Chief Secretary of the Ministry of Information and Broadcasting. Husain and I were keen to include in my film sequences of the labour movement and trade union organization. I had never seen this portrayed in any Indian film before. We talked of the Indian Socialist Party and its leader, Jaya Prakash Narayan, and wondered if he would ever find himself at the head of his country's government.

Azim Husain was one of the forty million Muslims who had, pledged their faith and lives to Nehru's belief in a society based on the respect of all religions. He was hostile to the concept of the purely Islamic state of Pakistan. The leading Mohammedan figure in the Indian Union was the greatly respected scholar, Maulana Abdul Kalam Azad, Minister of Education. I filmed this distinguished educationalist in cabinet the afternoon of October 16th, 1947.

The composition of this first independent governing body reflected Nehru's intention that the Indian Union should be a broadly based secular state, in which the dominant religion of Hinduism should not usurp a monopoly of power as had Islam in Pakistan. With Patel the conservative Hindu on his left, Jawaharlal had Maulana Azad seated at his right hand. The Sikh Baldev Singh was Minister of Defence; beside him sat a Christian Minister of Transport, John Matthai. Dr. Bhimrao Ramji Ambedkar, the Minister of Law, was an Untouchable. Facing him was the only woman member, the Minister of Health, Rajkumari Amrit Kaur.

Nehru and Patel were guests of honour at the Thanksgiving Day reception that I filmed at the United States Embassy: two utterly dissimilar men on whom so much depended. Nehru the aristocrat and Europeanised intellectual. Patel the practising lawyer from an orthodox peasant family. The one impulsive and emotional. The other practical and direct. Nehru the socialist and idol of the Indian intelligentsia. Patel the orthodox conservative drawing his support from the business community. The Prime Minister an agnostic and firm believer in the equal rights of all religions. The Home Minister a staunch Hindu by up-bringing and conviction. Small wonder that Delhi echoed with rumours of tension and hostility between the two.

But Nehru exhibited few signs of strain when, following my whirlwind day with the Mountbattens, I filmed him at the simple desk across which flowed the problems of three hundred and fifty million souls. Inscribing my copy of his autobiography he suggested that I read his later book which was in a sense a deepening continuation: *The Discovery of India* that he had undergone whilst imprisoned during the war. Throughout all his trials and tribulations Jawaharlal's family had always been a source of constant strength and, invited to his home, I continued this study of a truly remarkable man by filming him in conversation with his elder sister, Mrs. Vijaya Lakshmi Pandit, fresh from the recent General Assembly of the United Nations to which she was the Indian Union's delegate. Successively her country's ambassador to the Soviet Union, the United States and High Commissioner in London, this handsome lady provided Nehru with an invaluably personal diplomatic link with the world outside India—to which Patel was utterly indifferent.

The two statesmen were not even contemporaries, for at seventy-two Patel had been in his mid-forties when the twenty-nine year old Nehru had first fallen under Gandhi's spell. But one thing both enjoyed in common was the love of a devoted daughter. In the Sardar's case this was Maniben who had always accompanied him to gaol, and who now hovered by his side during my filming of her cold and impassive father. Although he lacked Nehru's contact with the masses Patel none the less commanded enormous power through his control of the Ministries of Home Affairs, Information and States, and, discussing policy and tactics with his secretary on the verandah of his house, something of this political force was captured by my camera, focused on his aloof and forbidding face.

All that had held Pandit Jawaharlal Nehru and Sardar Vallabbhai Patel together in harness had been their common passion for Indian freedom, and a shared devotion to the Gandhi whom each had served for nearly thirty years. With the former goal accomplished the Congress Party that the Sardar bossed with such ruthless efficiency had now achieved its object. Patel's increasing hostility towards Pakistan and the Muslim minority within the Indian Union was leading to an open break with the Mahatma.

Hoping by his presence and example to avert the fearful threat inherent in Patel's intransigence, Gandhi was living in his usual austerity at the nearby home of C. D. Birla, the Hindu millionaire publisher of the *Hindustan Times* edited by the Mahatma's son Devadas. When in England for the Round Table Conference of sixteen years before, Gandhi had lived with a group of British Quakers. One of these led me into the presence of this little man—perhaps the most Christlike figure of our century—for whom martyrdom was now but nine short weeks away.

The Mahatma was being helped on to a couch. With a smile towards me indicating that I was free to go ahead with my filming if I wished, he began his correspondence. For all his absolute mastery of the language spoken by those rulers whose abdication he, more than any other single man, had brought about, he did not address me with a single word of that or any other. This, it transpired, was his Day of Silence. Who was I to question it? Lord Mountbatten himself had been greeted with the same silent smile, when, six months before, he had presented to Gandhi his plan for the 'immediate transfer of power' to the Indian leaders. The Mahatma had scribbled, not spoken, his reply. His vow was not to be broken however momentous the occasion. The day of his greatest triumph was his Day of Silence. On Days of Silence he would scribble notes on the back of an old envelope. It was on an envelope that he replied to the Viceroy's proposals. I was shaken to see him in the flesh. The flesh looked so pitiably naked and frail. It was as if the spirit had nearly consumed it, in seventy-eight years of selfless living. Born in a tiny west-coast state, in an age when the dominion of the British Raj must have appeared impregnable for a whole era to come, Mohandas Karamchand Gandhi had now seen his country free for four months. He was still its epicentre.

It was hard to believe that he was not just an old, simple, happy man, enjoying the morning's sunshine. The only irreconcilable note in the picture was the garden around him. It did not belong to him. Nothing did. In these luxurious quarters Gandhi was still Gandhi. He lived with the simplicity of Delhi's Untouchables whose quarters were now crammed with outcasts from the Punjab.

What did his worldly possessions amount to? A cheap watch. A pair of spectacles. His sandals. And a spinning wheel, with which to weave the cloth that covered his nakedness. This was the man whose spiritual integrity had humbled the richest empire of modern times into voluntary abdication.

He owned no more than the refugees on the dusty and bloodstained roads of the Punjab—the arena in which was being played out the first trial of strength between India and Pakistan.

Twelve Million on the Move –
And an army of Twelve-year olds

The difference between cows and music is the gulf between Muslim and Hindu. The Hindus insist that cows should not be killed and that music should be played in the temples. The cow is a goddess for the Hindu and Music is food for the goddesses, and hence they must have both if Hinduism is to survive. Cow is food for Muslims, and quietude in the mosque is the very quintessence of Islam. An early Jesuit missionary

The British government had had to negotiate the transfer of power with two major Indian political organizations: the Congress Party of Gandhi, Nehru, and Patel—and the Muslim League of Mohammed Ali Jinnah. The former claimed to represent all India, of whatever caste or creed; but the latter had demanded a separate state in the northern provinces of east and west where Mohammedans were in a majority. Independence had thus created Pakistan on the one hand, and a Union of the remaining states and provinces of India on the other. Trouble had at once flared in the Punjab, the border province divided between the two. Half a million people had already perished in a fearful carnage and, although the killings were coming to an end, an immense movement of human beings was under way. The entire Muslim population of the East Punjab, the part of the afflicted province which had been awarded to the Indian Union, were moving into the Pakistan territory of the West Punjab; while the Hindu population of the West Punjab was moving in the opposite direction towards the hope of a similar sanctuary in the Indian Union to the east. By bullock cart and on foot, twelve million people were on the move in the greatest migration in human history.

One of the few trains still running, a train from the Indian Union, pulled into the station at Lahore. It was a passenger train; but not a single traveller left it. Behind the hiss of steam from the locomotive, another noise could be heard. At last, raving hysterically, the engine-driver leapt down on to the platform.

He was the only person on board left alive. Little could be made of his story; but the blood oozing from beneath some carriage doors, dried already into obscene scabs at the foot of others, told its own tale. Over a thousand Muslim refugees had boarded this train. All of them, to a man—to a child—had been killed.

And thus those that held the cow sacred, and would rather die than slaughter and eat its meat, butchered other Indians who would never dream of touching pork. And those who worshipped one God through the revelation of a single prophet, slaughtered in their turn those of their neighbours who prayed to a diversity of deities in a multitude of manifestations. Here was all the fury and passion of a religious war to the death—nowadays something impossible for we of the increasingly pagan and secularised so-called western world to comprehend. But once French and English marched to the limits of their own world to put to the sword the heathen usurpers of the birthplace of their own faith's founder; and a handful of men and women set sail in a cockleshell of a boat from Plymouth Steps to found a great new nation in a wilderness—just so they could worship their own

God as they pleased.

In an age which has lost faith even with itself, these bloody goings-on in the Punjab twenty years ago seem incomprehensible. But if you believe in a life after death, to be rewarded on the basis of what you have done with this brief moment of existence in this world, and, like the Crusaders before, believe that infidels should be slain, then life becomes largely a question of how well you can die—or kill —for the cause.

But Kali drank her fill at last, Allah called halt, and the killings came to an end. But there remained the refugees, homeless in their millions.

The trains started to run again, in comparative safety, thanks to the Gurkha soldiers of the Indian Army, who now travelled front and rear, mounting their automatic rifles in open sand-bagged trucks. In the freight yards of Lahore I

The Punjab, October 1947

filmed the loading and departure of one such train, and an old Sikh wandering to and fro, in bewildered silence, with the whole station to himself.

Every coach overflowed with refugees. Slowly the train got under way. The track swarmed with a moving mass of men, women and children desperately struggling for a foothold. All of them succeeded in clambering on. The train blackened like fly-paper. When it had disappeared, only this one old man, too feeble to have found a place on the couplings or the carriage steps, was left behind on the track. Quite lost, he stared at a dwindling dark shape—the last coach of a train which had taken his family away. The station around him was now entirely deserted. For a moment there was silence. Then the flies which this human activity had driven away descended on it, and settled once more—still thicker than the swarm of humanity which had displaced them. Their frenzied buzzing soon drowned the old Sikh's lament.

The movement of these millions was not limited to the trains. Greater refugee columns took to the roads. I filmed my first on the Grand Trunk Road between Lahore and Lyallpur. The first sign of the advance was a huge floating cloud of dust in the air. Vultures hovered in its upper reaches, or else, in the branches of sparse, skeletal trees, waited for the hungry and the exhausted to fall out of line. Below them, the tide of human misery rolled on. The men were on foot. Their women, their children and their few pathetic bundles were loaded on to bullock carts. Nine hours passed before the last of them had gone. My own transport—an ancient hired truck—groaned past them along the baked and rutted mud that fringed the road.

Through a miasma of dust I filmed the sun setting in a glow of crimson fire. The scene had a certain beauty, bitter, and infernal. I had seen migrations before, but never on such an Asian scale of misery as this. Here were people who had forfeited everything—their possessions, their homes, the land they had tilled for generations. All they now possessed was the rags on their backs, their little carts—and their lives.

But there were vast numbers whose plight was still more wretched. These at any rate had their bullock carts. Others had nothing. All they could do was to gather in the camps provided for them, and hope and pray that some means of mass evacuation would be provided. Near Lyallpur, I was taken to one of these camps, where two thousand Hindus, now isolated amongst Muslims in an alien Pakistan, sighed for the sanctuary of Indian Union territory, or as they called it, Hindustan. These were the people who had nothing, nothing whatever. Their tents were scraps of tarpaulin and rags and tatters of cloth. Over open fires, women cooked pitifully inadequate bowls of rice. Others were bathing their children. One, not far from the end, nursed an equally aged husband to whom fate had been kinder. He was dying, his head in her arms. Cholera had broken out and if both governments—India's and Pakistan's—had not united in the promptest possible effort to have serum flown into the Punjab, a major epidemic would certainly have followed. Everywhere I saw anguish and desolation. And everywhere I saw flies.

A week later, filming the other side of the story, I found myself in this camp's opposite number, near Amritsar. Here, it was the Muslims who awaited a passage to Pakistan. It was hard to believe they were a minority.

They numbered tens of thousands. What was now their refugee camp, the largest in the East Punjab, had once been an immense cattle fair-ground. Now it was chock-a-block with Muslims, squatting beside their bullock carts with the same mute, endless patience in their eyes as the beasts who drew them. They were waiting for safe conduct into Pakistan. On the outskirts of the camp, a growing number of graves stood, silent reminders of those for whom the journey was already over. I wandered amongst these patient Muslims with my camera. Their privation was every bit as great as that of the Hindus. But there was a difference. Here, one object at any rate had been salvaged from virtually every home: the 'nargile' or hubble-bubble pipe. While the womenfolk tried to feed and look after their starving children, the men puffed away, lost to a world in chaos. An archetype picture of humanity in distress: the men were left dazed. It was the women who coped. Here, in the East as in the West, survival was in their hands.

I stayed long in Amritsar, for Amritsar has an older claim to fame. In the midst of a warring Punjab here was the centre of Sikhism. It is a faith based upon a synthesis of the two major religions of India. Barely five hundred years old, it had been founded by an orthodox Hindu named Nanak, born fifty miles further west, near Lahore, in 1469. This original guru retained the Hindu doctrine of the trans-migration of souls but rejected the caste system—the largest single source of human misery I was to film in India, the cause of almost as much human suffering as even the religious strife.

The central shrine of the new faith arose by the healing waters of the Pool of Immortality, which is the meaning of 'Amritsar'. Persecution by the later Moguls proved the making of the Sikhs—the word means 'seekers after truth'; the seven-

The price of Partition

teenth century saw them organised into a great military fraternity, armed with their 'kirpan' daggers and forbidden to sever a single hair from their bodies or their heads.

The close of the eighteenth century saw the birth of a mighty leader; under Ranjit Singh (the 'Lion') the Sikhs developed nationalist yearnings. A Sikh state was envisaged, embracing all the Punjab, extending westwards to the borders of Afghanistan and northwards over the vast Himalayan regions of Kashmir. For a time, this Sikh empire actually existed—which is not only a matter of past history, but still a Sikh dream for the future. In the 1840's the British came into collision with the Sikh armies. A hundred years later, with the British gone, the Sikhs planned to carve out for themselves a separate homeland in the Punjab. History,

110

which is said to repeat itself, sometimes does not do so clearly in the west. In the east, its i's are often dotted with a recurring decimal point.

The Minister of Defence—so often a synonym for war—in the Cabinet of the Indian Union was a Sikh: Sardar Baldev Singh. Nanak's original vision had called for unity between Muslim and Hindu. But the Sikhs of the Punjab had been foremost in the massacre of Muslims, and all now looked to the Indian Union for support. Of all Sikh political leaders the most notorious was Tara Singh, whose devious diplomacy had been devoted to widening the breach between the Muslim League and the Congress Party. From Baldev Singh I had obtained a letter of introduction to this formidable figure. When I called at his house in Amritsar I was told, by one more grim, turbaned and bearded figure: 'He is not now to be seen. He is suffering from a heart attack'.

It was obvious what had caused it. Not only had the Sikhs failed to achieve a separate state of their own, for all Tara Singh's machiavellian manoeuvring, but their native land had now been divided between the Indian Union and Pakistan.

My meeting was postponed. In the meantime I was introduced in a singular way to the aims and objectives of these heirs to Ranjit Singh.

Ever since my arrival in Amritsar I had been fascinated by the beat of drums and the shout of military commands which came from the grounds of a large house quite close to the hotel where I was staying. One evening I asked a young Sikh what was going on.

'Oh', came the reply. 'That's the I.N.A.'

My interest deepened.

The initials I.N.A. stood for one of the most mysterious chapters of the Second World War. In August 1945 I was in the Far East, filming the Japanese surrender. In Saigon, where Field Marshal Tarauchi had had his headquarters, I discovered thousands of feet of propaganda and newsreel film, fruit of five years work by the Japanese Army Film Unit. Not a little curious to see the work of some of our Far Eastern counterparts, I screened this find. I watched the planes taking off for Pearl Harbour, and the *Prince of Wales* and *Repulse* disappearing beneath the waves. The waves had been simulated in a studio-tank, and the battleships were models. The result would have been quite convincing to an unsophisticated audience. Then there appeared on the screen a sequence of Japanese soldiers advancing into the Indian Frontier-Province of Assam. They had some strange, and to me wholly unexpected allies—in the shape of those same bearded Sikh troops at whose side I had marched in the desert, and whom I had filmed in action in Italy. This was the I.N.A.—the Indian National Army. It was an army that the Japanese had recruited from Indian prisoners of war to fight against the British in Burma.

I did not hesitate two years later. I wanted to meet these I.N.A. leaders. I was taken to an English style country house, where my guide seemed to be on the best of terms with everyone. Over a liberal whisky and soda in a comfortable living-room, I met 'General' Mohan Singh.

He was a small, dynamic man. I asked him what plans he had at this critical moment of Indian history. He smiled, as if he had something up his sleeve. To learn that, I should have to come back tomorrow. Today he spoke only of the past.

In 1941 he had been an infantry commander in an Indian Army battalion serving

Jinnah

with the British garrison in Malaya. Seventy days later he had watched the fall of Singapore.

'It is hard for you to realise what that meant out here', he explained. 'In Asian eyes, the meek surrender of this great imperial base meant the eclipse of the white man in the Orient. For Britain, it was only a defeat. To us it was a collapse, both military and moral'.

To the young company commander, it seemed only a question of time before the Japanese overran the whole of Asia and India, and drove the British out. He decided to assist them in the process.

'Yes', he said, 'I founded the I.N.A. From the sixty-five thousand Indian soldiers captured in Malaya, I prepared to raise an army. Colonel Niranjan Singh Gill—then the highest ranking Indian officer in the Indian Army—agreed to collaborate with me. The two of us were flown to Tokyo'.

Seated beside him, Niranjan Singh Gill nodded agreement. He was as big and burly as Mohan Singh was small and vital. It was an effective combination. By the end of 1942 they had a whole division ready for the field.

At a conference in Bangkok Mohan Singh was declared Commander-in-Chief. Niranjan Singh Gill, who had previously out-ranked him, became his chief executive officer.

'And yet both of you appear to have spent the next three years in a Japanese internment camp. What happened?' I asked.

'What I wanted', came the reply, 'was India for the Indians. I had suspicions that Japan only wanted India for the Japanese. They gave me no guarantees.

Driving the British out only to let the Japanese in meant nothing more than changing masters. I refused to collaborate'.

'And Subhas Chandra Bose took your place ?'

'Yes'.

Bose, a former President of the Congress Party, was convinced that Britain stood on the verge of total defeat. He hated them. He broadcast to India during the war from Berlin on behalf of Dr. Goebbels. After the Japanese entered the war he was taken to Tokyo by submarine. He was received by Tojo. They laid plans for a provisional government of 'Free India'. They initiated an I.N.A. campaign in Burma.

At the end of the war Bose was a wanted man. On his way to seek asylum in the Soviet Union, his plane crashed in Formosa. His death in this remote place, no less than the passions which surrounded his life, have combined to transform him into legend. Many Indians refused to believe that he had died. They are convinced that 'Netaji' will return. Fourteen years after these events I was in Kenya. In the heart of the Masai country, I met a Hindu trader. On the wall of his small store hung a single photograph. It was yellowed by time, but the burning force of those eyes had not faded. I recognised him immediately. It was Subhas Chandra Bose: the revolutionary, mystic, who in his most tragic hour still exhorted his countrymen 'Never for one moment falter in your faith in India's destiny'.

All this was now past history. There were no Japanese to suspect and no British to fight. The British had gone. Grave problems remained. What was Mohan Singh's role now? He told me to return in the morning.

I did. I loaded my camera. On a large sign on the gate of the house—the home of a wealthy Sikh—I now read: Desh Sevak Sena—National Defence Corps. Inside the grounds, I could make out the source of the drum beats and marching feet I had heard from my hotel. In their ranks, as many boys as young men were on the march. Some of them not more than twelve years old. They drilled in squads of thirty or thereabouts—all on the model of the once-hated British by whom the ex-I.N.A. men who officered them had been trained. The 'Colonel' in charge of this private army was named Dhillon. Dhillon had commanded a group of the I.N.A. in 1945, harassing General Slim's XIVth Army at the Battle of the Irrawaddy River. After his capture at Pegu, he had been brought to trial with three other I.N.A. 'quislings'—as they appeared in British, and Indian Army eyes—at the Red Fort in Delhi. The seventeen counsel defending them included Nehru. The sentence expected was transportation for life: but the climate of the times, the defeat of the Japanese and the imminence of independence for India led to greater clemency. All were allowed to go free.

Dhillon was a martial figure, and as I filmed him I could not help wondering how the survivor of such stirring times felt as he drilled his juvenile soldiers, armed only with wooden staffs. Boy-soldiers these might be. But they were anything but toy soldiers.

'They will be needed' pronounced my host.

War between Pakistan and the Indian Union was inevitable, so he declared. The government in Delhi was not facing up to the situation at all. Mohan Singh of his own initiative was recruiting an army to place at Delhi's disposal. At present he was recruiting it in the Punjab alone. It was here that the first clash with Pakistan was bound to come. Later, recruits would be drawn from all over the

Indian Union. Delhi could supply weapons, when the time came.

This military force had never been publicised. Sikhs remained Sikhs. To me it seemed that their aims, as fighting men and boys, were more directly concerned with their own nationalist ambitions than with those of the new Indian Union. Just before independence, attempts had been made to prohibit them from carrying swords, the ancestral 'kirpans'. Sardar Patel, the Deputy Prime Minister, had protested on their behalf. Mohan Singh claimed further that Patel supported his military force. Nehru approved, perhaps somewhat reluctantly. Gandhi had been told that this military youth-movement existed for self-discipline. This explanation, its proposers claimed, satisfied him.

I myself saw the grimmest implications in the movement. The enthusiasm of this private army, and the ambition of its sponsors, was a potent and alarming combination. As arms were raised in a Fascist salute, Dhillon's cry 'Enemies of our Country' met with the thundering response—'We will destroy'.

Armies, or youth movements in this case, are not fanned to fever heat without reason. It seemed clear to me that their objective was to seize out of chaos the entity of a separate and independent Sikh state. These men had no outlet elsewhere. The regular Indian Army wanted nothing to do with turncoats who had fought for the Japanese. They held them in contempt. And it is perhaps more than a little ironical that when war finally broke out between India and Pakistan eighteen years later, a Sikh Lieutenant-Colonel surrendered himself and his entire regiment to the enemy once again.

Tara Singh recovered sufficiently from his 'heart attack' during my stay to receive me. Before I met him I was able to visit and film the Golden Temple of Amritsar. Pilgrims were bathing in the sacred waters of the five-acre pool— their swords for once discarded—and at every turn, I was impressed with the fervour of their turbulent faith; a fitting preparation for my visit to the Master. Forty years earlier Tara Singh, a convert from Hinduism, had started a school for Sikhs. He had become its first headmaster, and been known as 'Master' ever since.

The President of the Akali Dal—the sword arm of militant Sikhdom—sat in the garden of a tiny house, finishing his mid-day meal. He was a venerable, patriarchal figure, with a flowing snow white beard. As soon as he had finished his meal, he sent for his secretary. He had a letter to write. He dictated it in English for the benefit of my camera, which for all he knew could record sound as well as picture. It was a fiery missive to Nehru. It deplored the division of the Punjab—the cause of all the Sikhs' misfortunes—and inveighed bitterly against Pakistan, chiding Nehru for too conciliatory an attitude towards this infidel state, with which war was clearly inevitable. He then sighed with visible satisfaction, and excusing himself as 'still a very tired old man' he went indoors. If he had not achieved his life's ambition, at least, by his diatribe, he had provided a finale for my filming this rarely appreciated torment of the Sikhs.

For simplicity in moving about, and ease of operation under tough conditions, I believed a clockwork camera to be more practical than electrically driven equipment. It was free from the encumbrance of batteries and recharging unit. But at the height of my Punjab filming this advantage was set at nought.

The spring broke.

This was catastrophe, and nothing less. In front of me was passing a vital sequence in the film, and all I had with which to record it was a piece of inanimate machinery. Shades of Ahwaz. So far as I knew, the only mechanics able to carry out the repairs were in Bombay. It would take me two weeks to get there and back with transportation in the state it was. Things have looked better than they did to me at that moment. I found that by turning the winding handle with the mechanism released the camera would run for about ten feet of film—sufficient for the shortest of scenes; and by judiciously winding the apparatus as it was running, I managed to prolong these few seconds sufficiently to complete the filming of the refugees' crossing of the Ravi river. I hoped that the inevitable shake as I turned the handle would not appear on the screen when the film was projected. I prayed for a more permanent solution the next day in Lahore.

In a tiny workshop above the shuttered showroom of the Singer Sewing Machine Company I tracked down a mechanic. He was a refugee separated from all his tools. He was at first pessimistic at the prospect but, on taking the camera to pieces, we discovered that the main spring had only snapped a few inches from the end. This was fortunate, for if it had broken in the middle we could have done nothing about it. As it was this most adaptable of craftsmen soon had the broken end of the spring shaped and fixed to the driving drum. The camera ran again as sweetly as ever—if not better than before.

I exposed five thousand feet of film in the Punjab.

I finally got back to Delhi by air—in a military plane from Jullundur. Then a flying visit to Bombay. There I had not only to despatch my material to New York and collect fresh supplies of film.

I was off to the newly formed state of Pakistan.

A Lonely Man in Karachi – And War in Shangri-La

No claim to the future, its joy or its sorrow,
Has he in whose soul no hot passion burns now;
Unworthy the tumult and strife of tomorrow
That nation to whose will today does now bow.

Mohammed Iqbal

Pakistan is a portmanteau word, not even coined till 1933. It combines, in its first syllable, an actual meaning (the 'Paks' are the spiritually pure) with one of those sets of initials applied with such facile felicity to every other institution of our world today. The P stands for Punjab, and A for Afghan (the Pathans of the North West Frontier) and the K for Kashmir. The suffix 'istan' is merely 'the land of' in Persian and Urdu.

Its first Governor-General, Mohammed Ali Jinnah, for much of his life held common cause with other protagonists in the struggle for Indian independence. It was not until 1937 that he came to accept a united sub-continent as an impossible dream. The religious antipathies were too strong and too deep.

In London, before my departure, Pakistan had no India House and India League. All that existed was a tiny office, six flights up the stairs of a house in the Victoria district, and Messrs. Hubert Williams and Partners. The former housed the one-room London bureau of *Dawn*—the newspaper founded by Jinnah in 1938—and the latter handled the Public Relations accounts of certain Indian Princes, and hoped to do likewise for the new Muslim state. Approaching Mountbatten had been easy. The way to the Governor General of Pakistan was more difficult.

Our first encounter took place in the Punjab where, after filming the new frontier post of Pakistan in the morning, I attended a garden party in one of the beautiful Mogul gardens of Lahore. The magnificence of the setting was reflected in the shimmer of innumerable pools. Fountain after fountain played as Punjabi ladies moved gracefully in the wide trousers, blouse and head-scarves of their national dress. Among them, in trim tennis-style contrast, was one English girl, the fair daughter of the still British Governor of the West Punjab. With faultless precision, a Gurkha drum major led a pipe band up and down the gravelled paths. And in the midst of this brilliant and scintillating affair moved a tall, gaunt, elegant, monocled figure, the leader of a vast country no more than eleven weeks old, and in the eyes, and hopes, of its enemies, doomed to founder well before it had reached eleven months.

Suave, immaculate, seemingly withdrawn into a world of his own, aloof, un-bending, of all men the least gregarious, and of all democrats the least demagogic, Mohammed Ali Jinnah might have come from a different planet from Gandhi. Yet not only was the burning faith of each identical in its integrity. Both had been born the sons of poor parents, and as young men both had studied law at London's Inner Temple. Jinnah's birthplace had been Karachi, then a small fishing port on the edge of the Sind Desert. It was now the capital of the State he had made. Few men have ever ruled with such patience. Jinnah never ceased to exhort the populace to avoid reprisals, to exercise restraint and to help the Hindu minority in their midst. Pure Gandhi. But on one tactic they always parted company.

'It is easier to go to gaol to fight for freedom than it is to run a government', Jinnah once declared. Always a believer in constitutional practice, this brilliant lawyer had avoided the frequent arrests and incarcerations which had become the accepted lot of the Congress leaders. Mohammed Ali Jinnah had always argued his case with complete legality.

This cold and complex man was at work on state papers when I filmed him. They were spread all around his immaculately shod feet, stretched out between despatch boxes lying open on the floor at Karachi's Government House. No one spoke. It was the same with Gandhi. The reasons were different. Jinnah had ever been indifferent to public relations. The integrity of his life and the justice of his mission were sufficient in themselves. A wealthy barrister at forty-one, Jinnah had married a beautiful Bombay girl of an alien faith twenty-four years his junior. Within ten years, this single venture into the intimacy of a personal relationship had crashed. One woman, however, remained devoted. This film sequence of the lonely fanatic who had created Pakistan ended with him in as relaxed a state as ever he could be: enjoying the company of his sister Fatima—the only person who had been permitted a share in the last twenty years of his withdrawn and lonely life.

The finely cut suit and silk shirt hung loosely. His tall frame seemed to be wasting away. It had been a long and bitter struggle. His will had at last emerged triumphant. But Jinnah was dying.

At dawn on the following Christmas Day I flew to Lahore. This was the last birthday which Jinnah was ever to celebrate on this earth. The aircraft circled over the roofs of Karachi as the rays of the sun rose out of the Sind desert. There was a wealth of history in Lahore, but not of riches, there or anywhere else in Pakistan—with the exception of the jute of East Bengal. The country had no iron, no coal, no hydro-electric power. The Ministries of the new government even lacked typewriters, pens, pencils. And there was a worse lack still—the 'know-how' needed to run a modern state. The Hindus who had previously administered the commerce and communications of what was now Pakistan had fled. Economic collapse threatened the state even before it was launched. Business houses and banks had lost all their key-men. Lahore itself had been a minor centre of film production. Where were the technicians? Where were the stars, producers, camera-men, camera-mechanics? All Hindu. All gone. Rioters had burned the studios down. Jinnah, and his Prime Minister, Liaquat Ali Khan, would have to work miracles if their vast territories were not to disintegrate. The one point in Pakistan's favour was abundant natural resources of food, of which the Indian Union was chronically short.

The position of Kashmir was even more complex and strategic than that of the Punjab to the south. Three quarters of the inhabitants were Mohammedan. Jinnah and the Muslim League had always seen it as an integral part of Pakistan. Its ruler, the Maharajah, was a Hindu. His great-grandfather had purchased Kashmir from the British after their war with the Sikhs: he had paid one million pounds for it in the good, solid money of the nineteenth century. He had undertaken to present annually to the British "one horse, twelve goats of approved breed, and three pairs of Cashmere shawls". Hindu interests were strong, and so were Sikh. Three days before the surrender of British power in India, a standstill agreement had been signed by which the control of postal, telegraphic and the normal economic services went to Pakistan. The Maharajah nevertheless refused to accede to Pakistan —or the Indian Union: whereupon the tribesmen of Pakistan's fierce North West Frontier had taken the law into their own hands. They invaded the state, and advanced on Kashmir's capital, Srinagar.

There were urgent talks in Delhi and Lahore. The Hindu Maharajah, too panic-stricken to equivocate any longer, declared his state's accession to the Indian Union. Now Governor-General of the Indian Union, Mountbatten accepted the new member state as part of the Indian Union. A Sikh battalion of the Indian Army was flown into Srinagar. They landed just as the invading tribesmen were about to take over the airfield. They flung the enemy back from the perimeter. The Maharajah's capital was saved, but he had already fled to the safety of Jammu in the south.

I had decided that my camera would be best rewarded in Srinagar—if I could get there. The only overland route was the one the tribesmen had followed. But at the time of the invasion I was in the Punjab, and could only go under Indian Union auspices. The new map of partition now itself came to my rescue. In the Punjab the Gurdaspur district had been awarded to the Indian Union. Through

Jinnah in the Punjab

this ran the only road into Southern Kashmir. This was tough luck on Pakistan. It was fortunate indeed for the Indian Union. Under instructions to repulse the tribesmen, General Thimayya, whose headquarters were in Jullundur, was planning to push up heavy tanks in support of the Sikh battalion already in action. I was flown to Srinagar in a heavily loaded C 47. By the time I landed Indian Union troops had driven the invaders back sixty-five miles, into virtually impregnable positions in the mountains towering thousands of feet above the Vale of Kashmir.

I drove through the vale. Little wonder that poets and travellers had found in its green tranquillity a Shangri-la, a heaven on earth. Now it was the setting for the highest war in history since the British invaded Tibet in 1904.

The invaders from Pakistan lost Kashmir at Baramula. They could have pressed on the remaining twenty-five miles to the capital before Indian Union troops were brought up to meet them. Instead, drugged with success and the intoxication of a 'holy war', they had paused at Baramula and surrendered themselves up to an orgy of rape and destruction. At the Franciscan Convent of St. Joseph, they wrecked the altar, cast down the crucifix and shattered the statues of the saints. They butchered a British family and left the town a plundered shell.

I drove through the town. Then I continued to Uri, the headquarters of 161 Brigade, whose artillery and infantry patrols were aimed at the guerilla force up in the heights. The film I proceeded to shoot was virtually interchangeable with hundreds of feet I had shot during the war in Italy. Once more, the ranging, loading and firing of twenty-five pounders. Trucks crawling along the side of a great gorge—in whose depths now thundered the mighty Jhelum river—bringing up supplies from the Punjab; the staff-briefings, the maps—it had a mournful familiarity. It was war, never ending.

Kashmir is close to the roof of the world. Snow and ice are never far away. Srinagar had only a grass-covered air-strip, which at any moment might close for the winter. I flew out on the last plane. I hoped, by hook or by crook, to reach the receiving end of Brigadier Sen's guns. I belonged to neither side. Though I sometimes had difficulty in convincing people of that fact, I was just a camera, strictly neutral.

In the three weeks it took me to reach Pakistan Army Headquarters at Rawalpindi, the Kashmir crisis had become a major international issue. Charge and countercharge had been flung between Delhi and Karachi. Eleven days after the tribesmen's original invasion, and barely forty-eight hours after the Indian Union had first moved its troops against them, Jinnah had proposed at a meeting of the Joint Defence Council in Lahore that he and Mountbatten—the respective heads of the two States now clashing over Kashmir—should call for an immediate ceasefire. If the tribesmen did not heed it, then the Pakistan Army should enter Kashmir to see to it that they did. An ingenuous suggestion, perhaps. Delhi countered: why not an immediate plebiscite, held under international auspices? Unfortunately Nehru happened to choose that very moment to declare that "the will of the people" was already being obeyed. Karachi claimed that the struggle in Kashmir was strictly indigenous in origin; the crisis had been brought about by the denial of any rights to the Muslim majority by fuedal and autocratic Hindu rule, a rule now backed by the Indian Union.

My problem was how to get to Pakistan's side of the war in Kashmir, when

Pakistan wasn't fighting—officially. There could be no question of my going up the line with the troops, because Karachi claimed that no troops were being sent. But I had to go.

Quietly finishing my dinner in Flashman's Hotel in Rawalpindi I looked across the deserted dining room and recognised a Pakistan Army Colonel who had been on the plane from Lahore. We talked over coffee. 'I'll get you into Kashmir', he said. 'Be ready at the hotel after lunch tomorrow'.

The following afternoon up drove a ramshackle truck. It was strictly civilian. It was driven by a young Muslim League Volunteer Worker. It would be an understatement to describe him as uncommunicative. I received the immediate impression that I was to ask no questions. We followed the main road north-east. My attempts at conversation were met by silence. By nightfall, we were on a mere track; it came to an end. My companion got out and walked. I followed. In a one-room stone house which had once been a frontier post, we made tea, opened some cans of food, filled the place with smoke if not exactly heat and passed a silent night. In the morning however, my companion found his tongue. Trucks were drawn up all round. Ammunition was being unloaded—on to camels—from every one. But as I set up my camera, my companion spoke, at last.

'No filming'.

It was all happening before my eyes. But the eye of my view-finder was not supposed to see what my own were blinking at. My camera and equipment were lashed on to a mule, and the journey continued. My escort and I now joined a stream of men—some in uniform—moving down into a ravine with stacks of allegedly non-existent arms.

Hundreds of feet below, the Jhelum, once more, thundered its way out of Kashmir into Pakistan. Here was the physical reason why the K of Kashmir was essential to the spelling, and existence, of Pakistan. With four other mighty rivers it irrigated the plains of the Punjab. Whoever controlled its headwaters in the Himalayas could turn off the life of Pakistan like a tap.

We crossed the racing waterway by a narrow wooden bridge, precariously slung high above the torrent. Terra firma on the far side was the battleground.

This frontier zone of what was known in Pakistan as 'Azad' or Free Kashmir, was patrolled by armed guards—rebels from the Maharajah's State Troops who, when Kashmir acceded to the Indian Union, had thrown in their lot with Pakistan. I thought it might be an auspicious moment to start filming; my cicerone might thaw a little if photographed in conversation with these freedom fighters. Not a bit of it. In silence, we toiled on.

The back door of Kashmir. It was not the usual tourist's entrance to the province, but infinitely worth all the effort it involved. All that day we climbed up a long, narrow, winding track and every time we stopped for water, or just for breath, we were greeted by one more vista of wild magnificence. We spent the night in a handful of huts clinging to a mountainside, and in the morning looked back, the way we had come. We were still below the snow line in spite of a steady climb of thirty miles. Behind us stretched vista upon vista of tree-clad slopes, framing the peaks and vales of our ascent. On the third day out from Rawalpindi we reached the headquarters of 'Azad Kashmir'.

The centre of Azad Kashmir was a village called Palandri. We had no sooner reached it than my guide, for the first time, spoke with enthusiasm.

'I will present you to the leader'. he said.

Sardar Mohammed Ibrahim. A short, dark little man, with a belt of cartridges and a pistol slung around his waist. No Tito perhaps, but the leader of a resistance just as fanatic. 'Bring your camera to the meeting. I shall be speaking this evening', he said. I explained that at dusk there would not be enough light for photography. He agreed to let me film him with his rebel government in the morning.

In a hut nearby I lay down on a *charpoy*—that seldom resilient network of cord suspended from a wooden frame that serves as a bed for most of India—and instantly fell asleep. I was jerked violently awake by the roar of aircraft overhead and the scream and crash of falling bombs. As I rushed outside a Spitfire shot over my head, its cannons blazing. I dived for cover into an irrigation ditch in a field below. As I hugged the good earth I realized that Ibrahim's open air meeting around the corner must have been, quite literally, a sitting target.

The Spitfires droned off back to their base in the Indian Union. I climbed out of my ditch and walked into the village. Twenty-seven Kashmiri peasants lay dead or wounded. It was New Year's Day 1948.

Ibrahim led me into the hut where he slept and planned his campaign. He told me the story behind the revolt. Nine months later, in New York, the spotlight of the world was to be turned on him as he spoke at the United Nations. The cause he pleaded there was essentially the same.

The people of Kashmir had wrested a few elementary rights from an authoritarian Hindu Government as long as seventeen years before. In effect they amounted to very little. Sheikh Abdullah, the leader who had secured this grudging award was soon languishing in the Maharajah's gaol. Sardar Mohammed Ibrahim assumed the leadership of the 'Muslim Conference'. On October 3rd, 1947, he had declared himself Prime Minister of the Provisional Government of Free Kashmir. The rule of the Maharajah, Sir Hari Singh, was alleged to be at an end. Equally defiant pronunciamentos were made for the benefit of Pakistani press and radio. Ibrahim then left for Poonch, this western province of Kashmir where he had now set up his headquarters.

Poonch, where Ibrahim had been born, had already risen in open rebellion. The Hindu oligarchy in Kashmir had taken a blood-thirsty lesson from recent events in the Punjab. They had launched an onslaught against the long suffering Muslim population. The few Muslim units in the State forces had turned on their officers, and deserted to fight with the rebels.

'I raised a force of thirty thousand', continued Ibrahim. 'The tribesmen from the North West Frontier were coming to our help'.

Ibrahim went on to tell me that the aim of the Hindu oligarchy in Kashmir had been to drive the Muslims out to Pakistan. Their place was to be taken by the millions of Hindu—and Sikh—refugees now flooding the West Punjab. He claimed that this exchange of populations—if not genocide—was a project decided upon at a meeting between the Maharajah of Kashmir, the Sikh Maharajah of Patiala—and Patel.

'Yes, I have received some supplies, and some financial aid from certain people in Pakistan', he admitted. 'Weapons for the revolt were smuggled across the Jhelum by raft'.

Military command of the rebels was in the hands of a certain 'General Tariq'. He remained a dim and reticent figure throughout our conversation. Ibrahim's

Nehru in Kashmir

role was primarily political. With four other Ministers—a Minister of War as deaf as a post—he shared the responsibility for the administration of five thousand square miles and 900,000 people, scratching a living from terraces of soil on the mountainous slopes of Azad Kashmir.

Facing him in Srinagar was another government, another Prime Minister. Sheikh Abdullah. This legendary Lion of Kashmir had been the first to raise the flag of revolt against the Maharajah. Although a Muslim he was a disciple of Gandhi, and a friend of Nehru. He believed in a Kashmir—and an India—free from this religious rivalry which Jinnah claimed could only be resolved by the creation of two nations. Abdullah had been released from the Maharajah's gaol two days after the tribesmen's invasion had forced that autocrat to join the Indian Union. Abdullah had now become the official Prime Minister. He too was determined to transform the feudal stagnation of the state. But time was to deal him a blow of terrible irony— and to justify Ibrahim's alliance with Pakistan. Six years later Adbullah was himself denouncing the persecution of Muslims on his side of the divided state. He called for a Kashmir independent of both Pakistan and the Indian Union. He was clapped back into gaol, for another twelve years, and this time by his own government.

A rebel patrol, and a primitive field hospital set up in a gully concluded this first filming of 'Free' Kashmir. I took my leave of Ibrahim, and thanked him both for his help and his confidence. Accompanied by my taciturn guide I set off for Rawalpindi. My companion seemed even more morose than ever.

As we circled down the mountain trail we passed others coming up. They were group after group of Pakistani soldiers. Only the badges of rank and insignia had been removed from their battle-dress. By sundown we reached the frontier. On the other side of the Jhelum the sun sank ever lower into the hills of Pakistan, but an endless discussion went on between my escort and the frontier guards. It went on and on. At last I joined in myself. I asked what reason there could be for this unnecessary delay.

'You are not permitted to proceed further', I was told.

I had by now become a crafty traveller, and this was just the sort of contingency I had foreseen. Forewarned is forearmed. I had armed myself with a letter from none other than Ibrahim which explained my business, and advised all whom it might concern to offer me no let or hindrance in my return to Pakistan.

I was just congratulating myself on my forethought when I saw, not without some disquiet, that upon these frontier guards the signature of their Prime Minister had no effect whatever. The very escort whose job I had always supposed to be to see me safely back to my destination was not merely unimpressed. He became belligerent—and led the attack.

I was seized and searched from head to toe. My film and all my equipment were taken away. Propelled by ancient muskets I was thrust into a fortunately empty cowshed. The door was slammed behind me, and bolted hard.

I lay on the mud floor and pondered my predicament. No-one knew where I was. No-one would miss me. The London bureau of *The March of Time* had heard from me as recently as Christmas Eve. They would expect no word or cable for at least a week. There was nothing whatever I could do.

I had been arrested and imprisoned. Why? I soon hit on a possible explanation. My arrival had practically coincided with that of the Spitfires. The Indian Union pilots had known the location of Ibrahim's headquarters and not only that: they had found the leader addressing a meeting when they arrived. I had been conspicuously absent from it. Didn't it follow that I might have been sending them a signal?

It was fairly obvious that this was the conclusion somebody had come to. But, surely, a little late in the day. Why had Ibrahim received me and talked, at such length, on the very evening of the attack? Why had he given me every facility for filming his guerillas in action afterwards? I gave up worrying and went to sleep.

Next morning I was let out of the hut as if I had gone there of my own free will for a quiet night's rest. My film and equipment were returned—but all without a word. We crossed the Jhelum. My guide deposited me back at Flashman's Hotel in Rawalpindi and left with the same churlish taciturnity as he had collected me five days before. That was that. I could only conclude that he had gone through all my equipment while I slept. (Fortunately the cans of exposed film had not been opened.) Failing to find a radio transmitter or indeed anything electronic whatever, he had concluded that I was nothing more than what I claimed to be, an innocent abroad with a camera.

Later in Pakistan Army Headquarters in Lahore I met members of the General Staff. A uniformed, red-tabbed Brigadier seemed somehow vaguely familiar. 'Brigadier-General Akbar Khan'. 'How do you do', said I, recognising him an instant later. This senior officer of the Pakistan Army was none other than the mysterious 'General Tariq' commanding the rebel forces in Kashmir whom I had glimpsed at Ibrahim's headquarters.

I discussed my adventures with the British General who at that time commanded the Pakistan Army. Sir Douglas Gracey was completely frank with me—and not for the first time I discovered a personality who was prepared to talk more freely to a character with a camera than he might have done to a correspondent with a typewriter.

The Commander-in-Chief believed that, acting on the Indian Union's complaint to the Security Council, the United Nations would order a cease-fire in Kashmir. Pakistan, as I was by now convinced myself, was in no position to comply. Resistance to the troops of the Indian Union in Kashmir had originated in an indigenous Kashmiri force which had risen against their ruler *before* he had declared his accession to the Indian Union. It was only his consequent accession which made the presence of the Indian Union troops legal in Kashmir. The Indian Union would then declare that since Pakistan refused to withdraw support, she would be justified in taking action herself. She would launch an invasion of Pakistan through the Punjab in order to bring about peace in Kashmir.

A pretty fair forecast of what did in fact eventually happen.

I lost no time in communicating the substance of this grave situation to the producers of *The March of Time*. Writing, January 12th 1948, that:

"India is on the verge of civil war . . . The atmosphere now is quite appalling, both sides are spoiling for a fight . . . While I was in Kashmir this second time a very bad outbreak of communal fighting occurred in Karachi, and eighty Sikh refugees were murdered by Muslim refugees from the Punjab. Coming as this did after a period of comparative calm and taking place in the capital of Pakistan, it has further inflamed feelings in the Indian Union . . . I therefore feel that there is rather a race against time to complete coverage before the whole show blows up. Accordingly I have revised my itinerary. The one area in which we must get coverage before this eventuality is Eastern Pakistan. If I leave it to the end of the trip as originally planned, hostilities may prevent movement . . . A customs and police check has already started on both sides. Therefore I plan to go over to Bengal immediately for this material, and hope to reach Dacca, the capital of Eastern Pakistan, in a week's time . . . My one and only hope is that I do not have to be measured for a War Correspondent's uniform".

This letter was barely in the post before news from Delhi electrified India and alerted the world.

At his daily prayer-meeting the evening before, Gandhi had announced that with God as his 'supreme and sole councillor' he would fast until death unless there was 'a reunion of hearts of all communities brought about without any outside pressure but from an awakened sense of duty'.

Behind this gesture lay not only the rapidly worsening relations between India and Pakistan. There was also an immediate and very definable event. The Government of the Indian Union had refused to hand over to Pakistan the latter's share of the cash balance of pre-partition India; no less than a sum of five hundred and fifty million rupees. Maulana Azad, the leader of the forty million Muslims mortgaged to the Indian Union later declared: "The fast was directed against the attitude of Sardar Patel, and Patel knew it". After three days of his ordeal, the rapidly weakening Gandhi announced that he would never break his fast unless this economic blackmail was revoked.

'The loss of Mahatma Gandhi's life would mean the loss of India's soul': these were Nehru's words. The next morning came an official announcement to the effect that the funds would be transferred immediately. Two days later Gandhi broke his fast and I took advantage of the breathing-space his example had secured. I flew across India to East Bengal.

The Prime Minister of East Bengal was Khwaja Nazimuddin, destined to be Jinnah's successor as Governor-General of all Pakistan.

After the strident street scenes of Karachi—all camels, donkeys and thrusting automobiles—Dacca, the capital, was as strange and novel as an Indian Venice. This was river-land, delta-land, the land criss-crossed by the tributaries of the Ganges and the Brahmaputra. All life and trade moved on water. The scene was dotted with boats, paddle-steamers—and mosques. There are more mosques in Dacca than in any other Indian city.

But there was wealth here, real wealth at last—jute. Three quarters of the total world supply of the golden fibre which had spun so many British-Indian fortunes was produced here. The creation of the Indian Union had very nearly trumped even this ace. The mills that wove the fibre were over the border, in West Bengal, in Hindu hands.

Pakistan was already planning its own processing plants, though there were as yet none for me to film. I followed the sorting, packing and compression into bales of an abundant crop as it was prepared for export. I took it for granted that it was all going to Dundee. Any other name stencilled on the bales would have seemed almost unreal. But there was one—Boston. America was a developing market too.

From Dacca I went, not by boat, but by narrow gauge railroad to East Bengal's only sea-port, Chittagong, where, a mere eighty miles from the Burmese border, Subhas Chandra Bose had first hoped to raise the flag of 'Azad Hind' four years before. There were Pakistani plans to turn this small port, on the sluggish mouth of the Karnafulli river, into an eastern Karachi.

This province of East Bengal had an honourable nationalist past. It was in Dacca that the Muslim League had been born 'to protect and advance the political rights of the Mussulmans of India'. This was in 1906. Forty-one years later, the League was mustering a private army for the protection of the state it had won. Its recruits swore loyalty not to the government of their country, but to the political party which dominated it. 'In the name of the All-Powerful, ever-present Allah', they swore 'to remain for ever under the flag of the Muslim League'. I heard, and filmed, this oath sworn by warrior after fledgling warrior at a parade and display given by these 'Muslim National Guards' in Dacca.

They pronounced it to a chorus of 'Pakistan Zindabad'—'Long Live Pakistan'— and 'Quaid-i-Azam Zindabad'—'Long Live the Great Leader'. They swore 'to make all sacrifices in obeying directions of the League for Pakistan and for the preservation of the freedom and prosperity of the Brotherhood of Islam'. I filmed these youngsters saluting, signing their copies of the oath and finally kissing the flag which a Guardsman held out to them. I remembered Mohan Singh and his private army in the Punjab. The more fanatical Muslims could never forget that the crescent flag of Islam had once flown over the Red Fort of the Mogul Emperor Shah Jehan in Delhi. By the same token, the Hindu extremist could never relinquish the vision of an India united by the obliteration of Pakistan.

Organized into the Rashtrya Swayamsevak Sangh, the Hindu exponents of a communal fascism were about to strike their greatest blow.

On January 29th I flew out of Dacca with my film of Pakistan complete. In Calcutta, I set about its despatch. The necessary formalities were completed by the afternoon of January 30th 1948. At the airport I saw the negative off on its flight to New York.

That same evening, in Delhi, the usual crowds waited in the grounds of Birla House for Gandhi's daily prayer meeting. The usually prompt Mahatma was late. At last he tore himself away from another quarrel with Patel and, as he stepped from the house to cross the lawn, a young Hindu came forward to greet him with the traditional 'namaste' salutation of joined hands. As the Mahatma replied, Nathuram Vinayak Godse pulled out a revolver and fired three shots. Murmuring 'Oh, God', Gandhi sank to the ground. Within a few minutes he was dead.

Thus perished the living symbol of Hindu-Muslim reconciliation and India's greatest son since the Buddha. India was brought to her senses, shocked to her senses. Even the most virulent of those clamouring for war with Pakistan paused in their plans. Sardar Patel suffered a heart attack, never to play an actively influential role again. By the manner of his death, Gandhi achieved the greatest miracle of his life: the peace between Hindu and Muslim for which he had always strived.

Sidetracked to China

The profound depression in which much of the world sank during the inter-war period; the spectacle of millions of unemployed, of ruined farmers, and of hungry people contrasted with the known potential of modern production—these events have convinced men that the world's resources must be better used for human welfare and that nations must work together rather than at cross purposes, or our civilization may go down to destruction. Charter of the United Nations' Food and Agriculture Organization

By midsummer 1948, after the first nine exhausting Indian months, both my camera and myself were in urgent need of rest and repair and, with filming effectively halted by the monsoon rains steadily falling until the end of September, I accordingly proposed our return to London for this purpose. This was approved, on the understanding that after this break I agreed to go on to China from India. Fine by me, and back home by the end of July I learned that this new venture was to be a film commissioned by the United Nations to illustrate and dramatise the work of their recently formed Food and Agriculture Organization.

My old UNRRA chief and friend, Bill Wells, was now Deputy Director of the UN Films Division; and in Paris his boss, Jean Benoit-Lévy, briefed me more on just what they wanted shot in China:

"Our film shall help the FAO, by clearly showing its limitations, to prepare the minds of the audiences for stronger and more powerful and all embracing measures to ensure food for all, according to Article 55 of the U.N. Charter".

Benoit-Lévy also told me that this film must be completed and ready for release by mid December. This was news both to me and *The March of Time*, and it was now already 27th September. I would have to get to China right away, and fast. Hurried cables were sent to New York.

In Bombay the Chinese Consul knew nothing of me, or this project. Still therefore without a visa for his country, I flew on to Calcutta, where I had already, nonetheless, booked myself for Shanghai on the first available plane. In Calcutta the Chinese Consul knew no more about all this than his colleague in Bombay. He told me that he must await instructions and confirmation from the Republic of China's delegate to the United Nations before he could act. I accordingly took advantage of the annual Dussehra holiday festival to fly to Delhi, where I arranged to film, on my return from China—if I ever got there—some of the F.A.O.'s attempts to stamp out the pests which were destroying annually thirty million tons of bread grains and rice: rats, insects and fungi were devouring enough food to keep fifty million people alive every year.

Back in Calcutta the good word had at last come from Dr. Ting Fu-tsiang at Lake Success, and three weeks after I had spoken with Jean Benoit-Lévy in Paris I at last landed in Shanghai.

"The Communist peasants would take over the lands, the Communist workers would demand a different labour system, the Communist soldiers would no longer fight unless they knew why they were fighting—whether Moscow wanted it or not."

Such had been the thoughts of André Malraux's Kyo in Shanghai on the night

Rice queue in Shanghai, 1948

of March 27th, 1927; and now 25 years later, I was to witness the five climactic weeks of communism's greatest post-war triumph.

> "For next Marchtime release ship urgently some coverage of Marshall Plan offices officials and activities . . . scenes Nanking exteriors government buildings and shots present Minister of War or Chief of Staff plus any scenes troops in action or on way to same you can get in Soochow region. Theme of picture is worldwide effort combat Soviet aggression on all fronts need film here by November 2 at latest so do your damndest : . ."

This cable reached me the moment I arrived in Shanghai. I hurried off to an office on Nanking Road: that of the United States Economic Cooperation Administration—the agency of the Marshall Plan. I had eight days in which to chronicle what was to be the last stand of Chiang Kai-shek's Nationalist Government on the mainland of China.

Jack Doughty, E.C.A.'s enthusiastic Information Officer, dropped all his own routine work and took me straight to the Ministry of National Defence in Nanking.

Once again I set up camera to record a general's exposition of strategy. Minister of War when Chiang Kai-shek first moved against Mao Tse-tung's Kiangsi Soviet Republic in 1930, General Ho Ying-chin outlined the course of the battle raging a hundred and fifty miles north of the capital.

Below the Yellow River the Communist Commander Ch'en Yi, after capturing Tsinan, had moved southwards towards the great concentration of Nationalist forces at Hsuchow. The defenders had abandoned this vital railway centre and junction, hoping to fall back unscathed with all their equipment to the defence of Nanking. But with the help of his one-eyed colleague Liu Po-cheng, Ch'en Yi had surrounded the escaping garrison. Heavy fighting was in progress as the

Coal-miner at Pengpu, China 1948

Twelfth Army Group, moving up from Hankow, endeavoured to break through to its relief.

Railhead was at Pengpu, a hundred and ten miles north of Nanking. Doughty and I boarded another train to find the battle. Constantly held up on the single track, we were halted in station after station as other trains passed in the reverse direction, crammed with refugees fleeing from the area that we hoped to reach. Open coal trucks clanked their way south, whole families with their inevitably pathetic bundles and belongings clinging to their filthy tops and sides. Germany, Poland, the Punjab—and now China, the same scene passed before my camera. The displaced persons whose wanderings chart so much the course of this fearsome twentieth century.

North of Pengpu all was confusion. Two Nationalist armies in one army group had already surrendered without fighting. What remained of the original four hundred thousand defenders of Hsuchow were scattered across these great open plains. They were out of touch both with their command and themselves. We continued our journey to the coalfields of Hwainan, whose product in shipment had already provided the means of escape for so many fleeing families.

The miners were still working normal shifts. But elsewhere most of China's coal was already in communist hands. The Economic Cooperation Administration was being forced to purchase and ship petroleum from Saudi Arabia in order to maintain Shanghai's power supply. Cotton supplies were also short in the city's great textile mills. Doughty's Mission was attempting to shore up the fast shrinking Nationalist fabric. From the bleak faces of the miners in the Hwainan coal pits, to the dexterous fingers of young girls at work on the looms, my camera was to catch two aspects of the Chinese industry soon to be placed at the service of the world's most populous communist state.

Contributing to the military defeat of Chiang Kai-shek was a galloping inflation, which the two thousand million dollars worth of aid that his government had received from the United States since the Japanese surrender only seemed to intensify. Ten weeks before our return to Nanking from our abortive attempt to locate a battle, a new currency had been issued. The 'Gold Yuan'. Its rate of exchange set at three million to the old Chinese dollar—and four to the American. For a short while the plan had seemed to have a chance of success, but with the fall of Tsinan public confidence had finally evaporated, and the inexorable economic laws of a situation in which a government's income was less than fifteen per cent of its expenditure soon rendered the reform valueless.

The helpless Minister of Finance was Dr. Wong Yong-wu; and, having filmed him in discussion with the economic advisers of the American Mission who, with their own grant of a further four hundred million, were hoping still to stave off the inevitable, Doughty and I were once more forced aboard the creaking Chinese railroad system by the heavy thunder and torrential rain that had halted all flying to Shanghai. I had by then barely forty-eight hours left in which to complete this hurried assignment and get my film away across the Pacific.

The journey was an endurance test, relieved only by innumerable glasses of weak tea served by an attendant, who brewed this insipid beverage in a corner of the wooden-seated coach in which we attempted to sleep. We were jerked awake as troop trains, speeding in the opposite direction towards the vacuum of Hsuchow, forced us to a halt. The two hundred mile journey took us ten hours. At seven the

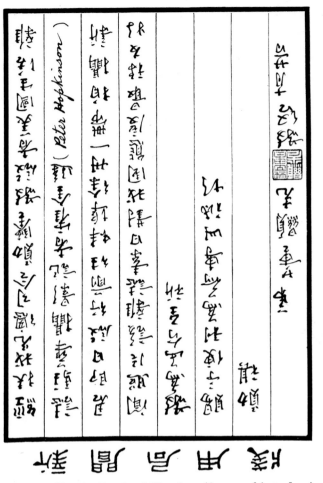

China 1948—Permit to film the Battle of Hsuchow (Letter of introduction to General Kin Fu)

next morning we unloaded my equipment at Shanghai's main station. We were to film Doughty's Mission Chief.

A former Mayor of San Francisco, Roger Lapham had inherited an impossible situation, and its grimmest aspect was hunger. Barely a mile from his office some of Shanghai's three million hungry had already rioted for rice. Reserve stocks were being released, and in the city's seething slums, to the accompaniment of a carpenter hammering away at ornate coffins for sale just across the street while the carefully rationed grain was weighed and distributed, I filmed the face of famine.

Then I moved westwards towards Nanking.

From the remote fastness of Tibet, through the Red Basin of Szechuan, the Yangtze makes its way past Chungking, Ichang and Hankow to Nanking, and in the crisp sunlight of an early November morning a river steamer bore me along its banks to the island of Pa Kua Chou.

Raising money from a bank in the nearby capital the farmers of this delta community had been able to purchase ten tractors, five seed drills, ten disk harrows, ten ploughs, three combines and four irrigation pumps, convinced that this new equipment would so improve the yield of their land that they would be able to repay the original loan with the proceeds of their next two seasons of crops.

But before even the first sowing that I had filmed had taken root the bank's interest rates, the land, the Yangtze, and all of China had passed into communist accounting, and this microscopic little experiment in cooperative farming was swallowed up in the mass regimentation of Mao Tse-tung's communes.

Once there might have been a chance.

While I had been filming for UNRRA in Russia, Canada's Grant McLean had been covering the work of that international organization in China. In the truce of 1946 he had made two major expeditions into communist territory and, in Yenan, filmed the elusive Mao Tse-tung himself. Barred from the United Nations year after year, Mao's China was to be denied the international aid that the F.A.O. was still optimistically attempting in Chiang's ever-shrinking estate as 1948 drew to a close. In what little time was left, I pressed on with the filming of activities that could always serve as a pilot project for such a programme of assistance to underdeveloped agricultural countries.

Nearly all the non-tillable land in some provinces of China had been denuded of trees and shrubs, which had been destroyed in warfare or cut down by a people bereft of any other source of fuel. Four million seedlings had been raised in forest nurseries near Nanking and transplanted as the raw material of the reforestation needed to control soil erosion and flooding. Seventeen million miniature pines, cedars, oaks, sycamores, willows and poplars were growing in other nurseries, preparing to follow the thirty thousand already planted along the waterways and dykes of the Yangtze delta, where irrigation ditches were being dug, sluice gates installed, and flooded fields drained by pumps imported by the F.A.O.

Irrigation, drainage and flood control projects of this nature had been drawn up to improve over a hundred thousand acres of land in ten Chinese provinces. It had been estimated that the completion of these schemes would have resulted in an increase of food production by more than nine hundred thousand tons a year at a cost of less than a dollar a ton. The living standard of a million and three quarter people would have materially risen for an outlay of less than half a dollar a head.

Entirely dependent on the cow and water buffalo for the draft power with which to till her ricelands, the loss of a million head of cattle a year through rinderpest had long been a major cause of China's hunger. The virulence of the disease was the principal handicap to the establishment of a healthy livestock industry. Without this neither meat nor milk could ever be made available to her famine-haunted people.

Preserved in dry ice and flown from Africa, an original strain of rinderpest virus had provided the basis for a vaccine developed at Nanking's 'National Research Bureau of Animal Husbandry', where F.A.O. scientists, with their Chinese colleagues, were now producing sufficient to immunize 20,000,000 head of cattle a year—which would have meant, if those twelve months had been vouchsafed them—the total elimination of the disease from all China south of the Yangtze.

Developed by the F.A.O. in India, another vaccine successfully immunized poultry from the Newcastle's Disease, which was killing millions of chickens every year. At a rural inoculation centre, baskets of chicks were brought from sometimes as far as thirty miles by farmers anxious to take advantage of this free treatment.

Eggs from Australia and high-laying poultry from the United States were being multiplied at a chicken farm near Nanking in order to further improve the native breed. Root stocks of an improved variety of sweet potato had been imported from the United States in order to increase both the quality and quantity of China's third most important food crop.

UNRRA had sent to China machinery for the local production of insecticide, together with a supply of easily assembled sprayers with which the farmers could rid their fields of the pests ever eager to devour their crops. On this foundation in Shanghai, the F.A.O. were assisting in the establishment of small-scale factories for this two-fold manufacture.

A land of great rivers and vast coastline, China could always look to her waters for food, and in the past had led the world in the cultivation of fresh water fish. But what had previously been productive culture ponds had been destroyed in the war and were now lying idle. An ambitious project existed to collect fifty million young fish fresh from spawn and transport them to these areas of potential propagation. It had been planned to charter specially equipped junks and river boats for this purpose; and, at a Fisheries Research Laboratory in Shanghai, technicians studied specimens collected from nearby breeding pools.

So passed a delightful seventeen days of filming in the crisp light of the autumnal Chinese landscape. A brief period quite detached from the political and military struggle to the north that had now decided China's destiny, and whose consequences were no longer to be ignored. The F.A.O. offices in Shian Road, so eager and active when I first arrived in Nanking three weeks before, were now fast emptying as all the staff and specialists hurried their evacuation.

For it was all over at Hsuchow. The final nationalist army and the ultimate nationalist conscript had surrendered. Chiang was finished—he had no troops left. There was now nothing between Mao Tse-tung and the Yangtze: he could enter Nanking and Shanghai whenever he liked. To the south, there was nothing to halt his advance to Canton—from whence the Kuomintang had set out to redeem China twenty-one years before.

On the slopes of Purple Mountain, near the tomb of the first Ming Emperor, above the fields in which I had filmed the cutting of sweet potato slips, a vast and imposing structure awaited the coming of China's triumphant communism. Designed in the style of the ancient imperial tombs it housed the mortal remains of Sun Yat-sen, the founder of the Republic and the Kuomintang that had originally proclaimed his Three Principles of the People: Nationalism, Democracy and Socialism. Dead of cancer two years before his lieutenant Chiang Kai-shek had marched north from Canton, his widow was now about to become a vice-chairman of the Communist Central People's Government Council.

"On completion F A O China coverage try spend day or two shooting current turmoil Shanghai" read my latest cable from New York.

That great commercial metropolis now awaited its fate in an atmosphere of calm but expectant normality; my five remaining days were passed in the relaxed comfort which, at least so far as I was concerned, was such a conspicuous feature of my own Chinese experience.

International capital had developed a mudbank on the Yangtze estuary into one of the world's greatest ports and commercial centres. Now Shanghai's large foreign business community viewed the coming of the communists with a mixture of relief and equanimity, so sick were they of trying to live and trade under the inefficient and corrupt bureaucracy of the Nationalists.

Despite Britain's early recognition of the new government in Peking, the foreign business community were soon to regret this equanimity. Amongst Shanghai's large White Russian population there was however no such false optimism. Having fled the excesses of one communist revolution thirty years before they viewed with dismay and despair the approach of another.

No one family had done more to develop the magnificent facade of Shanghai's waterfront than the Sassoons, who had emigrated from Baghdad to Bombay a generation before the outbreak of the opium war. Their many interests built up in China after the First World War had been actively promoted by Sir Victor Sassoon, to whom I was indebted for so much of the comfort of my own stay. Some years before the outbreak of the Second World War E. D. Sassoon and Company had constructed Shanghai's tallest building, the Broadway Mansions which were host to and housed the Foreign Correspondents Club. From the flat rooftop, a few paces from the end of the corridor outside my apartment, a glittering carpet of light nightly reflected the simmering city far below. A white-coated room boy brought breakfast in the morning with a copy of the British owned *North China Daily News*. Afternoon tea could accompany a reading of the American owned *Shanghai Evening News*.

On the other side of the Pacific my complete film of these efforts to combat hunger in China was greeted with delight. I received the following letter from the film's Associate Producer:

> "I screened your . . . coverage of the F A O this morning with Bill Wells and we were both very impressed. I think you did a really marvellous job: the quality is good and you got exactly the scenes we need , . . the China coverage (was) of such wonderful quality . . ."

I was therefore all the more surprised, when I finally saw the completed film—released by Columbia as *Battle for Bread*—to discover that while my correspondent's name featured in its credits, together with those of the Executive Producer, the Commentator, and the gentleman who arranged the music, none other appeared. Audiences viewing the film might therefore have been forgiven for assuming that what London's *Daily Cinema* described as a "brilliant documentary" had come into being without benefit of any direction or photography whatsoever. My name did not appear.

Six Men of India

Action rightly renounced brings freedom, action rightly performed also brings freedom. Both are better than mere shunning of action. Take either path and tread it to the end: The end is the same. There the followers of action meet the seekers after knowledge in equal freedom.　　　　　　　　　　　　　　　　　　　　The Bhagavad Gita

I returned to Delhi to resume work on the Indian film.

"For the moment, as you realize, you are pretty much in control of the India story, and we are depending heavily on you to use your judgment as to what is important and what isn't . . . I don't want you to pull out of India until you have really covered it, but, on the other hand we realise that we could keep you there for the next five years and still not shoot everything available . . . I think you ought to do a take-out of a day in the life of an Untouchable and a day in the life of a well-to-do high caste Hindu. I don't think these should be too detailed, but we ought to get an idea of how both of them live, work, pray and amuse themselves if they do".

Thus, seven months after my first landing in Bombay, and ten weeks after his cable had announced *The March of Time*'s plan for a feature film of India, in reply to my own airmailed proposals, I had been assured and apostrophied by the producer in New York. To have at last exchanged the inadequacies of the occasionally frenetic telegram for constructive correspondence with this remote figure was a great relief; and to the task of reflecting these two polarised extremes of Hinduism I now directed my camera. But for how long was I to be "in control of the India story"? Just, and only, during its interpretation and filming? Or up to and including the editing, and the writing of the commentary—in which attitudes could be adopted, opinions expressed, prejudices paraded by persons with no experience of the subject, no commitment; and perhaps, as was to happen with the Russian film, a deliberate desire subsequently to distort, to manipulate?

My proposed Indian film was not the first full-length feature to be essayed by *The March of Time*. In the early days of the war *The Ramparts We Watch* had reminded then neutral Americans of the issues at stake. Ten years later *The Golden Twenties* had nostalgically surveyed the Jazz Age. A year later I was to be present at the Washington première of *Modern Arms and Free Men*, another such documentary feature on the strategy of nuclear annihilation.

The first stage in making such a film as a feature length documentary of India is research, study, research. One must read all one can, see all one can, talk to, and listen to, every person one can; absorb oneself in the story, its atmosphere, history, art, culture, and politics. And then, tentatively at first, proceed to the drafting of an outline on paper: organizing and synthesising ·everything in the shape and pattern of a film, with a beginning, a middle, and an end. (But not, as Jean-Luc Godard has reminded us, necessarily in that order.) This is the first rough sketch, a charcoal drawing as it were, of the portrait to follow.

Stage Two takes the camera—and tape recorder—out of its case, and translates this document, this script, this blueprint into its own wonderfully exciting medium of pictures that move. But not merely a series and collection of isolated still photographs that happen to contain movement. Each separate image should be composed in relationship to the whole, to each other: each should carry its own meaning, but at the same time possess a significance only in association. And at the time of filming, one must always be ready to adapt to circumstance and improvise; to take advantage of, and incorporate the spontaneous.

Stage Three takes place in small, air-conditioned rooms, far from the noise, dust, and clamour of the location, all of which are now on film—but in hundreds of different and disjointed strips of film, just as they left the camera in the arbitrary order of filming. Sometimes there may have been many attempts at the same scene, the same action. Everything is viewed, assessed, and examined. And steadily,

Jaipur—The Games Room

shot by shot, scene by scene, it is all assembled. And now new associations appear: overtones hitherto hidden emerge in novel and unexpected juxtapositions. It is here, on the editing bench, and in the recording studio, that the film finally takes on its ultimate shape, emerges with an organic life unique to itself.

All three stages of creating an entire film are inter-dependent. But with costs of production astronomical—far above the financial reach of most individuals—rare was the film maker who could command control throughout. With enlightened sponsorship it still sometimes happened, to a degree, in documentary. But whoever pays the piper, ultimately calls the tune. The maker of *Nanook of the North*, *Moana*, and *Man of Aran*, Robert Flaherty, got away with it just once in twelve years, with Standard Oil, in his *Louisiana Story*. Eisenstein was forced to leave all his Mexican film behind him, and never got his hands on a single frame. What would happen to this film of mine I wondered; whose hand would finally edit?

"India—Long Version", as it was called when in production, was finally designed to interpret in detail the vast panorama of the sub-continent through the lives of six of its citizens. The Untouchable and the Brahmin. The Maharajah and the Peasant. The Anglo-Indian schoolmaster and the young Hindu intellectual. Included were scenes that I made later of young Indian students studying hydrodynamics at London University, and others at the feet of Harold Laski at the London School of Economics. Concluding with scenes of Nehru's first visit to the United States.

I chose my Maharajah with care. By March 1949 ten days remained for me to film a Maharajah still supreme master of his hereditary realm. Under Azim Husain's auspices I had more than an introduction. His Highness Saramd-i-Rajahai Hindustan Raj Rajendra Sri Mararajah Driraj Sir Saurai Man Singhi Bahadur, Lieutenant-General, thirty-ninth ruler of Jaipur bade me be his guest. An enthusiastic aviator with a charmed life, he flew me into his capital city in his personal DC 3. I was installed in the luxury of the State Guest House, and for the first time in my life, had peacocks to parade on the lawn.

Jaipur itself had scarcely caught up with the airplane. Much of it was still eighteenth century, and ancient carts and carriages drawn by white oxen, ambled along amongst the automobiles in its streets.

Beside a lily pond, rippling under its fountains, sat the ruler of two and a half million subjects, with just another one hundred and sixty three hours to go, taking tea. His daughter, the Yuvrani of Baria, joined the group. The Maharani—unquestionably one of the world's most beautiful women—filled the cups for her husband and her new son-in-law, the young Yuvraj of Baria. In a glittering ceremony which had cost four million dollars, lasted nine days, and been attended by ten thousand guests, this minor princeling had just been married to the Princess Miki. With the exception of the Maharajah's two young sons, who were at school in England, the family circle was complete.

The Maharajah, a strikingly handsome man in his late thirties, wore a sports jacket, open necked shirt and slacks. Three days later I filmed him in the beribboned regalia of his State Forces uniform in conclave with his Prime Minister and the Dewan of Jodhpur, speculating over the extent his privy purse would assume in just one week's time. The figure agreed upon for the next seven years was eighteen hundred thousand rupees a year, as a fee for the Governorship of the new combined state of Rajasthan, with a further five hundred and fifty thousand for a personal allowance. Sardar Patel obviously did not intend to pauperise his 'Rajpramukhs'—the princely figureheads of his streamlining of states.

Not every former ruler received such a golden fare-thee-well. India was littered with out of work princes. Their palaces became hotels. Their jewellery, automobiles and dancing girls, their voraciously hungry herds of elephants, their orchestras and private zoos, together with all the paraphernalia of their previously sybaritic existence, were taken over by the state. This chill draught of democracy did not dampen Jaipur's spirits or cause him to lose his insatiable appetite for sport. As a Rajpramukh he would still remain the custodian of much of his former princely glory, and I followed him from the tennis courts to the polo ground. Here he umpired an exciting seven chukkers of the game in which he was an international champion. A recent third plane crash had kept him from playing himself.

Housekeeping on such a scale was nothing less than a military operation. Each department of the royal household was administered by an officer of the State Forces. I filmed a corps of gardeners tending the regimented lawns and flower beds surrounding the Maharajah's palace. Then I moved through to its luxurious interior.

A host of turbanned servants flicked the minutest speck of dust from the surface of innumerable cups won at polo, including a magnificent trophy awarded to the runner-up in the Prince of Wales Commemoration Tournament at Delhi in 1922. Beside an autographed and silver-framed photograph of the aide-de-camp who had accompanied the future Duke of Windsor on that occasion and who had become the last Viceroy and first Governor-General of the new Indian Union, bowls of flowers were carefully arranged. In the billiard room the spotless green baize was made ready for play beneath the head of a rhinoceros shot in the forests of the Marahajah's brother-in-law at Cooch Behar, affixed to the wall alongside the skin of a tiger hunted and killed in Jaipur's own domains. In the armoury, the guns that had laid these beasts low were taken down from their racks, inspected and cleaned. From the stables a string of some of the one hundred and twenty polo ponies were led out to exercise while, at the airfield, one of the fast single-seater planes which had almost cost its dashing owner his life, had its propellor swung and engine tested, as the DC 3, which had flown us into this private world, was towed to rest within its hangar. In the garage a Buick, a Packard, two Bentleys, a Delahaye, several hunting jeeps and the favourite Cadillac convertible were greased and polished, as one of two stately Rolls-Royces had its tank filled in readiness for the conveyance of fellow princes arriving for the inauguration of Rajasthan in two days' time. The Maharajah's personal pennant mounted on its radiator cap flew

The Untouchable at home

138

The Brahmin at work

above the world famous trademark.

For the ceremony of the merging of this state with the new state of Rajasthan, the jackets of the Maharajah's scarlet uniform were brushed before my camera. The chief of his personal wardrobe staff supervised the pressing of his trousers and the polishing of his spurs. Squatting on the floor amidst row upon row of boots and shoes a servant cleaned his footwear, dwarfed by the thigh-high giants which shod an officer of the British Life Guards—the regiment in which the Maharajah held an honorary commision. From a cupboard was taken a box that enclosed a gorgeous turban, to which a plume of fine spun silver was affixed. From a safe in the wall diamond encrusted decorations and medals were made ready for display. Of the fabulous collection of state jewels I saw no more than the Maharajah had hitherto seen himself—and he had never even set eyes on them.

High above the city, behind the battlements of Nahargarh, the Tiger Fort, lay a great treasure, alleged to have been brought from Afghanistan a thousand years before, and guarded by a criminal tribe of outlaws whose loyalty in their trust had never once been broken. Once in a lifetime, and only once, a ruler of Jaipur was permitted to enter the fortress, gaze upon its hoard, and choose for himself just one object from its riches.

The present Maharajah had not yet availed himself of the opportunity. In an uncertain world he believed perhaps that here remained one adventure that he could always anticipate. His predecessor had brought out a solid golden bird, studded with rubies, that stood a full sixteen inches high. If I could not photograph the treasure, at any rate I could film the fort. I climbed to the craggy heights it crowned mounted on an elephant. When I returned I lined up my camera just in time to film the Maharajah, his study desk strewn with deeds and documents, signing away dynastic rights that stretched back into the creation of the Hindu world.

The ceremony of the accession was held in the Durbar Hall. In all the glitter

Filming the Maharajah of Jaipur surrendering his powers

of its chandeliers and its gold and silver thrones, Sardar Vallabbhai Patel, the architect of Rajasthan, cut an odd figure in his plain white dhoti. He had very nearly failed to appear altogether: engine trouble had forced his plane down in a dried-up river bed just outside the city. To the relief of many, and doubtless the disappointment of a few, he had emerged unscathed. In his last public appearance before his death, he administered the oath of allegiance to my Maharajah.

This was Patel's supreme moment. 'Rajasthan' crowned a feat of organization and diplomacy which made him the Bismarck of India. He had gathered five hundred and sixty two princely states into the fold of the Indian Union. Yet his face betrayed not a flicker of emotion.

To find a day in the life of a Brahmin of high caste, I had travelled far south to Travancore. Travancore had rarely been exposed to alien influence. Conquerors had always invaded the subcontinent from the north, and before they reached this 'deep south', forest and mountain had usually stopped them. Travancore and Cochin—now Kerala—were Indian states where Hinduism was preserved in all its purest form.

It even had a 'juggernaut'—if it had discarded the human sacrifice once attendant upon such ceremony. On solid wooden wheels, twice the height of the hundreds of panting disciples who milled around their barely moving circumference, an enormous chariot the size of a double-decker London bus, supporting a pagoda-like structure a hundred feet high, was dragged, inch by painful inch, around the precincts of the temple at Suchindram. Assisting the many straining at its forward towing ropes, others hung from great beams of wood sweated into place beneath its groaning rear axles which, having contributed their own primitive leverage to its shuddering onward movement, fell with a crash to the ground. Then they were lifted and brought forward for another effort once again by elephants following the chariot.

140

Carrying my camera down into the midst of this nightmare progress I remembered that in earlier epochs its attendant fanatics would have flung themselves to death beneath its enormous wheels, their blood and bones laying a sacrificial carpet for the advancement of what was in fact Juggernaut: the great symbolic car in which rode an image of Krishna, the charioteer. It was he who had consoled his Prince, aghast at the thought of an impending battle, with his recital of the 'Bhagavad-Gita' or Song Celestial.

I next attended a more intimate religious rite: the 'puja' or private service held within a house on the eve of its owner's pilgrimage to a Hindu shrine. I found a small, bare room packed with some thirty people. Two Brahmin priests officiated. The deity now being worshipped was a minor one, represented by a small painting of a woman's head. It stood among flowers at an improvised altar, scarcely visible in the smoke and shadows, rather than the light, which came from oil lamps and which, for filming, I had to augment with photofloods.

I had taken care to feature the elder of the two officiating Brahmins, and at the conclusion of the 'puja' I achieved the introduction for which I had been hoping. Rama Shastri was one of southern India's leading scholars of Sanskrit. He spent part of every day in the manuscript library of the University of Travancore. He agreed to my filming his research into this classical language of ancient India.

Teaching had long been the prerogative of the Brahmins. Almost daily Rama Shastri held classes of instruction in the courtyard of his simple little house. From Sanskrit text my camera moved to the faces of young Brahmin boys, as the Pandit—the wise man—read to them from the Vedas. This formidable depository of Hindu tradition was in himself a genial and charming old gentleman, whose innate dignity and kindness I recorded in the gift of a flower to each of his acolytes at the end of their lessons. Now I took the final hurdle with a rush.

'Would he mind my filming an aspect of his own domestic and personal ritual?'

Jaipur—The Guest House

141

Jaipur—The Palace

Not in the least.

Every day began with worship. At dawn my camera was set up outside the temple—a perpendicular thrust into the sky, reflected in the waters of the surrounding tank in which the devout attempted to wash away the impurities of material existence.

My Brahmin lived in a street in which only others of his caste resided. As even in such a short walk home he might have been defiled, a pot of holy water waited on his doorstep—and in front of my expectant camera—for the washing of hands and feet before he stepped inside. Eating nothing before these morning devotions, the first of two daily meals now awaited him, prepared by a completely invisible wife. This wholly vegetarian diet consisted of fruit arranged in a formal pattern on a banana leaf on the floor of an otherwise empty room. Although this food, prepared by the hands of a wife of the same caste, could not have been defiled, nevertheless before eating Rama Shastri three times sprinkled it with holy water. This ritual and preparation complete he fell to with a hearty appetite, popping the pieces of fruit into his mouth without his hand ever once touching his lips.

"'Untouchability' is abolished and its practice in any form is forbidden. The enforcement of any disability arising out of 'untouchability' shall be an offence punishable in accordance with law".

In its section on fundamental rights so reads the Constitution of the Indian Union, framed itself by the Untouchable who had risen to serve as its first Minister of Law; and, in my search for one of the fifty million of these so-called 'scheduled castes' whose sufferings and support had led him to such eminence—and through whom we could tell the story of their degradation—I flew on to Madras, the commercial centre of southern India.

I was searching for one of the 'Children of God'—as their great champion Gandhi had called the Untouchables. Without the existence of these outcasts—

Jaipur—The Gardens

their very presence an abomination and defilement to those with caste—carrying out the menial tasks and occupations beneath the notice and dignity of their caste-endowed superiors, the whole complex social structure of Hinduism would collapse.

Thagadore was a basket maker. From scraps of wood his hands fashioned an existence for himself, his wife, and their four children: their world a huddle of huts on the outskirts of the town, where they passed their days in a segregated colony of fellow outcasts. In its centre the well where his wife, Amananachamal, daily scrubbed the pots in which she cooked their food so dearly bargained for, its cleansing water powerless to wash away a stigma which the new Constitution was theoretically to abolish: its revolutionary legislation however already changing the life of their younger son, now a bewildered ten year old in the classroom of a school hitherto forbidden.

While Thagadore sought the materials of their livelihood, and tried to obtain a fair price for the handiwork in which he was assisted by his elder son, and Amananachamal struggled to provide them with at least one square meal of rice a day, this younger boy, free from such cares and perhaps heir to a brighter future, played with his friends a form of low caste cricket. Batting with a stick, he adroitly hit out at pieces of wood pitched towards him, striking them first to the ground, and then, on the rebound, swiping them hard to the boundaries of his little world. Unable to visit, let alone afford, any place of entertainment, his parents once in a while were also able to escape the monotony of their dispiriting days in the visit of a band of strolling players who, travelling from village to village, and traditionally everywhere vagabonds themselves, brought the magic of their rhythm and dance to an otherwise ostracised community.

Previously the proselytising faiths of her conquerors had been the only avenue of escape open to such of India's helpless Hindu outcasts, and, in the days of the

Mogul Empire, many Untouchables had embraced the spiritual democracy of Islam. Thagadore and his wife had been converted to the religion of the apostle Thomas who, only forty years after the Crucifixion, and fourteen hundred years before Francis Xavier first landed in Goa, had been martyred by the Brahmins at Mylapore, only a few miles away from this same Madras; and no more moving scene than any I made in India was that of Thagadore and Amananachamal, kneeling on the floor of their one room hut, beside the sleeping figures of their baby daughters, as they prayed to their common Mother of God.

Whilst others looked to diminutive images hiding in a simple shrine at the entrance to the village, the same dark Indian beauty could well have served as the model not only for the cheap postcard of the Virgin that kept vigil over the sleeping children, but also for the flower bedecked feminine deity that had held court over Rama Shastri's puja—so similar was their appearance in the flickering light of a Hindu temple lamp which Thagadore had placed beside this object of their own supplication.

Another Christian community I had decided to film was the Anglo-Indian. In Calcutta, my camera recorded the prowess of these Eurasians in the marshalling yards, control cabins and express trains of the fourth largest railway network in the world, carrying the mail which I had filmed them sorting alongside their despatch of cables in Bombay's Central Post Office.

Terence Belletty was a schoolmaster in a Calcutta Jesuit school, teaching the English language that was the very essence of his Anglo-Indian identity; and, constructing a sequence around these 'Hostages to India', I portrayed a way of life which, even at the best of times, had never been more than a pathetic reflection of an English middle class fast vanishing from the Indian scene: shifting my camera from the father's blackboard to another classroom in this same school, where one of his three sons was already being confronted by a linguistic threat to their

Jaipur—The Living-room

Jaipur—The Durbar Hall

survival.

The government had decreed that English must be replaced by Hindi as the lingua franca of the Indian Union. The ten-year-old boy was dutifully attempting to master this language derived from the Sanskrit of Rama Shastri's erudition. This xenophobic move was in time to be soft-pedalled, with the realisation that the new Constitution's plan to have thus completely dismissed the foreign tongue by 1965 was impossible in a sub-continent of more than two hundred different dialects, where only one person in ten could read and write in any of its eight major languages.

Leaving Donald to grapple with the intricacies of these Hindu semantics, my camera brought into focus the hands of his sister on the keyboard of a typewriter in the secretarial school where Chloe was learning shorthand. With religious prejudice barring most Hindu and Muslim women from such commercial activity, virtually all India's typists and stenographers were Anglo-Indian girls; and in Hyderabad's Osmania Hospital I had filmed an example of their similar monopoly of the terribly under-staffed nursing profession, such low caste defilement out of the question for orthodox Hindus and beyond the pale of the Mohammedan purdah.

But despite such an ominously unknown future it was a very happy gathering that I filmed in their four room apartment, at the top of three flights of stairs in a Calcutta neighbourhood almost exclusively Anglo-Indian. The cares of a large family, which included a mother-in-law as well as a baby son, Daryll, had in no way depressed Ruby Belletty, After their evening meal—tomato soup, the roast beef of old England and Hindu horror, fruit salad and cream—Terence endeavoured to correct his form's homework to the accompaniment of a duet on the piano by his wife and elder son, Denholm. Dishes were washed by the servant that the income of an Anglo-Indian schoolmaster was still able to afford.

Leader of the 'All-India Anglo-Indian Association' was Frank Anthony, who had arranged my introductions to the Bellettys through its Bengal branch. Now I filmed his speech to a crowded meeting, where he advised his audience of fellow Anglo-Indians that, although they had loyally served the strategically vital communication system of British India during the war, they should forget the British past and identify themselves with the Indian future.

To a minority which had prided itself upon its 'Englishness' such a pill was hard to swallow. For to the Anglo-Indian, although in most cases he would never see it, England had always been 'home', despite the fact that the British—who had fathered him—held him in contempt; and because the Indian—who had mothered him—despised his mixed blood. Attempting to placate their fears, Anthony pointed out that in the new Legislative Assembly the community was guaranteed a definite number of seats from which to advance its interests— a concession made to no other minority. To these worried people actions spoke louder than words. Calcutta Corporation was already dismissing them from its telephone exchange as fast as it could train Bengalis to take their place, and at a lower scale of salary fully acceptable to the latter, but ruinous to the former— who needed to maintain a semblance of European living standards if they were to survive as a separate community at all. From the social club that in the past had seen many a gay dance and happy bingo night, my camera moved to one of the soup kitchens with which the Association was attempting to keep alive the twenty-five per cent of its members already out of work.

Another minority, almost, one might say, another business club, a thousand miles away, right on the other side of the sub-continent, were the Parsis of Bombay. Descended from early Persian settlers, this tight little community suffered none of the religious inhibitions which tied other Indians to a prehistoric past. With the result that, though small in numbers, they had forged ahead in business and commerce. They were to the forefront in India's highly developed film industry, then second only to Hollywood in volume of production, producing at that time more than two hundred and fifty feature films a year.

Bombay's leading motion picture tycoon was a Parsi, Keki Mody. From a conference in the luxurious office to which he had just returned from a tour of the United States, my diminutive clockwork camera was conducted to his lavishly equipped 'Central Studios'. As it had been elsewhere in the pioneering days of its early development, the cinema was the staple entertainment of India's poor and hungry masses; who enjoyed in the elaborate fantasies of Hindu mythology that passed across the screens a momentary release from the misery of their own daily struggle for survival. Satyajit Ray had yet to emerge with a trilogy of films to shake the world, and, at this time, when he was still working in an advertising agency and an enthusiastic member of the Calcutta Film Society that I was called upon to address, Shantaram was the acknowledged leader of progressive Indian Film production.

Master of his own studio and central figure of a cooperative production unit, Shantaram had been almost alone in making films that reflected to any degree something of the life beyond the stifling sound stages of this booming motion picture industry. In the unoriginal flattery of his competitors the surfeit of mythological pictures was giving way to just as lavish a cycle of what were called 'socials'. The attempt of the Madras Board of Film Censors to prohibit the portrayal of

Hindu gods and goddesses upon the cinema screens of the more orthodox south could only encourage the production of more contemporary subjects. The set on which I filmed Shantaram riding his camera crane was at least a recognisable replica of a Bombay street—and not the enchanted glade of Krishna's courtship fabricated by a studio art department.

An astonishing feature of this highly skilled and efficient industry was the practice of many of its artists to work in several productions at one and the same time. The billboards that I had filmed above the 'House Full' notices of the neighbourhood cinemas spoke eloquently of their great appeal, and the Suraiya whom I filmed at 'Famous Studios' playing the lead in *Bari Behen*, under the direction of Kashyap, was similarly starring in seven other films in simultaneous production; and I could not but sympathize with the eight production managers attempting to synchronise their schedules around her much sought after presence.

From the monsoon rains sweeping Bombay's Marine Drive, upon whose crescent

Jaipur—The Wardrobe

of lights I had gazed from the Parsi Towers of Silence on Malabar Hill the night of my arrival in India, I next descended into the midsummer heat of Delhi's blistering airport. Exchanging the easy informality of the Parsi-owned Taj Mahal Hotel—barred only to white South Africans—for the exclusivity of the English style country club that called itself the Cecil Hotel.

This cosy refuge from the overwhelming squalor of India's misery was the home of most of the foreign correspondents assigned to the coverage of her newly won freedom. Presided over by the formidable and Swiss-born Miss Hotz, its luxurious insulation from the realities of life outside its high stone wall was the cause of varying degrees of guilt amongst this almost always conscience directed community.

The only contact between the Cecil's swimming pool, tennis courts, lawns and rose gardens—which included a little cemetery for departed residents' deceased dogs—and the India beyond its gates were the servants and bearers of its fortunate guests. These, hailing mostly from distant villages, remitted their relatively princely salaries to families that still lived in a Vedic age. The vast majority of the Indian Union's peoples were quite untouched by the embryonic industry only just beginning to infiltrate a way of life unchanged for thousands of years—and the success or failure of the Congress government was wholly dependent on the degree to which it could succeed in raising the living standards of these three hundred and fifty million peasants.

Believing that a fully developed sequence of village life was absolutely basic to any film of India, I had reported to New York my conviction that:

"It is most important that we have a thorough documentary take-out on the Indian peasant . . . I should like to try to get as thorough a story as possible on how the peasant is born, lives, works, plays, marries, prays, dies. These people are really the future of India, and if India is to progress, they must be lifted out of their centuries old torpor. We could also show the basic tenets of Hinduism in the village, where they are clearer and more traditional. The Hindu joint family system. The Hindu regards the family as one large composite unity and, on marriage, the son brings his bride back to his own family, where they all live together. This has certain advantages as all resources of the family are pooled, but it means on the land a process of fragmentation, as the existing holdings are divided equally amongst sons. This of course is an obstacle to the more efficient working of the land".

Sixty miles from Calcutta, and ten miles from the nearest road, Barrabpur was in the heart of Tagore's Bengal that was to be so beautifully filmed by Ray seven years later. By Land Rover and foot, early in the May of my second Indian Summer, I reached this rural location to which I had looked forward so long. Believing that only by living in such a village, and becoming accepted by its people, could I ever hope to establish the understanding essential to their sympathetic filming, I had overcome the initial stumbling block of my almost total ignorance of Bengali—or any other Indian language—by first approaching the American and British Quakers who, working on a veritable shoestring, were doing all they could to help the Indian peasant. I journeyed with an English-speaking Hindu social worker assigned to aid the villagers in the development of community self-help, who offered to act as my host, guide, and interpreter. Depositing my film and equipment under one of the two charpoys that constituted the sparse furnishings of the mud-floored hut which was to be our home, I set about exploring this tiny corner of an India virtually unchanged since the days of the original Aryan invasions.

The mournful blowing of conch shells and the wailing of women signalled the beginning of one twenty-two year old's greatest day—and the opening of what was to be the highlight of my village sequence: the wedding of the peasant Jatin and Sishubala, his bride.

In the courtyard behind their hut the mother poured water over the head of her only son, and, after this ceremony of purification, placed a garland around his neck, passing her hands across his face in blessing. Moving my camera to the home of his fourteen year old bride, I joined the priest who, seated under a canopy, intoned the litany of age old Hindu ceremony. Emerging from the hut the two children—for they were but little more—bowed to the Brahmin, and than sat at his feet. Invisible behind her veil, Sishubala was but a decorative doll beside the trembling figure of the husband whom she had never seen before. Meeting for the first time the wife whose name he did not even know, Jatin bowed his head as the ancient Vedic litany droned over their now combined destinies.

To reach Jatin's neighbouring village I had carried my camera four miles across a countryside already sodden with the threatening monsoon, at one time wading through flood waters four feet deep. My original plan had been to film the village during the previous November, at the height of good weather. The interruptions and priorities of the China films had forced my postponement of its filming until this period of steady downpour, and now all further camera work was brought to a halt.

For days I lay in the hut while the torrents streamed down outside, seizing what breaks I could to film the villagers drawing water from their now overflowing but still stagnant pond, roofing their huts with straw, and dragging their bullocks through the steaming fields still worked with the primitive tools fashioned by the blacksmith and his son. Realising that what I had envisaged for the Indian village was no more, or less, than the substance of a full length film in its own right, and that I had secured in Barrabpur all that the next five months of rain would ever grant me, I made my water-logged way back to Calcutta, where I planned to record the training of the community development workers with whom it was hoped to transform the countryside.

The rural revolution which the Congress government hoped to effect by such democratic means, was the essential corollary to the great schemes of hydro-electric development and irrigation that Nehru had described to me so enthusiastically at our first meeting. At an All India Exhibition designed to illustrate the pattern of tomorrow, I had filmed the visitors' fascinated absorption in a large relief model of the Damodar Valley Project. Based on the example and practice of the Tennessee Valley Authority—and sited in a sub-continent where only a fiftieth part of available water power had yet been harnessed—this vast undertaking was planned to irrigate scientifically vast areas of Bengal and neighbouring Bihar, at the same time generating power for the concentration of heavy industry already established and planned for this area in the successive five year plans of the future.

Calcutta, host to this ambitious trade fair, was also staging an exhibition of working models of the railway system. New locomotives and rolling stock were being purchased with a thirty-four million dollar loan from the World Bank. The University was bursting at the seams with traditionally unruly students, desperate to play their own part in a transformation now sweeping Asia. From the reading room of the library packed with young Indians devouring its well-thumbed volumes, through physics and electronic laboratories, I moved camera and lights to a lecture hall where a class of young men listened to an outline of psychology beside the Hindu girls who, not so very long before, would not only never have so sat in such unchaperoned masculine proximity—but would not have been expected to interest themselves in such intellectual pursuits at all.

For their degradation of recent centuries the women of India had the Muslim invasions to thank. Previous to the descent of Islam upon the sub-continent—with its institution of feminine purdah putting an effective end to their emancipation—they had enjoyed a status equal to that of the men with whom they had shared every achievement since the glorious days of the Mahabharata. In the purely Hindu stronghold of Travancore they had always gone unveiled, not only playing a prominent part in public life, but actually governing the state itself. In this matriarchate of the traditional south they had ruled by hereditary right—the succession to the throne and the large estates going always to the female line. To the fore in the freedom struggle of recent years had been such Congress stalwarts as Sarojini Naidu, now Governor of the United Provinces, and Rajkumari Amrit Kaur, Nehru's Minister of Health. His daughter was in turn to become Prime Minister, at a lower point in India's fortunes.

Rallying centres of this struggle to regain their position and self respect were the 'All India Women's Conference', and the Bombay offices and meetings of this militantly feminine organization. If it had any say in the matter at all, the Sishubalas of the future would have the right to choose their own husbands. I had already filmed its illustrious president, Lady Rama Rau. This handsome lady was not only

Jaipur—The Gun Room

consort to the Indian Union's then Ambassador to the United States, but also the mother of Santha Rama Rau, whose travel and writings were to bring a wider understanding of India to the English speaking world.

These energetic women were tackling the problems of the still dormant countryside in their own practical manner, and Karuna Gupta led me to one of the basic educational training schools which the Conference was maintaining near Calcutta. Past my camera with a song, a hundred village boys and girls marched out to the fields where they were taught the correct way to plant and harvest local vegetables. Sitting in the shade of banyan trees, even the youngest joined in the spinning of cloth on the 'charkha' that was Gandhi's great symbol of self-help. In the evening of my days' filming, they joined in the acting of a play by that great humanist and writer Rabindranath Tagore, a pioneering educationalist whose work and inspiration had been drawn from the strength and vitality of this same Bengal.

150

The prejudice that had barred women from professional life was dramatically demonstrated in the medical profession which, in a population of more than three hundred million—and increasing at the rate of more than ten million a year —could only muster seven thousand trained nurses. At its Calcutta Industrial Centre the 'All India Women's Conference' was busily training Hindu girls in the care of the human frame and its unfortunate ailments previously left to the non-caste Anglo-Indian.

Basic to the teaching that these girls would take to the villages was the prevention of disease so frequently engendered by malnutrition. From their deft bandaging of each other's imaginary concussions, my filming progressed to dietary demonstrations in the kitchens, where they were taught how to cook rice without sacrificing the vitamin content so often thrown away with the water in which it had been boiled. The training of rural schoolteachers was no less urgent a task underway at 8 Bethune Row. My sequence of a new feminine generation asserting their right to active participation in their country's affairs ended impressively with the sari-clad forms of Calcutta's women police prone on a rifle range as, with efficient deliberation, they sighted and hit their targets. This Amazonian development I had only seen equalled by Sheikh Abdullah's arming of Kashmiri Muslim girls in Srinagar. Bose's Indian National Army had mustered a regiment of women named after the Rani of Jhansi—the Boadicea of the Marathas who had been the foremost leader of the Indian Mutiny of 1857.

The Bengali letters, formed into words by the hands of children in the teacher training classroom, took the form of questions in the half-yearly examinations that I filmed at the Gokhale Memorial Girls School. From such a college, named after the leader of the Congress Party Moderates of forty years before, Indian girls were now emerging as at least the intellectual equals—and no longer necessarily the domestic slaves—of the young men similarly graduating from Calcutta's University.

Satyabrata Chatterjee was a twenty-eight year old Brahmin but, in common with most of the youth of his caste brought up and educated in such a free-thinking atmosphere, he was no longer an observer of the religious orthodoxy of his ancestors. He was employed as a sub-editor in the Calcutta offices of *The Statesman*, the long-established and leading English language newspaper. A previous editor had been forced to resign as a result of his inability to equate an impartial reporting of the Kashmir conflict with his expected support of the Indian Union. Chatterjee was a typical example and product of the new India of Jawaharlal Nehru, free of the inhibiting cant of the past and searching for intellectual roots in a future which he and his generation would largely determine.

Bringing my marathon assignment to an end with a study of this alert young man of my own age and enthusiasms, I filmed his editing of copy; supervision of type; relaxation and work at home with his parents and sister. In a seemingly always crowded coffee house, I followed his interminable arguments with friends on the subjects of art and socialism. I fled at last, after twenty thousand miles, and the better part of two years' voyaging over the surface of this vast Indian question-mark, to the nirvana of the Palm Beach Hotel at Gopalpur—where I awarded myself four days respite from an India of which I was surfeited.

Tossed about in the breakers of the Indian Ocean, I looked back over the fifty-six thousand feet of film which had passed through my camera since my arrival in Bombay twenty months before. I was still haunted by doubts as to what would happen to it in New York.

In Bangalore, three days after my filming of the Kolar Gold Fields at the beginning of this second year, I had been dumbfounded by a cable that announced:

"Must have all untouchable material New York not later than January twenty please report prospects".

Prospects were a great deal more than fair. I shipped all the southern Indian sequences in their entirety. I had then been informed that:

". . . Must complete two reeler for current release but you finish schedule as longer picture still planned for later . . ."

None of this made any sense at all to me, and to New York I wrote:

". . . it seems to me a pity that you are now making a release after waiting over a year, when there only remain about twelve weeks work to bring in everything we have ever visualised . . . I cannot see how the latter will make a separate picture. To my mind it is a question now of either releasing the existing material and leaving India at that, which in any case will be a very thorough take-out, or waiting a few more weeks and incorporating the remaining subjects".

And to London:

"I have learned . . . quite by chance . . . that India is to be next month's release. I must say that this is a bit odd; I would have thought that I might have been let into the secret some time ago . . . In New York's reply it is stated that my programme is unaffected by this. This is palpably absurd, as the major proportion of future coverage I have planned only has significance in relation to existing coverage which is now going to be released separately".

I received in due course a typewritten memorandum from New York. The twenty minute release had been successfully completed. The Associate Producer informed me that: "It is our intention to make a 'featurette' on India some time in the future", which would "in all probability run around five reels". I had therefore resumed work on what was still to be an apparently integrated full length production, far from reassured as to its final outcome. But, sitting beside the swimming pool of the Cecil Hotel on the eve of my departure to Jaipur, I had read a copy of an infinitely more encouraging letter from Unni Nayar, an old friend from the Indian Army, and then Public Relations Officer at the Indian Union's Washington Embassy:

"This morning, some colleagues of mine in the Embassy and I had the privilege of seeing ASIA'S NEW VOICE . . . I should like to tell you that our opinion is that it is a good film and that you have managed to compress within . . . twenty minutes a great deal of the salient points concerning modern India. Let me congratulate you on this film which I am sure will be welcomed in India . . ."

Such a tribute made everything seem worthwhile. Refreshed by the bracing breezes of Gopalpur, I boarded a Tokyo bound plane of Pan American World Airways, in the next stage of an eastward journey that I confidently hoped would bring me, after I had finished filming *MacArthur's Japan*, to New York for the editing of the Indian feature.

PART THREE: Borders of the American World

A Conflict of Principle – And the Promise of Pakistan

The only real tragedy in life is the being used by personally minded men for purposes which you know to be base. All the rest is at the worst mere misfortune and mortality: this alone is misery, slavery, hell on earth.
George Bernard Shaw

Uppermost question in my mind when I finally reached New York was the fate of the Indian feature. It had been announced in the trade press as a forthcoming special release, and the film was run for me in *The March of Time* projection room, complete and ready for recording.

The fifty minute film ran silently on the screen before me, without a word or whisper from any sound track.

The regular *March of Time* short release on India, *Asia's New Voice*, had opened with scenes of the collapse of Chiang Kai-shek in China, and its commentary had stated that with "the way . . . left clear for communism to swallow up the largest nation in Asia . . . hope of saving Asia for democracy centred in the new state of India",—an implied equation of Nehru with Chiang Kai-shek that enraged Krishna Menon when he first saw the film. Neither Nehru nor the United States had fallen overwhelmingly in love with each other at the time of Nehru's visit. India's Prime Minister had made it crystal-clear that his policy was to be one of non-alignment in the struggle between the United States and the Soviet Union. The promotion of an ambitious and long film, which paid tribute in the words of its commentary to a people led "by the wisdom and inspired leadership of Jawaharlal Nehru, one of the world's truly great men", could hardly be reconciled with the current editorial policy of *Time* and *Life*. Nehru had failed to replace the fallen idol of Henry Luce's oriental affections. My film was shelved.

This stillborn production had lacked only music and commentary. The latter had been written, revised, and readied for delivery by Lowell Thomas—when all had been halted, and the production abandoned.

For years I had had the satisfaction of capturing with a camera the spirit and action of a world in ferment. I had not had any control or say whatsoever in the ultimate use to which such labours might be put. I was frustrated and demoralised. I felt party to deceit. The exploitation of some of my Russian film in ways contrary to its original intention in the spring of 1950 – and this after months of failure to elicit any word at all on what might be happening to the Indian material – had led me to express my desire to part company from an organization in which I increasingly felt my own contribution and standing to be little more

153

than that of a hired mercenary.

Back in London from India, and before flying to China, I had met Stuart Legg of the Crown Film Unit. Legg had worked with John Grierson in Ottawa during the war, when Grierson was engaged in the establishment of the highly successful National Film Board. In his *World in Action* Legg had developed an effective rival to *The March of Time* on Canadian screens. He had hoped to produce a similar series in England, as a contribution to the programme of film production initiated by the British Government's recently formed Central Office of Information. He was anxious that I should join him. We had corresponded, and now we met again.

Fifteen years before, each *March of Time* had consisted of three separate and dissimilar items. With the 1938 release of *Inside Nazi Germany* the whole of one issue had been devoted to a single story—and banned in the Britain of Neville Chamberlain's "peace in our time". The Central Office of Information had lately been producing a regular magazine film similarly made up of a trio of stories.

Lahore—The Shahi Mosque and Tomb of Iqbal, Pakistan 1950

Stuart Legg was now proposing that I take over production responsibility for 'This is Britain'. A few evenings later I met John Grierson, who three years before, had urged me to publish my experiences and impressions of *The Russians Nobody Knows*—a task only finally discharged in the pages of this book.

The success of *Drifters* had led to Grierson's creating a film unit and founding a movement. Arthur Elton, Paul Rotha, Stuart Legg and Edgar Anstey had been amongst the first disciples. With the dissolution of the Empire Marketing Board, the General Post Office had provided the sponsorship. The G.P.O. Film Unit had in turn become the Crown Film Unit. The war's vast release of money and energy had made the documentary film an accepted and memorable feature of the regular cinema programme. Returned from Canada Grierson was Director of the Films Division of the Central Office of Information. From a pub nearby its Baker Street offices I had next found myself at the Savile Club in Brook Street, being assessed by Ralph May, in charge of the Crown Film Unit.

In the midst of these negotiations, and immediately prior to my completion and signature of the document required for such official employment, a cable had arrived in London from *The March of Time* in New York:

> "Can you fly Hopkinson . . . Rome to make us coverage on early
> Holy Year pilgrims for updating our Vatican feature fullstop . . . have
> covered here today departure Cardinal Spellman on SS Atlantic due
> Rome March second . . . your contact William McCarthy Hotel
> Hassler Rome who accompanying pilgrimage . . ."

At the beginning of the war, before Mussolini had joined in for the kill in France, Jean Pagès of the Paris office had secured for *The March of Time* an exclusive and never previously granted permission to film "The Vatican of Pope Pius XII". Cinema-goers had enjoyed the unique experience of a guided tour of the hitherto enclosed world of the Vatican City. Now the same Holy Father had declared this mid-century year of 1950 to be a Holy Year of "purification and of sanctification, interior life and reparation, a year of great return and great forgiveness". *The March of Time* had obviously sensed an opportunity to produce what would appear to be a new feature film of the occasion by the re-editing and 'updating' of all this original material.

A few days later in Rome I was handed a telegram:

> "Would you consider proceeding from Rome to Pakistan approxi-
> mately three weeks shooting completing your original coverage . . ."

The day before, a letter had been despatched from New York to London "no doubt alerted to the project of making a *March of Time* on Pakistan", in which it was explained that, having run "all the material . . . shot by Hopkinson . . . within the last two years . . . our problem now is to get some additional material which will show the constructive work being done by the Pakistanis."

This had me in a quandary. The discussions in London had indicated my joining the Crown Film Unit within a week of my return from Rome: but I welcomed the opportunity to complete a companion piece to *Asia's New Voice* in which, by default of a presentation of its own case, Pakistan had appeared to be no more than an unfortunate aberration of independence that had led to disaster in the Punjab and hostilities in Kashimir.

The evening of the next day had brought a reply to my request for guidance from Ralph May at the Crown Film Unit's Beaconsfield Studios: "Advise make

Pakistan trip contact me on return".

The most striking achievement of Pakistan to which I so unexpectedly returned in the Spring of 1950, two and a half years after its creation, was the simple fact that it was still there—it had survived.

Jinnah was dead: but, within ten days I had visited his tomb, filmed his successor, and recorded the bustling industrial development of his birthplace; the expanding capital of a country that was currently host to the Shah of Persia—the ruler of the ancient Islamic land on its western frontiers with which Pakistan was soon to be allied in military defence.

A State guest, with everything that I might order in the Palace Hotel 'on the house', I none the less cashed some travellers cheques at the New State Bank, whose existence was proof of the Muslim's determination to master the financial intricacies of a trade that he had formerly allowed the Hindu to monopolise. The new Pakastani rupee was itself a symbol of national probity.

The Foreign Secretary was Mohammed Ikramullah, who sat at the left hand of Prime Minister Liaquat Ali Khan when I filmed the members of the cabinet in conference

Pakistan now had a population of 80,000,000; almost wholly unable to read or write and increasing by one and a half million every year. At a village school my camera caught something of the rapt attention that the children brought to a lesson in elementary Urdu.

Throughout this province of the Western Punjab where, two and a half years before, I had followed the bloody migration of its peoples, the ears of corn were

Tribesmen of the North West Frontier, Pakistan 1950

now high in the fields. My camera dwelt on scenes of a rural simplicity and elegance difficult to associate with the background of that bloody nightmare. Through countless irrigation ditches the waters from Kashmir raced amongst the now ripening crops. As pots were filled and meals prepared, cattle were led home to a multitude of villages. At the end of the day, a band of wandering minstrels entertained the farmers on the banks of a wide canal.

Based on these fundamental units of its society Pakistan was to promulgate a new type of constitution twelve years later. A dispute about grazing rights gave me the opportunity to film the procedure of such a village 'panchayat' deciding the merits or otherwise of a plaintiff's case. Grouped under the trees, while an elderly and bespectacled scribe made notes, the council elected from amongst the villagers themselves sat in debated judgment. Such 'Basic Democracies' would be called upon to elect the general members of a future National Assembly.

Here in the Punjab was Pakistan's greatest wealth and strength. The annual crop of more than three million tons of wheat alone was still providing a surplus of over half a million tons of exportable foodstuffs. From the sale of these cash crops the Ministry of Finance was able to budget for further industrial development. Within two years there was to be a deficit and a crisis in this initially healthy balance of payments, and Pakistan was to need every grain of the million tons of wheat offered by the United States and every penny of the £10,000,000 loaned by Great Britain.

Meantime, in association with the Commonwealth's Colombo Plan, Pakistan was drawing up a six year development programme. No more dramatic project was taking shape than the harnessing of the great rivers of the North West Frontier Province. I flew from the Punjab, and over Rawalpindi, at 8,000 feet, looked down on to the wild landscape through which I had climbed my way two years before towards the disputed mountains of Kashmir. Here, in this most northern corner of the Indus plain, a few miles to the west of my crossing of the Jhelum, the site was to be chosen for a new national capital, Islamabad.

Now, in what was for me territory untouched during my previous visit to an infant Pakistan, the three days passed in this wild North West Frontier became the highlight of my return. Here I was in the most legendary of Indian landscapes: the turbulent and romanticised setting of *Bengal Lancer;* of the Kiplingesque heroics of *Wee Willie Winkie* and *Gunga Din;* of a host of fabled tales once the very essence of a Britain confident of an imperial mission.

The passes that had sullenly witnessed Sir Bindon Blood's systematic destruction of village after village, house after house, the burning of the tribesmen's crops and the wrecking of their reservoirs, now provided the foundation for the spillways and powerhouse of a new hydro-electric project which would generate a hundred thousand kilowatts and bring under cultivation ten thousand acres of land still farmed by these same proud Mohmands. From the filming of this new source of power and livelihood, and by way of a new sugar factory standing huge and gaunt in the open plain outside Mardan, I drove past the martello-type towers that guarded the fields from these once predatory people into Jamrud, and the beginnings of the Khyber Pass.

Bounded by the snows and peaks of the Hindu Kush this savage landscape had provided a bleak arena for the tribal fights and feuds of the Afridi, the Khatak, the Orakzai, the Bangash, the Wazir, the Turi and the Mahsud—and the training

The Khyber Pass, Pakistan, 1950

ground for many a future British general.

Climbing for more than three thousand feet, from the plains to the defile that was the historic gateway into India from central Asia, the road twisted and turned through crumpled and steep ridges and fortresses. A stream of brightly painted trucks sped past us on the way down into Pakistan and, with radiators steaming, groaned their way upwards towards Landi Kotal and Afghanistan: a two way traffic in which the Pathans were revealing hitherto unsuspected gifts of retail trading—and a means of locomotion that had precipitated them into the gates of Srinagar three winters before.

I set up my camera on the slopes of the last of the hairpin bends that had lifted us to the summit, and then framed and focused the frontier post into Afghan territory. Despite the airplane's obliteration of distance, this was none the less a strategic location of the first order. Between these narrow cliffs, up from the Kabul river, had entered into India Alexander the Great and, sixteen hundred years later, from Samarkand, Tamburlaine. Here Kim and Hurree Babu had played the 'Great Game' of political intelligence in nineteenth-century British India—and Kipling's 'Dread Power of the North' was now more active than ever on the other side of the border.

Dispute about the dubious nature of these Himalayan borders, and the need to secure support for her claim to Kashmir, was to bring Pakistan an unexpected ally thirteen years later. In Peking, on the 2nd of March 1963, Pakistani Foreign Minister Zulfikar Ali Bhutto was to sign an agreement which defined the frontiers of Sinkiang and Kashmir. By such action, and the surrender of more than seven hundred square miles of territory, China implicitly endorsed Pakistan's right to Kashmir—and thus sided with her in this mutual struggle against the Indian Union. Tired of what she believed to be a lack of British and American support for the justice of her cause, Pakistan was thus to take the first momentous step away from an alliance which, in those March days of 1950, she never even doubted.

I filmed Pathans in tribal dress dancing outside Peshawar and met them in the bazaar at Landi Kotal—their rifles slung amidst its plenty both of fruit and ammunition. They seemed happy enough to be citizens of the new Muslim state. But Kashmir was never far from their thoughts, and, at a great 'jirga'—a tribal gathering—that I filmed on the side of a hill near the Khyber, loud were the denunciations of Jawaharlal Nehru.

Relations between Pakistan and the Indian Union were now at their worst since the terrible days of January 1948, and the object of the tribesmen's wrath was now about to meet Liaquat Ali Khan in an attempt to halt what was freely canvassed as yet another drift to war.

The devaluation of the Indian Union's rupee a few months before had led to the halting of coal deliveries to Pakistan, and an embargo on the shipment of jute from East Bengal. At the time of independence the presence of Gandhi, and the absence of such a third catalytic agent as the Sikhs, had saved the 12,000,000 Hindus of Pakistan's far eastern province from the threat of massacre, which had decimated their co-religionists in the Punjab. In an ominous parallel now, a million Muslims from West Bengal were on the move across the frontier into Eastern Pakistan, and one and a half million of the latter's Hindu citizens were fleeing to the Indian Union. Behind it all lay the bitterness of Kashmir.

The determination of these two men to avoid at all costs such mutual self-destruction was reflected in the harmony that they reflected together in our film. Though attitudes on Kashmir remained completely irreconcilable, the economic disputes that had led to this exchange of populations were resolved by agreement. This led, in time, to the guarantee of the sources of the common Punjab irrigation in an Indus Waters treaty, which was finally negotiated and ratified under the auspices of the World Bank.

In a letter to Nehru four years later, the then Prime Minister of Pakistan, Mohammed Ali, announced that:

> "We have sought military aid from the U.S.A. so that, given this assistance to strengthen our defences, we may be able to devote our domestic resources increasingly to the development of our economy. We believe that by doing so we can better serve the cause of peace in this area . . . We do not have, we cannot possibly have, any intention of using this aid for the purpose of settling the Kashmir dispute by force".

A year before his assassination at the hands of a fanatic, this reassurance was to be anticipated by Liaquat Ali Khan in his own summing up to *The March of Time's Promise of Pakistan*.

> "We will never allow our freedom to be taken away. We shall fight aggression wherever it may be. And Pakistan shall cooperate with all those countries who want peace in the world and progress of mankind".

On an Island in the Pacific – Time Marches off

Europe is a dying system . . . The lands bordering the Pacific with their billions of inhabitants will determine the course of history for the next ten thousand years."

General Douglas MacArthur

From Pakistan, which had become the United States' latest ally, I flew back to London to the new appointment that I had every good reason to believe awaited me at the Crown Film Unit.

"The situation arising from the revised estimates for film production for 1950-51 has forced upon us some drastic alterations of plans. I had a suspicion of this when you cabled me from Rome but the actual situation is far worse even than I feared and I am afraid there is no possibility of proceeding for the present with the question of your appointment . . . This is a great disappointment to me. I am sure you would have been able to contribute a great deal to the quality of our productions and I would very much have liked to have you on the staff. I only hope that this is not a very serious blow to you".

Thus, after four weeks of further vacillation, my own future seemed jeopardised by a Labour government's parsimonious attitude towards the documentary film developed by previous Conservative administrations: an unimaginative pursuit of fiscal solvency that was in fact to lead to the complete and absolute liquidation of the Crown Film Unit itself two years later.

Flung back into the still welcoming arms of *The March of Time*, this apparently disastrous flirtation with the official film makers of my own country was in no way held against me. Before very long I received a summons to New York, and was aboard a Stratocruiser on my way at last to a meeting with the directors of the organization for whom I had been working for nearly four years.

Now the red carpet was out. Over a final drink on my first evening, Producer Richard de Rochemont proposed that I take charge of a special *March of Time* release, returning to New York after its filming, to supervise its editing and production. The subject was to be the British troops fighting alongside those of the United States and the United Nations in Korea.

This story had been ignored by the documentary film makers of my own country. My first assignment of this trip was however somewhere else in the Pacific: Formosa; for a film to be part sponsored by the United States Economic Cooperation Administration. Researcher Nancy Pessac prepared a seventeen page preliminary briefing covering the island's topography, population, history, economy, politics, and armed forces—in the light of President Truman's statement of nine months before when, forty-eight hours after the invasion of southern Korea, he had "ordered the Seventh Fleet to prevent any attack on Formosa", and, "as a corollary of this action", called "upon the Chinese Government on Formosa to cease all air and sea operations against the mainland".

We studied reports of the Chinese Nationalists' training, organization and

New York, 1951. Author planning Formosa *with March of Time Producer Richard de Rochemont*

supply of guerillas, still, it seemed, active on the mainland, breaking off from our work to join in the Sunday morning Easter parade on Fifth Avenue. In conference with Dick de Rochemont, and associate producer Sam Bryant, we hammered out our story line. This was to be no whitewash job on Chiang Kai-shek. We aimed to draw a distinction between the Formosan people and the Nationalists who had descended on them, and it was decided that I would go to Hong Kong to record in picture and sound statements from members of the "Formosa Republican Government in Exile", and interviews with representatives of a possible 'Third Force' such as the exiled General Chang Fa-kuei, who claimed to be able to offer China a future neither Communist or Nationalist.

With confidence in the integrity and calibre of my producer and his associates, thoroughly briefed, and with the very latest portable lighting equipment supplementing a new camera, I flew across the United States to San Francisco. In the luxury of the Mark Hopkins hotel, I had thirty-six hours free at last in which to relax and recover from these first three immensely stimulating American weeks. Hesitations and doubts about the nature of my employment had vanished in the warmth of my welcome. The promise of partnership in the production of my future films had made all the difference. Now that I was no longer separated from it by *The March of Time's* insipid and, at least so far as I was concerned, superfluous European direction, New York had ceased to represent two impersonal words whose apparently peremptory demands had often seemed unreasonable. I wished I had been there long before.

All of us, including Richard de Rochemont, were of course employed by 'Time-Incorporated', which owned *The March of Time*—and 'Time-Inc' was owned by

Henry Luce. On the subject of China Luce had a one-track, if not a closed mind. Once described as the "single most powerful influence on the minds and opinions of America", Luce had been born of missionary parents in China in 1899. T. S. Mathews, one of his erstwhile editors, believed that the dichotomy resulting from this foreign birth and initially alien schooling partly explained some of Luce's "most strongly held convictions: his feeling for America, a kind of patriotism more usually felt by converts or late-comers (in a less intelligent man it might have been chauvinism); his feeling for England, a complex of love and envy, admiration and contempt. If he had been British he would certainly have been proud of the Empire, an extreme Tory, protesting furiously at its liquidation. As an American, with an imperial sense of America's future, he was glad to see Britain's competition dwindle".

Certainly, like Confucius, he believed that "Heaven has entrusted me with a mission". In the editorial pages of *Life*, he had recently sounded a clarion call: if the nineteenth had seen Britain master of the seven seas, this was to be "The American Century".

Mathews adds: "His feeling for China I never altogether understood. I believe he loved the country and the people, and I have heard him really eloquent on the subject. And yet, long before China's defection—or kidnapping, from his point of view—into Communism, he must have misunderstood China just as badly as his hero Chiang Kai-shek. Luce was stubborn and headstrong, but facts and logic could usually persuade him; on this issue alone he went beyond the bounds of reason. At the climax he pitted his faith in the China he had known against the present facts reported by his principal correspondents on the scene; it was a heavy responsibility for a journalist to take, but he took it".

Formosa was not the first Chinese offshore island regarded by Mao Tse-tung in Peking as still in the hands of a hostile power that I filmed. The British Crown

Formosan Election

Formosan Ballot-box

Colony of Hong Kong had already been host to my camera two years before.

Driven out of Canton in 1839 by a Chinese government determined to stamp out the opium trade, the British had discovered only a few hours away a great land-locked harbour, and an island that was then completely defensible by sea power. His primitive navy blown to pieces and his feudal armies scattered, the Emperor had been forced to concede not only trading rights at five treaty ports along the Chinese mainland, pay an indemnity of over twenty million dollars for the imported opium stocks destroyed, but also yield to Great Britain this "large and properly situated island" off the coast, "from which Her Majesty's subjects in China may be alike protected and controlled".

Exactly a hundred years to the day of Hong Kong's foundation, its British government had surrendered to the Japanese crossing its borders in the wake of Pearl Harbour. Only a month before, the Secretary of the American Treasury had proposed a more peaceful shift of sovereignty, suggesting that Britain be persuaded to sell her colony back to China. The United States could loan Chiang Kai-shek the capital with which to carry out what would have been one of the most ironic transfers of real estate in history. In private conversation with Stalin before the fifth regular session of the Yalta conference, Roosevelt had suggested that the Russian need for a warm water port in the Far East could be met by making Dairen, at the top of the Kwantung peninsula, a "free port", under some form of inter-national control. He had explained that as a precedent for such a solution he hoped that the British could be persuaded to give Hong Kong back to China, and that the Chinese would then make it into a similarly constituted and internationalised trading centre.

Not having become "the King's First Minister in order to preside over the liquidation of the British Empire" Churchill had lacked enthusiasm for such proposals. The unexpected suddenness of the Japanese defeat had seen Sir Cecil

Formosa

Harcourt entering Hong Kong with units of the British Pacific Fleet in order to proclaim British control once again. Chiang Kai-shek had protested but, in the event, the Admiral had accepted the surrender on behalf of both his own and the Chinese governments.

By the time I reached Hong Kong in 1949, the Nationalist government had been virtually ejected from the Chinese mainland and Mao Tse-tung's victorious troops were about to reach the shores of the South China Sea and the borders of the colony itself.

In case these proved to be no deterrent, and they kept on coming, General Sir Francis Festing could call upon more troops than his unfortunate predecessor of eight years before. The British Army Public Relations Officer was an old friend from Algiers in 1943. I set about filming the defensive positions in the willow-patterned setting of the Golden Dragon Hills.

This fortified perimeter stretched along what were known as the 'New Territories' : three hundred and fifty nine square miles of the mainland opposite the island, acquired by Britain in the great scramble of 1898, and leased for ninety nine years as a convenient extension for supply and defence. At Lo Wu, across the unimpressive waters of the little stream that was now about to become in effect a "bamboo curtain", the refugees were already beginning to make their way—soon to become a flood that would reach millions.

The Foreign Correspondents Club of China was now amongst these dispossessed, evacuated from Shanghai fallen to the communists in May 1949. I had made straight for the new location of what had been the comfortable and friendly quarters of my previous Chinese winter. This establishment was but a shadow of its former self. After the first few nights spent on one of several camp beds in an otherwise empty room, I loaded equipment and film and took the ferry to Kowloon, to the adjacent town on the waterfront of the so-called 'New Territories'.

Number Seventeen Chung Shan Road, Shanghai, had also been abandoned to the communists. The *Time* and *Life* Far East bureau had contracted to Room 305 of the Peninsula Hotel. I rejoiced to find Harriet Wong installed by day in its sitting-room, as ever the most efficient of office managers and certainly the most attractive of refugees.

I spent the better part of my time loading and unloading camera and accessories on and off ferries plying between the island city of Victoria and the Kowloon of the New Territories. I was in no mood to enjoy the fabulous combination of the exotic and the orderly that makes Hong Kong so unique an indulgence. My presence, at that time, was but proof that any hopes I might have entertained of being present at the editing of the Indian film in New York had proved in vain. My one desire was to complete the filming of this report of a colony at the crossroads as soon as possible—and get home.

I filmed the training of the local police by their British officers. I filmed their patrolling of the bedraggled street of the little village bisected by the frontier, their search for contraband amongst the multitude of junks moored along the waterfront. I filmed the Spitfires dispersed around Kai Tak Airport, their cannon loaded and their fuel tanks full. I filmed the checking and sighting of torpedo tubes and anti-aircraft defences on board the warships anchored in the bay. I filmed the funicular railway leading to the incomparable view from the eighteen hundred foot Peak; I moved through the jangling streets of red rickshas and green, double-decker tramcars. My camera led me into the epicentre of this teeming enterprise—the board room of the Hongkong and Shanghai Banking Corporation and a meeting of the colony's Chamber of Commerce under the chairmanship of Sir Arthur Morse.

Overlooking St. John's Cathedral, the Supreme Court and the Cricket Club the 'taipans' sat around the table in what was—until the communist Bank of China

Filming in Formosa

rose twenty feet higher next door—the tallest building in Hong Kong. These 'merchant princes' directed businesses founded by the Jardines, the Mathesons, the Dents and the Henrys of the Opium War. Although the narcotic which had founded such fortunes had not been officially outlawed from Hong Kong until 1945, the trading experience and adaptability of such men was to lead the colony into the greatest boom that it had ever known. Meantime it was widely believed that Britain's China policy was in fact largely influenced by the interests of this group.

The diplomatic recognition of Mao's Government in the following year was held to be largely dictated by Britain's desire for trade. This had been unfulfilled by recent experience in the Shanghai from whence most of these tycoons were evacuating their interests. In a sense, relations between Great Britain and China were back where they had been before the war of 1840. Trading across her frontiers was no longer free, but depended upon the desires and wishes of Peking.

I spent both spring and part of summer 1951 in the lovely tropical island of Formosa. Like a luxurious tobacco leaf suspended on the waters of the Pacific, it lies strategically poised between Japan and the Philippines. I never tired of driving along its beautiful coast line and the mountain roads of the interior, of filming in its fields and forests. This one time Manchu colony was now an oasis of Asian well-being. Its rice crop was unrivalled. It numbered fourteen thousand square miles of fertile abundance.

My filming began one morning as I slid open the window of a Japanese-style inn seven thousand feet up in the very centre of the island. Mist wreathed the mountain peaks and rose from the surface of 'Jih-yuehtan'—the 'Sun Moon Lake' of tourist attraction, whose one hundred and fifty million cubic metres of water had been harnessed by the Japanese fourteen years before. From this fragile vista of oriental grace, its foreground animated by the passage of peasants with their cattle, my camera moved to the camouflaged power stations fourteen hundred feet below. I set up lights alongside their closely guarded hydro-electric generators and switch boards. The United States Economic Cooperation Administration had already provided one and a half of the ninety eight million dollars that it was bringing to the assistance of Formosa during this current year.

Making *Battle for Bread* on the mainland of China, I had come across a 'Joint Commission for Rural Reconstruction': an agency set up by the Chinese and American governments to assist and sponsor agricultural development. Mao Tse-tung had pulled the rice fields out from under its feet before it ever had a chance to do anything, but now on Formosa it had come into its own. E.C.A. had made over to its operations more than two million dollars, and it was underwriting a rural revolution widely hailed as unique in Asia.

Peace, bread, and land had been the basis of the Bolshevik's original appeal to the Russian masses. To millions of Chinese long suffering the exploitation of rapacious landlords, the communist promise of land reform had been a major factor in their rejection of Chiang Kai-shek. From the outset of its operations the J.C.R.R. had attacked this basic agrarian problem on Formosa, where more than half a million farming families were trying to make a living on only two million acres of arable land. Mostly tenant farmers, they had in the past been forced to surrender sometimes as much as three quarters of their crops to their landlords. With the proceeds of the remainder barely sufficient for the purchase of seed, fertilizer and equipment, the Formosan peasant, however hard he worked, could never hope to save enough to become the owner of the land he tilled.

Legislation had now been passed—binding on all of China if Chiang ever got back, and there were any landlords left to compensate—cutting land rentals to barely a third of the main crop.

In the village of Kwei-Jen Hsiang, near Tainan, in the south of the island, I found a farmer whose life could tell this story—the centrepiece of a report on the work of the J.C.R.R. and the E.C.A. on Formosa that was basic to my assignment. The railroads were being rebuilt. Irrigation systems developed. Harbours restored. Old industries rehabilitated, new ones pioneered. Agriculture transformed. Livestock imported to improve the native strains, now almost immunised from the cholera that had been such a scourge. Outside the Commission's laboratories girls worked in the fields, straw hats and cloth on their heads shading their complexion from the rays of the sun—their smiles made vivid by the lipstick which was such a striking symbol of this rural prosperity.

From the installation of Japanese-built and E.C.A.-purchased electrical equipment at Sin-tsu, to an oil refinery processing petroleum piped up from Kaohsiung; from the 'Cheluchien Sugar Factory', to the quaysides of Keelung, I filmed the length and breadth of this tight little island in the Pacific.

Formosa had become a haven not only for Chiang Kai-shek, but also for Chinese cuisine. Chefs from every great school of China's gastronomic versatility had sought refuge there just as he had. The Fukien school specialised in the subtle use of cooking wines. Shantung menus favoured delicious roast meats. Honanèse food was distinguished by rich seasoning. Szechuanese meals were heavily spiced. A Mongolian barbecue served slices of beef and vegetables boiled in sauces mixed by the customer according to his own taste from an assortment of exotic condiments, such as ginger-juice and sesame oil. In Tainan I dined Cantonese style, enjoying

U.S. General William Curtis Chase who planned the defence of Formosa

Formosan farmer

many a 'sweet and sour' combination of delicacies.

The Japanese had been ousted from Formosa in 1945. Chiang Kai-shek then appointed his own General Chen Yi as Governor: and the next two years marked the hey-day of the corrupt and incompetent. A six-fold increase in the price of foodstuffs and a breakdown in the public health services, with epidemics of cholera and bubonic plague, finally led to an insurrection. Chiang was beginning to realise that Formosa might soon represent the last bastion of Nationalist China. He replaced the General by a former Mayor of Shanghai, K.C. Wu, who had been educated at Princeton. A 'reconstruction committee' was set up. One great handicap was that few of its officials could speak the local Formosan dialect.

At the beginning of the previous year President Truman had declared that:

"The United States has no predatory designs on Formosa or on any other Chinese territory. The United States has no desire to obtain special rights or privileges or to establish military bases on Formosa at this time."

Eighteen months later, Major-General William Curtis Chase was landing with a Military Assistance Advisory Group of one hundred and sixteen officers and enlisted men. For the Korean war had changed everything, and Chase was now committed to train and fashion into a first-class fighting machine an army of no less than half a million Chinese.

I was involved in many aspects of this undertaking. The most novel piece of new equipment I filmed was something that in the past no Chinese soldier had ever carried—a pay-book. The pay might not be much more than a dollar a month. But at least the days of the war-lords, who, from a lump-sum allocated to them, often failed to provide even food for their soldiers, let alone cash, were finally over.

Some still found it hard to accept that such a state of affairs had ever existed.

Sun Li Jen—Commander of Chinese Ground Forces Formosa 1951

When the Formosa film was finished, in the first draft of the commentary, we said that "it was no longer possible for a General to abscond with the pay of an entire army". Against this, in the margin, and in the neat handwriting he had been taught in a British school in China, Henry Luce expressed his displeasure. The line was changed to read "all soldiers now have pay books, and permanent records are kept as proof that they have received their pay".

I met 'Tiger Wang'—General Wang Shou-ming. Like so many of the Nationalist leaders graduating from the Whampoa Military Academy of 1924, he had been trained in aviation by the Russians. The Kuomintang had originally been patterned on the Communist Party. The very Russians who had aided Chiang Kai-shek in the early days of his march on Shanghai and Nanking were now supplying his adversaries on the mainland with modern jets. Formosa had then only obselescent P 51 piston fighters.

Chiang's navy was a real hodge-podge of equipment. Its cruiser, *Aurora*, presented by the British, had deserted to the Communists—only to be sunk by the Nationalist air-force on its way to Tsingtao. It was from a formerly American destroyer escort that I did my seasick-struck best to film its restricted sweep of non-Communist seas. On the bridge Admiral Hser Chen-hsing conferred with Commander Bundy of the U.S. Navy. Somewhere beyond the horizon, the great battle cruisers and aircraft carriers of Admiral Harold H. Martin's Seventh Fleet effectively insulated Formosa from involvement in the Korean conflict still raging close to the borders of China.

Chiang's somewhat shaky navy was doing its best to deny Mao trade with the outside world. His air-force was being employed to blackmail a China that was still hungry. At Chai-yi, bags of Formosa's abundant rice, emblazoned with the Nationalist flag, were loaded into transport planes. Filming their flight into the

169

sunset, I followed the first lift of their flight over the mainland, on which they were to be dropped.

On this same runway the following day, I filmed the loading of those old C 46s with a more lively cargo also, it was hoped, to be sometime dropped on the mainland. A brigade of tough-looking paratroops climbed aboard, and, having flown with one plane-load and filmed them as they leapt from its open door, I returned to the target area on Tainan's southern plain and awaited the arrival of the rest overhead, in order to film this practice jump from the ground. Minutes passed. The General Staff became increasingly anxious; and at last word came that they had been dropped ten miles away by mistake, to the very considerable loss of face of their General who, standing beside me, had arranged the entire operation specially for my camera.

Well within the range of its lenses however were special assault troops, storming up through the surf of a beach near Tsoying—simulating the return to the mainland to which Chiang was committed.

Despite President Truman's call to the Nationalists that—pending a peacefully negotiated settlement—they should "cease all air and sea operations against the mainland", Chiang's agents moved frequently across this narrow stretch of water to and from China itself. In an office in the 'Long Live Chiang Kai-shek Hall', from which he controlled the Kuomintang's political apparatus within the army, I filmed General Chiang Kai-min as he interrogated two such emissaries recently returned. Standing by a map one of these anonymous figures pointed out pockets of resistance in southern China. The cargoes flown from Chai-yi by night were not always as innocuous as rice.

Sometimes they originated with 'Western Enterprises Incorporated'—the cover name for the United States Central Intelligence Agency on Formosa. After the collapse at Hsuchow, fifteen thousand men of the 93rd Division, led by General

Nationalist Chinese Prime Minister Chen Cheng (Formosa 1951)

170

Formosa 1951—Waiting . . . .

Li Mi, had taken refuge in north east Burma. Here they prepared for an offensive back into China—only to be driven out once again along with all the other remnants of Chiang's 8th and 26th armies. For more than a decade these guerillas had wandered around the explosive borders that Burma shared with Siam, Laos and China, a source of some embarrassment to the Burmese Government. Ferrying supplies to them in this way from Formosa, a Nationalist bomber had been shot down by the Burmese, who protested directly to Washington.

Back in Formosa these agents were attached to a 'Revolutionary Implementation Centre'. I followed them to its headquarters in the mountains near Taipeh. Founded by Chiang two years before, this establishment offered a five weeks' course to selected military and political personnel in preparation for their return to the mainland. For the first seven days they studied the methods and aims of their communist enemy—the next two weeks were concentrated on the Nationalists' own plans for China's reconstruction. Then came a further seven days' study of local government on the island, with a final week for their instructors to analyse their reactions to the problems with which they would be faced.

The dean of this faculty of optimism was General Yao-hueng Wang. I attended a lecture on the actual strategy and planning of this nationalist come-back. I was positively invited to film a large map of the mainland on which superimposed arrows marked the course and development of such wishful thinking. In close-up the instructor's hand traced the development of hypothetical battles around the towns of Lienking, Fooching, Changlo and Foochow on the other side of the Formosa Straits. At the Taipeh Broadcasting Studios of the 'Voice of Free China', I filmed the transmission of a radio play devoted to the sufferings of a doctor forced to work under communism. It was beamed to whoever might have access to a radio set in a China long suffering an appalling shortage of adequate medical care of any sort whatsoever.

But I was still unable to arrange a meeting with the epicentre of this entire story—the Chiang Kai-shek who, attempting to hide his bitter humiliation at being excluded from the signing of the Japanese Peace Treaty, had retired to his house outside Taipeh, refusing to meet or talk with any correspondent or journalist whatsoever.

Almost equally shy of publicity, and certainly the most retiring of the foreign communities on Formosa, were the British. Small wonder. Not only had they recognised the communist enemy government of China. They were doing their level best to trade with it. I had been surprised to discover, in the same building as Chiang's Information Office, a plaque announcing the presence of a 'Royal Naval Liaison Officer'. At the British Consulate in Tamsui, the reception in honour of his Sovereign's birthday did at least give Lieutenant-Commander Davidson the chance to don his uniform.

Apart from Chiang, there was little left for me to film when, sitting down to lunch one day in the 'Friends of China Club', my companion asked me if I had seen the latest edition of the *New York Times*. I had not. He passed it over. Preserving a composure and upper lip as stiff I hoped as any Royal Naval Liaison Officer on Formosa, I read to my amazement that three days before Roy Larsen had announced "the discontinuance of *The March of Time*".

The decision was necessitated, this devastating report went on to inform me, by "rising production costs and the desire of the publishing company to devote creative facilities . . . to the production of material for television". Here was a bombshell indeed. There had been no threat or suggestion of this, so far as I knew, when I had been in New York twelve weeks before; although even a visitor such as myself could hardly have failed to notice an intense amount of inter-office intrigue.

The final paragraph of this shattering announcement went on to state that: "the series will be brought to a close, it was learned, with a pictorial study of Formosa". Well, what do you know?

Within forty-eight hours two cables had reached me from New York. From the first I learned that: "because change in situation necessary we now omit shooting in Korea"; and the second told me that I must "cover Chiang if possible but return New York by twenty fourth".

It was now July 12th. I had ten days in which to get Chiang. That very afternoon patience, tenacity, and this ultimate urgency brought its first reward. I was led to what had been one of the army's administrative buildings in Taipeh, and ushered into a small office which had become the headquarters of the 'Women's Anti-Agression League'. I was introduced to its still very beautiful President, Madame Chiang Kai-shek.

Twenty four years before our meeting, this daughter of a wealthy banker had married Chiang Kai-shek, then at the summit of his powers and success. Now his gracious lady, after my filming was completed, asked me to convey her regards to Mr. Luce. She did not ask me to call on the younger of her two sisters, married to one of the richest Chinese in the world, and domiciled in the United States. She could not ask me to call on the other, still living on the mainland, the widow of Sun Yat-sen—the founder of the Chinese Revolution. But she did promise to intercede with her husband on my behalf.

Just in the nick of time so far as I was concerned a personality that Chiang could in no way wish to ignore now arrived on the island. It was also a personality with whom he could not refuse to be photographed.

Accompanied by Madame, and host to Thomas E. Dewey, leader of the United States Republican Party, the Generalissimo walked out onto the terrace of his home. As my camera purred, I studied this controversial figure—the sixty-five year old converted Methodist, leader of the Kuomintang, President of the Nationalist Government of China, and Commander-in-Chief of its armed forces. Chiang Kai-shek was then in the prime of a life which had led him from the heights of the wartime coalition of Roosevelt and Churchill to the ignominy of exile in the former residence of a sugar refiner. To Chiang Kai-shek Formosa could never be a St. Helena. He was entirely convinced that in the Republican Party—which would talk bravely of "unleashing" him from this Elba in the following year of a victorious Eisenhower—he still enjoyed unqualified support. He willingly exposed himself to my camera by the side of a Republican representative in whom he reposed such faith.

With one day now left to me on Formosa, one other member of this famous family still remained to be filmed—Chiang's elder son, the widely feared and mysterious heir-apparent Chiang Ching-kuo. Even he I finally ran down in the grounds of the Air Force Club in Taipeh, at a meeting arranged by the spokesman of the Ministry of National Defence, General Chiang Yi-ching.

Chief of the Ministry's Political Department, Chiang Ching-kuo controlled the network of 'Commissars' strategically placed throughout the army, and never received a journalist. His ambition and his reticence too were clearly traceable to his one-time stay in Moscow where, during the early days of his father's alliance with the Communist Party, he had embraced both its methods and principles—and married a Russian-born wife who was still with him. Believed by many to rival the moderate and progressive, but older, Chen Cheng, who had initiated the programme of land reform, he was, within the year, to bring about the downfall of the island's popular and widely respected governor, K. C. Wu. And Wu, exiled to the United States, was to declare that all the worst features of Kuomintant misrule had been established in a Formosan police state operated by the Chiangs.

The following morning, this lovely island that had been my home for over three months, slipped away as I flew north to Japan and Hokkaido; eastwards to the Aleutians and Alaska; and south to Edmonton, Minneapolis and New York. With me I carried the final twelve hundred of the eight million feet of film that *The March of Time* had amassed over the years.

Paying tribute to its achievement, Bosley Crowther, the film critic of the *New York Times*, expressed "more than a sentimental sadness over the passing" of *The March of Time*.

> "Out of the turbulent Nineteen Thirties, out of those restless years of social change and evolution and growing tension in the world, it emerged with all the eagerness and confidence of the new journalistic approach, pacing off with the . . . innovators and waving . . . on . . . those toilers in the vineyards who have sweat blood over documentary films."

"Meanwhile", this faithful servant and historian of the cinema concluded:

> "It is a shade ironic that, in these most critical times, the film most watchful of the onward march of history should itself be compelled to march off."

On a Smaller Screen – A Greater Opportunity

The best way to sell the goods is to put a man in the home. The nearest you can get to that is television.   A statement to the Pilkington Committee

But all was not lost.

A beer company came to the rescue as the sponsor of *The March of Time* in television; and great hopes were held in what was to be a fresh approach to the reporting and interpretation of world affairs in this exciting new medium.

About to go on the air in October, in the final week of June 1952 nine programmes were already planned for immediate production, in a schedule which demanded a fresh half hour film for every one of an initial twenty-six weeks. I had plunged into an analysis of the subtleties of presentation and technique demanded by this tiny, more personal screen. The generalised nature and distant pictorialism of so many sometimes superb documentaries—undeniably impressive when projected on the large canvas for which they had been designed—failed to convey any impact when reduced to the exigencies of transmission on what was after all no more than another piece of furniture in the living room. The anonymous voice of an impersonal commentator—that basic hallmark of the seventeen year old *March of Time* —was obviously out, but out. Simple, little stories, built on an individual's experience, that in themselves highlit the larger issue, seemed to me then the pattern of this future approach.

A little film that I had shot for *The March of Time* on behalf of the E.C.A. before they had sent me off to Formosa gave me, on reflection, some pointers to this new, more personal approach. The central figure around which that story had been told had been a very illustrious figure—in fact a First Lady.

Early the year before, the Norwegian government had invited Mrs. Eleanor Roosevelt to unveil a newly erected statue of her late husband. She had landed in Oslo, as always punctual to the minute, to be confronted immediately by three weeks of further European invitations, and myself and camera doing our best to keep up with her perpetual momentum.

From the unveiling ceremony itself, we had been whisked to a reception by the Foreign Minister, to be airborne within two further days of hectic sightseeing for Sweden. From a break-neck tour of the factories and social institutions of that model welfare state, the former President's wife had flown on along the rim of the Soviet world to Helsinki. At Rovaniemi, on the Arctic Circle, I filmed her excitement at the spectacle of a midnight sun which refused to sink beneath the horizon; whence, as we watched, it began a stubborn climb back into a sky from which it was never absent in summer and sadly missed in winter.

But the cold air of this northern neutrality was as nothing to the frigidity with which I had been regarded by Mrs. Roosevelt's filial escort. To her accompanying son Elliott my presence was an invasion of privacy, and something to be dispensed with as quickly as possible, by fair means or foul. Readily agreeing to the production of such a film of her tour in Washington before her departure, his mother had not appreciated that this necessitated the company of a cameraman travelling along all the way on what had been originally planned as a family holiday. Elliott had done everything in his power to trip me up, passing out false times of departure at all our stops, in the hope that I would be left forever somewhere behind. The entire operation became, in fact, a battle of wits between the two of us. However I enjoyed the advantage of a staunch ally in Malvina Thompson, personal secretary to Mrs. Roosevelt; whom I was to film in one of our many airplanes taking the unfailing dictation of the column "My Day" which was, at that time, syndicated to more than three hundred newspapers three hundred and sixty five days in the year.

In their off-duty hours I could at least relax with the captain and crew of the United States Air Force plane which was flying us around. In Finland our hosts invited us to the intimately convivial atmosphere of a *sauna*, which Elliott refused; and in which, at that time, I would willingly have boiled him alive.

Back we had flown once more to the lands of the Marshall Plan and the model cooperatives of the Danish countryside, and a meeting with Mrs. Eugenie Anderson: until the appointment of Henry Luce's consort to Rome, the United States' only woman Ambassador. There we had transferred ourselves into automobiles, and driven into Holland—and to a moving welcome in the little town from which one Claes Martenszen had sailed to New Amsterdam in 1636. Once settled in the New World this Dutchman had decided to be known by the name of this, the village from which he had emigrated—Rosenvelt—and here I filmed the three latest generations of this illustrious American family against their original European background, for travelling with Mrs. Roosevelt and her son Elliott were two of her many grandchildren.

The late President's maternal ancestors, the Delanos, had come from Luxembourg, and so that little Duchy had been next on our list. There his grandchildren, pursued as ever by my camera, visited the old castle of the Delanois, now a hotel. On we had driven, to Bastogne, and the site of the encircled General McAuliffe's classic refusal to surrender; to the nearby grave of George Patton, resting place of this most dashing commander of a victory which had made his country then the new master of western Europe; to Paris, for a call on President Vincent Auriol, and a tour of Versailles. Elliott and I had then exchanged farewells of reciprocated relief. The next item on his mother's programme was to be an address to the Headquarters Staff of the United States 3rd Air Force just outside London. I had flown ahead of her, and routed out *The March of Time's* British crew and their sound recording equipment. Knowing that Mrs. Roosevelt would invite questions from her audience, I had then prevailed upon a G.I., carefully placed within camera range, to rise immediately to his feet and ask her what impressions she had formed of European recovery.

Mrs. Roosevelt rose to the bait exactly as I had hoped and planned, and launched into an enthusiastic reply. This provided the film with the perfect climax and summing-up that it needed. Later that same day, at a press conference at the home of Lady Reading where she was staying in London, further interrogation had been forthcoming from British journalists. What, she was asked, did she think of the attitude of the American airmen serving overseas whom she had visited that morning? Whereupon this dear sweet lady had replied that she had been most impressed by the intelligent nature of their questions.

My Trip Abroad had been the most successful of all the films of European recovery televised by the American Broadcasting Company. Now, two years later, in A.B.C.'s Frank Freeman I found a good friend and a wise counsellor, as I embarked on a crash programme of finding out what worked, and what did not, in television. Simultaneously with these researches I enjoyed America. At last I was able to meet Bill Wells once again and reassess our work with the UNRRA which had passed into history; over long weekends in Connecticut trying to see our way into a clouded political future. Closer to the hot, stifling summer of New York City I enjoyed equally pleasant visits to the Larchmont home of Brandt Enos, *The March of Time's* former treasurer now striking out on his own, and centre of as happy and united a family as any man could ever wish to see. The American theatre was at the height of its great mid-century series of musicals, and Gertrude Lawrence was playing her last part in *The King and I*. Hospitality and enthusiasm were unbounded.

Before my plane took me back to Europe and further east, I had one final duty to perform. As the maker of what had become the last theatrical *March of Time*, a certain amount of unsolicited and posthumous glory had fallen upon myself, and the drive to the airport led by way of an apartment on Central Park South.

For as long as *The March of Time* had itself been on America's screens, Mary Margaret McBride had been broadcasting to that country's homes. For fifty tough, unscripted minutes, in a live programme over the American Broadcasting Company's wavelength WJZ, I spoke of Formosa in particular and my filming over the previous ten years in general. I parried as best I could such provocative and leading questions as to my opinions of General Douglas MacArthur and Madame Chiang Kai-shek. The essential tributes to the virtues of Eclipse Spring Mattresses and twelve other sponsors were dutifully interpolated by my industrious interviewer.

And now, as well as observing, my camera asked questions too. It interviewed the high and the mighty, who spoke to it always succinctly and sometimes sincerely. Aneurin Bevan anguished over the threat of nuclear fallout. The year before he waged war against Egypt, Anthony Eden talked of peace. In Cairo Mohammed Naguib spoke of his country's revolutionary aims; and in Bonn it recorded an appeal which quite literally broke its spokesman's heart.

His right arm lost in his Kaiser's war of 1914, his left leg amputated after years of disease and privation in a Nazi concentration camp, the leader of Germany's Socialist Party apologised, in halting sentences, for his inability to "speak English well enough". In German he continued, that autumn evening of 1952, to tell us that:

> "The division of Germany is the real source of power for communist politics in Europe. The re-unification of Germany is of far greater importance for the peaceful reconstruction of Europe than the integration of a fragment of Germany with other European nations".

Five hours later Kurt Schumacher was dead. What remained to him of life had been exhausted in that final testament of faith.

Cairo, if one could get used to the disappearance of the British, had changed little since the war had ended seven years before. Higher up the Nile, and the narrow strip of green fertility which meanders with it, was a rural Egypt which had not changed since it was depicted in the wall-paintings of the Pharaohs' tombs.

Blindfolded oxen still trudged for ever around and around a hoof-hardened ring of earth, to drive an ancient creaking water-wheel; and in the fields the fellahin still laboured from dawn to dusk for five piastres a day—eighteen pounds a year. One third of the precious land they tilled had belonged to one fifth of one per cent of Egypt's population.

But at long last, change—reform, development, pioneer-work for education and health—was only just round the corner. At a United Nations rural centre, at Sirs El Layam, forty miles from Cairo, I interviewed Dr. Abbas Ammar, one of the pioneers helping to bring it about. The new rulers of Egypt came largely from villages themselves. The confiscation of great estates, with the restriction of land ownership to two hundred acres, could have had no more ardent advocates.

This time, however, Egypt, for me, was but one of six countries which I was endeavouring to put on the screen to make a record of the troubled Middle East of the early fifties; for a *March of Time* now in television. Today, as the commentary put it, history was being made where history began. I filmed the new state of Israel and the then divided city of Jerusalem. From the shell-blasted walls of the Monastery of Notre Dame de France to the shattered stonework of the Jaffa Gate, and from the ancient ramparts of the Citadel—built on the site of Herod's palace—I focussed my lens down the barrels of Arab bren guns— themselves sighted on the King David Hotel occupied by a bitter foe. I walked to within a few yards of Jewish Jerusalem. But the city was then more implacably divided than even Berlin, and four weeks were to pass before I was able to film it from the Jewish side.

I took my camera to the harsh, calcined desert where an angel had once appeared unto Joshua. I could not bring back pictures of a desert in flower, but at least my film could show Seyyid Musa Alami digging for water—and at last finding it, fresh water, uncontaminated by the proximity of the Dead Sea. The refugees of

Author with General Naguib, Cairo 1952

eight hundred villages had been settled here, and under the guidance of the Arab Development Company, they were producing fruit and vegetables and selling them as far afield as the Persian Gulf.

Near the ancient city of Sidon I filmed less fortunate Arab refugees: eleven thousand of the Lebanon's one hundred thousand, crowded into a make-shift tented camp on the sea-shore; living, dying and being born into an existence whose problems they believed only the extinction of Israel would solve.

In Persia I filmed the clash between Anglo-Iranian Oil and the personality of the hour—Mossadegh. I was ushered into the tiny bedroom of a modest home, where I was confronted with the man then more talked about than any other in the world—clad in grey woollen pyjamas, sitting up in the plain iron bed in which he was wont to take refuge whenever the situation assumed a particularly hazardous and complicated turn. Rapidly camera and lights were adjusted, in order to do justice to the torrent of words with which the microphone was soon bombarded.

Mossadegh could not understand why Britain's socialist government—pledged as it had been to the nationalization of its own country's resources of fuel and power—had not been able to appreciate and sympathize with Persia's desire to do likewise.

"The Iranian nation", he said ,"never expected from the beginning that all the endeavours of the British government would be spent in supporting a profit-loving company which, for fifty years, has interfered in all aspects of the life of the Iranian people".

The next destination, if ever the suspicious Persian authorities let British subjects reach it, was Kuwait.

Kuwait, which the Iraqi revolution's leaders were soon to covet, lay south of Basra in the stifling heat at the head of the Persian Gulf. Arrived there via Bahrain, I soon had my camera mounted on the derricks drilling into the depths of the apparently boundless Burghan field. In the harbour of Mina al Ahmadi I filmed the loading of tankers, carrying away 24,000,000 barrels a month—an output from this one tiny Sheikhdom which eight years later was to provide Britain with more than a third of all her imports of crude oil and petroleum products.

But where was all the money going in this miniature state that had become so desperately necessary to Britain's well-being? A new water distillation plant was under construction, and I dutifully filmed it; hospitals and schools were on the drawing board, but there was then as yet no comprehensive development plan or, for that matter, even a budget. But all this was soon to change, and change fast. Within a decade this small piece of desert was to be transformed into a multi-storied modern metropolis, an Arabian Manhattan, a Wall Street of the Middle East. The wealth that Kuwait derived from oil was to become, in the words of a former president of the World Bank, Eugene Black, "one of the world's greatest financial forces". And even that was an understatement. By 1968 those formerly Bedouin Sheikhs had deposited in various banks a greater sum of money than Britain's own catastrophic balance of payments deficit.

By now I had reached the absolute deadline for the completion of the film—"when you estimate final shooting this assignment"—and, pausing in London only long enough to fail to find a satisfactory replacement for an overcoat forgotten in Teheran, I landed once more in New York in a snowstorm at the end of November; to receive a tremendous welcome from *The March of Time*.

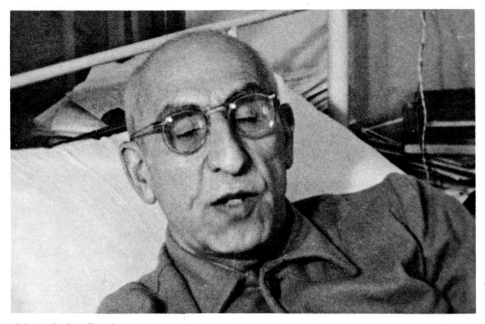

Mossadegh—Persia 1952

After three weeks of screenings and conference, I found myself destined for nothing less than a world tour during the following year: seven subjects had been scheduled for my direction. But once the warmth of my welcome had worn off I became keenly aware that all was far from well with *The March of Time* in television.

The icy winds of a heavy overdraft on this good intention were in fact whistling down the corridors of 369 Lexington Avenue. Deposits had by no means balanced the unrelenting necessity of a weekly withdrawal. Indifferent photography and inadequate sound recording, combined with the lack of experience in many of the new staff and an indecisiveness in direction, had militated heavily against the promised series—and the vast library of the old *March of Time* was being rapidly ransacked in an endeavour to stay on the smaller screen. Hoping to make an initial splash with their first programme on *The State of the Nation*, its producers had been dismayed to read 'Variety's' comment that "the show was too mixed and diluted to bear much interest".

As the one whose work had consistently secured the highest measure of success and audience-response, I found myself courted and lionised. This exuberant state of affairs came to a climax in an invitation to lunch with John Shaw Billings who, with Roy Larsen and Henry Luce, was one of the triumvirate then running the empire of Time-Incorporated.

Envious and agog were others at *The March of Time* as I set out for this meeting with the mighty, held in the company's private dining room on the sixty-fifth floor of the R.C.A. building in Rockefeller Center. Gazing out of the window before the arrival of my distinguished host, I was shaken to see that we were literally above the clouds. A low ceiling completely shrouded the lesser pinnacles of Manhattan below, lending an air of ominous unreality to the proceedings which followed.

Warned that the great man only listened and did not talk, I found myself being skilfully questioned on my experiences in Russia six years before. This interrogation also revealed that my film, sponsored by UNRRA in Byelorussia and the Ukraine, and still retained by *The March of Time*—was being re-edited as yet another stop-gap programme in the ill-conceived television series.

This was too much. What had been a unique and sincere endeavour of international cooperation between Russian, American, and British, was now, it seemed, to be once again twisted into the tensions of the Cold War then at its grimmest. This was now the America of McCarthy, of the witch-hunt: a truly air-conditioned nightmare. It was far from the America of the Founding Fathers; or for that matter, the America that I love. What did all the glamour of working for such a high-powered organization count for against my own lack of faith in its competence and integrity?

For the second time in two years, I resigned from *The March of Time*.

My decision had been hastened by the demonstrable failure of its new TV series. Around a luncheon table in New York's Bedford Hotel, Roy Larsen conducted a post-mortem. I was the first called upon to speak. In my opinion, to have attempted an interpretation of the entire and complex world of the Middle East in twenty six minutes was absurd. It would have been far better to have concentrated on developments in one country like Egypt which reflected the whole area: and even on one particular individual in that country whose way of life, and the pressures to which it was subjected, could represent the Arab world in microcosm. A broad panorama on the huge scale that we had attempted might be all very well in the pages of *Life* magazine—from whence most of the new direction had sprung— but in television it could only result in a lack of clarity and impact.

Larsen had seemed to agree. He then proposed that I myself appear on screen, narrating the next stop-gap crash programme to go on the air—nothing less than a rehash of my Indian film conceived as a full length feature four years before.

Mouthing a commentary whose banalities stuck in my throat, I was interviewed by Westbrook Van Voorhis. At the conclusion of every *March of Time* for the past seventeen years, in accents of doom and delight, Van had continued to remind the world that TIME MARCHES ON!

As indeed it did for me. The editors, the writers and, I hope the charming young ladies of the research department were all sorry to see me go. They could not have been more sorry than I was myself to be turning my back on such a fine group of people.

The sparkling Christmas Day of 1952 found me back in London—and out of work.

A Retreat into the Greatest Screen of all – And a Flight to Egypt

The prosperity of the East is now dependant upon the interests of civilization at large, and the best means of contributing to its welfare, as well as to that of humanity, is to break down the barriers which divide men, races, and nations. Ferdinand de Lesseps

The Cold War may have waxed warm in the upper echelons of Time-Incorporated, but over on New York's East River, in another great building, cooler councils prevailed.

For more than a year the United Nations had been suggesting that I take over the production of a series of films devoted to its programme of technical assistance throughout the world. Before leaving New York I had agreed to do this—providing the international organization could clear the way for my employment through its own complicated channels of multi-national bureaucracy.

But with the United Nation's necessity to balance its recruitment evenly amongst all the many nations that made up its strength, nothing had so far been finally settled, and two days after my return to London I put in a telephone call to the Dorchester Hotel. While his successors had been successfully putting *The March of Time* out of business Richard de Rochemont had been producing one of television's greatest successes—a five part life of Abraham Lincoln from scripts written by James Agee. He had suggested that I get in touch with his brother Louis, then at the Dorchester in London.

A legend was Louis de Rochemont, with Roy Larsen the original founder of *The March of Time*, which he had left during the war in order to apply its techniques of realism to the feature film. He had served an apprenticeship as a newsreel cameraman and began making films on his own at the age of eighteen, selling his idea of a film of the Harvard—Dartmouth football match of 1916 to Roy Larsen's father. With the entry of the United States into the First World War he had joined the navy. He resigned after the armistice to produce documentary films on his own. Assistant Editor of International Newsreel in 1923, he had become European Director of Pathé News four years later. With the advent of sound he joined Movietone, and in the 'Magic Carpet of Movietone' freed the newsreel for the first time from its unimaginative reporting of events. He developed it into that quest for inner significance which was to lead to *The March of Time*.

His younger brother, Richard, my old boss, had been European Manager in the early days, and he had taken over executive responsibility for the production of *The March of Time* when Louis left for Hollywood.

The arrival of Louis in that centre of hokum and ballyhoo had resulted in a new type of American feature film—the story taken from real life and filmed entirely on location. *The House on 92nd Street*, *13 Rue Madeleine*, and *Boomerang* had so impressed the British documentary director Jack Lee that he had been moved to write an ecstatic eulogy of their producer:

"Long before the war Harry Watt and a handful of other documentary producers in this country were moving away from the purely lyrical or literal or expressionist styles of documentary and insisting more and more on story and human values . . . At the same time that Watt and his contemporaries were struggling to get their two-reelers shown on a single cinema screen, de Rochemont was making a film a month assured of exhibition in thousands of the world's cinemas. This was *The March of Time* series. Clear, brief, incisive, these films were without parallel in America or indeed in England . . . and through them all ran Louis de Rochemont's faithful observance of the responsible journalist's rule that facts are sacred . . . It is said that Louis de Rochemont is not liked in Hollywood—that he is the object of a witch-hunt. I can well understand it. To many he is a dangerous man. To the lazy, settled mind-in-a-rut he is a challenge and a menace".

Certainly to Darryl Zanuck at 20th Century Fox Louis de Rochemont was a disturbing influence. They parted company. Louis returned to the east coast and set up his own company. With "The Earth and its Peoples" he made the most comprehensive series of geographical and ethnological films yet to be produced; and with *Lost Boundaries* the first film to dramatize the predicament of the negro in white society.

Now this "menace to the mind that is content to sit back in a studio chair" was on one end of a telephone, and I was on the other.

"My brother asked you to call me?" "Yes". "You've just resigned from *The March of Time*?". "Yes". "Well, you'd better come round to the hotel this evening".

At the appointed time I presented myself at the Dorchester. No de Rochemont. One hour, two hours went by. At last an unmistakable figure bore down upon me. "Why did you leave—what's the matter with *The March of Time*?" And, over a drink, I did my best to explain the inadequacies of conception and execution which, in my view, could only lead to the series' suspension. Chewing his lips, its original progenitor listened to my analysis of its contemporary shortcomings. Leading me back to the lobby, as he had to go out to dinner, he paused by the bookstand. There he bought a copy of the current *Atlantic Monthly* and thrust it into my hand. "There are three articles here—Spain, Middle East, Hong Kong. Write me a script on each as you would see them as a film for television. I will pay you seventy five dollars for each. Goodbye."

No sooner said than done. Within fourteen days scripts of all three, plus two more that I threw in for good measure, were on their way.

"Scripts generally good but technique needs further discussion and improvement stop can united nations job be delayed for two weeks without prejudice to you stop very much want send you hong kong via middle east and india but not in position to make firm offer until fifteen february".

It was now the end of January, and the United Nations Films Division was expecting me to take up my appointment at once. But the more I studied this cable the more encouraging it seemed to be. The chance of working with a man with such a record of achievement as Louis de Rochemont was surely too good to miss. "Obviously he is a lover of truth and freedom and liberty", Jack Lee had

182

written. Deciding to take a chance, for better or for worse, I let the United Nations pass me by.

One month later I was sitting in de Rochemont's study, at his home in New Hampshire, planning the production of *Our Times*. This was to be, as the New York Times reported, a new series which "will not be nature studies or scenic travelogues, but we hope they will be topical subjects bearing the fire and controversial aspects of the early *March of Time* issues . . . We're thinking of turning out about twenty twenty-five minute colour subjects a year. We're convinced that there is a definite place for such films in theatres—and we're also not forgetting that colour television is not far off".

Louis celebrated his signing of my contract as the European Director of *Our Times* with lunch at the Waldorf. We moved on, with a bottle of brandy, to the apartment he maintained in Manhattan.

The brandy flowed, goodwill abounded.

"We ought to have my brother here", said Louis. "He brought us together".

"Great idea".

A phone call and, in a little while, Richard joined us.

More drinks were poured. This was obviously an historic occasion.

"I always thought", said Dick, "that you two should get together. You're both a couple of bastards who only care about making pictures!"

Back in London I pressed on with the writing of blue-print after blue-print for *Our Times*. 'Roadblock to Peace – Berlin'. 'Europe's Pacemaker – Germany', 'Grassroots France', 'Red Mission' (a reconstruction of the life of a French worker-

Germany, 1952. Filming over the 'Iron' Curtain at Mödlareuth

priest). I wrote stories on Scots Nationalists, high-speed flight, the Duke of Windsor.

"Let us see and hear what people really think of the United States", Louis had said during that halcyon weekend of ideas and planning in the spring of New Hampshire. In "America on Trial" I had prepared a script of the British point of view.

Senator Joseph R. McCarthy was doing much to destroy faith and confidence in the United States during this crucial period of the Cold War. In the autumn of the previous year Charles Chaplin had sailed from New York to London for the premiere of his latest film *Limelight*; and, in the courtroom setting of this enquiry into the American image, I had a young British student ask a Defending Counsel:

"How about the greatest artist the cinema has ever produced— Charlie Chaplin. Your treatment of Chaplin is an absolute scandal. One of the founders of the American cinema and its most respected world figure and you hound him out of your country. And why? On the basis of charges never proved and never even pressed. He supported left wing causes and had a bad moral record. So have hosts of people in Hollywood. You give him a re-entry permit when he leaves and then the day after he sails you cancel it and say that he cannot re-enter except and until these charges are heard. After he had lived in America for over forty years and helped to lift the American film to its heights".

Explosion in the Dorchester dining-room. My employer and host choked at the very thought of this sequence. Chaplin was a subversive red who should have been

The village of Mödlareuth split in half by the division of Germany, 1952

With John Peters filming the 'Iron' Curtain on the Leipzig Autobahn, Germany 1952

thrown out long ago. A reaction not at all in character with a "lover of truth and freedom and liberty", and an outburst all the more surprising in the light of Louis' earlier announced intention to devote an entire *Our Times* to an attack on McCarthy and all he stood for. (Which, in the event, was finally mounted with devastating effect by Ed Murrow and Fred Friendly in their series *See It Now* the following year.) Attempts on my part to bring the conversation back into a more balanced perspective were petulantly slapped down, and the first meal and conference that we had had together for over three months meandered their way into a very uneasy and inconclusive close.

Silence for two days. Then a message. Would I be at the Dorchester at ten the following morning. This sounded promising: an hour early enough for much to be achieved but, as I entered the lobby of the hotel, I was immediately confronted by the sight of Louis in the act of paying his bill. "I'm catching the *Queen Elizabeth* this afternoon—you can come down with me and we can talk on the way". And so, as the boat-train sped south from Waterloo Station, through an old Hampshire to Southampton, I finally achieved a constructive discussion of my scripts, and an implication of their not too distant production—a promise sealed at the Ocean Terminal in a toast once again to *Our Times*.

> "We now ready schedule production stop due special and very interesting developments all equipment must come from here and requires you have special training its operation stop when can you conveniently arrive new york regards louis".

Handed a letter from Louis immediately on arrival in New York my spirits—then at their zenith—were immediately plunged into the lowest of depths by the words of its opening sentence:

> "We are placing *Our Times* on the shelf temporarily to undertake

a series of shows for Cinerama"

Cinerama. That crass and elephantine process which, in its original format, thrust the cinema right back into the cul-de-sac of the fairground from which Griffith had liberated it forty years before. The most monstrous of all the technical gimmicks with which showmen hoped to line their pockets by luring back an audience lost to television. The way to lick this competition from a tiny twenty-one inch screen was obviously with the most enormous screen possible, an eye-filling ear-splitting juggernaut of a picture encompassing as nearly as possible the entire peripheral range of human vision itself. Heart and soul had gone into the writing and planning of *Our Times*. Here at last I believed had been a truly original opportunity to interpret on film the complexity and promise of the second half of this fabulous twentieth century. And with what would its potential producer replace it—*Cinerama Holiday*.

"The second production in Cinerama [which] lacks the technical surprise of the first and offers little to take its place . . . *Cinerama Holiday*, in turn, is just an over-sized travelogue . . . [in which] the trouble . . . is that it employs such mighty means to such an insignificant end"—as *Time* magazine was to write in due course of this latest extravaganza of Louis de Rochemont.

Soon after its opening in a Broadway theatre on the 30th of September 1952, I had been to see *This is Cinerama*. Rushed down a roller-coaster and gondoliered through Venice, I had enjoyed the illusion of a flight across the United States, after attending a performance of *Aida* at La Scala Milan and a curvaceous water carnival in Florida. This grab-bag of synthetic sensation was to run in this one New York theatre for nearly two and a half years, breaking all records; but the financial structure of this sudden bonanza was unequal to the demands of its amazing success.

The process itself had been developed by a veteran of cinematic special effects, Fred Waller, who had first applied it during the war in the construction of an aerial gunnery trainer. Seated in the mock-up of his cockpit the approach of enemy aircraft was thus projected all round the fledgling airman's field of view. Lowell Thomas, who made his name *With Lawrence in Arabia* – and who was to have recorded the commentary of my Indian feature—soon realised its commercial possibilities and, as an officer of the newly formed Cinerama Corporation, with Dudley Roberts, invited Louis B. Mayer to join the board. That Hollywood Rajah, after twenty-seven years as the despotic production chief of Metro-Goldwyn-Mayer, had recently been ousted in the confusion of an industry fighting for its life—a turmoil in which Cinerama was certainly the largest of life-rafts. Largely on the strength of his participation a loan of more than a million and a half dollars had been secured with which to meet the costs of floating the enterprise. With money still needed to equip more theatres with which to tap further the rich promise of this first film—which was to finally gross more than twenty six-million dollars—a New York lawyer friend of Mayer's had brought in the Stanley Warner Theater Corporation.

With him to Cinerama Louis B. Mayer had brought his properties for filming: *Blossom Time*, *Joseph and his Brethren*, and *Paint your Wagon*. Walter Thompson, who had put together the fleeting and superficial history of the cinema which introduced *This is Cinerama*, had suggested to Stanley Warner's Si Fabian—who was now in control—Louis de Rochemont as the producer of their second spectacular. With his record he seemed uniquely suited to the production of a feature film with a plot, as opposed to an itinerary, in the new process. Like myself with *Our Times*, they were doomed to disappointment. *Cinerama Holiday* was to be yet another magic carpet of missed opportunity. It was to be nine years before Henry Hathaway, George Marshall and John Ford used a vastly improved technique to tell the story of *How the West was Won*.

Meantime, in this September of 1953, I was summoned once again to New Hampshire where, like a child with a new toy, Louis was photographing a rural fair in Cinerama, in order "to familiarize ourselves with the equipment". However disillusioned I might personally feel at this abrupt abandonment of *Our Times*, my contract still had the better part of five months to run, and for me there was no escape—although "the producer in his sole discretion (might) terminate this agreement for any reason whatsoever."

I determined to enjoy the scenery, the experience, and the always lively company of the New York to which we all soon returned, to the very best of my ability. This decision was vastly reinforced and relieved by Louis's announcement that he was planning a film of the Suez Canal to which I would soon be assigned.

Cinerama's workshop and development centre was to be found in a converted indoor tennis court on Long Island, and out to Oyster Bay I would daily commute, to be introduced to its technical mysteries by Harry Squire, the veteran cameraman who had photographed the first film in the new process. The camera was in fact three cameras in one, each equipped with a wide angle lens, and each lined up and interlocked to record a separate third of an overall one hundred and sixty five degree panorama. Each separate strip of film projected by three individual projectors—one in the centre and another at the corresponding angle on either side of the specially equipped theatre—were thus combined into one great curved image sixty-four feet high. The main and fundamental drawback to what was at times undoubtedly a tremendous impression were the joints between each segment of picture projected in parallel: the 'match lines' which, under certain circumstances, could result in hilarious optical distortions. Feeding the pigeons on the square of Saint Mark in the Venice of *This is Cinerama* a woman had appeared with three legs; in a sequence which Louis would shoot in Notre Dame de Paris a choirboy would sing with three eyes.

Before me to this Long Island retreat near Teddy Roosevelt's old home had come technical experts from Korda's revived London Films; Time-Incorporated had considered it an investment; and, at the time of his death, no less a film maker than Robert Flaherty had been experimenting with Cinerama. So who was I to cavil, even if the plans shaping for Louis de Rochemont's own essay into the new process were a far cry from anything that the grand old master of documentary might have done had he lived.

In an article on their impressions of the United States by a visiting French couple, Louis had found the point of departure for the monument of unoriginality that was to be *Cinerama Holiday*. Through the eyes of two such similar young Europeans the triple-eyed camera would size up America. At the same time, following the descent of a young American pair into Europe, it would do justice to the sports, pastimes and scenery of Switzerland and France. I became a casting director.

Louis had convinced himself that he had completely taken over Cinerama, and while we were awaiting the completion of the arrangements for the sponsorship of the Suez film, I was despatched to Switzerland in search of possible talent. The Swiss National Tourist Office instantly appreciated the advantages of such a show in Cinerama. Its director at once flung out a net for the attraction of young couples who might be its stars. On the cold lakeside of a wintry Zurich I filmed tests of the most likely of the many attracted by such a proposition. From Zurich itself Emil and Rosemarie Hitz, Oscar and Ruth Frehner, Kurt and Margrit Klipstein, Fred and Beatrice Troller; from Neuchatel Jacques and Lucile Staempfli; from Geneva Adrian and Catharine Rohner—my own preference. Louis's mantle of acceptance fell on the Trollers. That twenty-five year old commercial artist and his buxom young bride proved to be the lucky ones.

Three weeks later I was welcoming their counterparts: John and Betty Marsh from Kansas City, and getting this young dentist and his wife off to Paris where, with a vast concourse of imported equipment and technicians, the film itself finally rolled on the second day of January 1954, with an exterior view of Notre Dame. The tomb and the hat of Napoleon—'why didn't he try it on for size'—the Mona Lisa and the Louvre, an artist's studio and the 'Lido' night club were the clichés of the tourist's Paris which Louis de Rochemont was busily trisecting into Cinerama. I was once again banished to Switzerland, along with my ill-concealed disenchantment. 'They opened *This is Cinerama* with a ride down a roller-coaster—we'll put the camera in front of a bob-sleigh'; and so, at St. Moritz, I discussed and arranged such a mounting. Fresh from the ski slopes of Davos the camera was now set up in the passenger terminal of the airport at Zurich, ready to film the 'arrival' of the young American couple in Switzerland. But the Director of the Swiss National Tourist Office had barely time enough in which to forget his few lines of greeting before it was discoverd that the crew had run out of film. Frantic phoning to Paris located a fresh supply of Eastman Color negative which, flown in the next day, recorded this most embarrassing of receptions. In a state little short of mutiny a long-suffering unit was then loaded on to a train, and I accompanied them back to Paris where, having drawn up and submitted a schedule and budget of the costs of filming Suez—assuming the editing and final sound recordings of the film in New York—I awaited the next word from a Louis who had become more than ever an irritable and unapproachable sphinx. After five days, in which little happened beyond the final break between the director of these European sequences for Cinerama and their producer, a few handwritten lines from the latter asked me to return to London, where, he informed me, we would meet either the following Monday or Tuesday, "to discuss future projects".

So, back once more to a room at the Dorchester where Louis—inevitably, just about to leave for New York—asked for a new budget for Suez, based on its possible completion in London. This accordingly drawn up and despatched, I hopefully prepared myself for an early return to Egypt.

The film was planned in two parts. The first would illustrate the historical background, the construction, and the great gala opening of the Suez Canal in 1869. The second would dramatize the contemporary operation of this jugular vein of international trade, its unceasing traffic of the ships of all nations sailing its short cut to and from Europe and Asia, its waters carrying the oil of the Middle East to Britian and France—in the action and terms of the present.

In 1937, under the aegis of Darryl Zanuck, 20th Century Fox had spent two million dollars telling the first half of this story in Hollywood: as the architect and builder of the canal Tyrone Power battled with sandstorms and passion in his struggle to link the two seas.

The Hungarian John Halas had come to England the previous year. With his wife Joy Batchelor he was now Britain's most active producer of the cartoon and animated film. One of the many who had enjoyed the sponsorship of the Economic Cooperation Administration, he had drawn such a film demonstrating the folly of frontiers; for Louis de Rochemont he was now completing his adopted country's first full-length animated cartoon: the *Animal Farm* of George Orwell's bitter and satirical vision. Together we went over the sketches for the first part of our film, into which the brushes and pens of his artists would breathe colour and life.

At last de Rochemont's office reported that, after a conversation with Galal E.

Suez Canal 1954—our Egyptian Aide whose aim was to kill three Englishmen

Hamamsy, Press Counsellor at the Egyptian Embassy, "there seems to be complete agreement as to the procedure to be followed in clearing the scenario and the film with Egyptian officials. There is no necessity for the Embassy to obtain physical possesion of the film at any time. All that is involved is for a representative of the Embassy to be present when the rushes are screened in order that the Government may be assured that the film adheres to the scenario, as approved."

Our own representative in Washington had, at Mr. Hamamsy's request, outlined the story of the film:

> "I emphasised that it was to be a documentary, would deal at some length with the historical and geographical background of the canal, including the engineering difficulties involved in its construction, and would point up the vital significance of the Suez . . . as a link in the trade routes of the world. He observed that as long as the film was a documentary there could be no question of disagreement, since it would be a matter of historical fact. Mr. Hamamsy predicted that there might be certain difficulties in so far as the British were concerned. He indicated, however, that the Egyptian Government would handle any necessary arrangements in this regard".

A perusal of this correspondence by the Egyptian Embassy in Berne—and perhaps meantime word from Cairo—cleared the air. My new passport received its first visa, and with the Egyptian Minister's good wishes for the success of my mission, I left the following day, by way of Geneva in a DC 6 of Swissair. Asleep on my shoulder during the long night flight to the Middle East was the attractive head of Rakia Ibrahim, placed in the next seat by an attentive stewardess who thought the film director—now well known to her airline—would enjoy the conversation and company of the Egyptian movie star.

It was wonderful to be back in Egypt. The clamour and music of its streets was always a tonic, the very smell of Cairo itself a stimulant. After my frigid Swiss winter, the drive out to the Pyramids was little short of a homecoming. In the Mena House Hotel that had been the setting for the 1943 conference between Churchill, Roosevelt and Chiang Kai-shek, I took possession of a room. Soaking myself in anticipation and splashing about in the waters of the swimming pool.

The Ministry of National Guidance—ominous description—was housed in part of the Abdin Palace, and to this former abode of Farouk I now took the folder of drawings and text which constituted the scenario for which approval was sought. I carried it through miles of corridors and acres and acres of gilt drawing-rooms, once royal apartments, which now served as offices for the government of Egypt's revolution. Abu al Saud, the Under-Secretary, received me graciously, took possession of the dossier, and promised me the earliest possible consideration of its proposals and merits; while, over a cup of coffee, I politely enquired after the health of President Naguib whom I gently let fall, I had met and filmed on the occasion of my previous visit to Cairo.

Taking a wrong turning on my way out, and peering from a window in an attempt to get my bearings, I beheld a very familiar sight. Drawn up in much the same formation as may well have been the tanks with which the British Ambassador had threatened the King of Egypt in these same premises twelve years before, I saw a group of electric generators, throbbing away as they supplied power—to a film unit in action. Following the course of their cables I came upon, of all people, Gregory Ratoff, costumed and capering as Farouk in the former king's bedroom. This one-time graduate of the Moscow Art Theatre, after a tempestuous Hollywood career spent shuttling between the direction of other actors and the playing of larger than life-size Russians, was now both director and star of an extraordinary affair entitled *Abdullah the Great*. In suport of this tale of a king who loses his throne to a popular revolution, led by the idealistic young officers of his own army, the Egyptian government had made freely available all the formerly regal bric-a-brac and domiciles of their own fallen monarch—throwing in a few regiments of their own troops as extras for good measure.

Storming and shouting, hurling his tarbush from his head to the floor in a rage, Ratoff was every inch the image of the crazy Russian film director that he had so frequently played; and, back at the hotel, I was joined at the bar that same

North of Suez

evening by the two young people who provided the romantic support in this most curious of location-made films: Kay Kendall, the strikingly beautiful British comedienne, soon to be sadly missed, and Syd Chaplin, second son of that great comedian's marriage to Lita Grey: the former cast as a Canadian—the political situation depriving her of her own nationality in this piece of make-believe—much coveted by Abdullah, and the latter the dashing young officer who was to overthrow the tyrant.

Poor Ratoff—a man of very real talents, harassed, persecuted and foresaken by his backers—his film was to finish up as one of the cinema's minor oddities and little short of a fiasco. How pleased I was to see him again, eight years later, and just before he died, contributing a magnificent cameo as a refugee bound for Israel in Otto Preminger's *Exodus*—absorbed in a game of chess on the deck of the ship which was attempting to run the re-enacted blockade from Cyprus.

In Egypt's abundance of sunshine, exotic backgrounds and cheap labour, Hollywood had suddenly discovered a location worth cultivating. Metro-Goldwyn-Mayer had recently starred Robert Taylor in *The Valley of the Kings;* and also ensconced in Mena House was none other than the director of *Scarface*, *The Dawn Patrol*, and *Only Angels Have Wings*. With no less a writer than Nobel-prizewinner William Faulkner polishing his script in another room, Howard Hawks was almost ready to commence the filming of his *Land of the Pharaohs*. Followed everywhere by his dachshund, Alexander Trauner was busy designing the sets for this ambitious life of the builder of the great pyramid; while, already arrived, were the advance scouts of the greatest showman of them all—Cecil B. DeMille, who was about to ascend Sinai and, for the second time of asking, deliver himself of *The Ten Commandments*. The company and atmosphere of the hotel bar of an evening owed more to Beverly Hills than it did to the Middle East.

Believing that the "twelve to fifteen" days which I had been told the Egyptian government would need "to clear the scenario" might pass all the quicker with some assistance from myself, I set about pulling a few strings of my own. Back in another wing of the Abdin Palace I renewed my acquaintance with Captain Riad Samy, still personal aide to the President, General Naguib; telling him of my purpose and hoping that a word from on high would not pass unheeded in the salons of national guidance on the other side of the forecourt. Dinner with the Public Affairs and Information Officers of the American Embassy gave me a chance of informing them of the project. Calling at the offices of *Akhbar El Yom*, I enlisted the support of its twin editors, sealing this friendship with the brothers Amin at a lunch with Mustafa at the Semiramis Hotel.

Barely a week after our first meeting Abu al Saud was handing me back the 'scenario' of Suez with his government's blessing. Production was approved, and I set off back to Switzerland with the good news. Over my first breakfast back at Zurich, in a Paris edition of the New York *Herald Tribune*, I saw headlines reporting a state of emergency in Egypt and the arrest of General Naguib.

The following day confusion in Cairo was still further confounded. Naguib was reported back as President, and one Gamal Abdul Nasser was now Prime Minister. What did all this mean to our plans? Was the agreement that I had brought back now worth any more than the paper on which it had been typed? I assured Louis de Rochemont that it was still binding. Once the dust had settled in Cairo, we would be able to go ahead with the film of Suez. Meanwhile I was given a second, and even more rewarding reprieve from the banalities of Cinerama.

A letter from New York informed me that I had been nominated by the Overseas Press Club of America for its annual award of the "Best Photographic Reporting from Abroad on Foreign Affairs", and enclosed an invitation to the presentation banquet at the Waldorf-Astoria.

In New York we hurried the completion of the arrangements for my own expedition to Suez. A Mitchell camera was overhauled and checked by experts, and put on a plane for Cairo. Joined by assistant cameraman John Peters, and sound recordist Malcolm Stewart in London, I swiftly followed it. It was now April 1954, and Britain still maintained a huge military base in Egypt.

Both Stewart and Peters, like myself, were British, one of them a Jew, and in appearance, if one stopped to think about it, almost aggressively semitic. (What he looked like had not bothered me—that he could operate his equipment and fit in with my somewhat idiosyncratic ways of working was all that I cared about.) From the moment that filming began the Egyptian Government assigned to us a member of what was known as the 'Tourist Police'. His task, so we were informed, was to help us in any way possible. But obviously he was there in fact to make sure that we filmed nothing derogatory to Egyptian sensitivity. Fair enough.

One day we drove along the banks of the Canal and, as we passed British Headquarters at Fayid, he turned around from his seat alongside the driver, faced the three of us sitting in the back of the station-wagon, and asked me a question.

"Peter—do you know what is my dearest wish before I die?"

"No, Shukri. What is it?"

"To kill at least three Englishmen".

And there we were. Three holders of British passports right beside him. And one of them, to add insult to injury, a Jew, who since the creation of the state of Israel, was an even more mortal foe. We were making the film for an American producer, and so Shukri had assumed us to be American citizens.

When the filming was finally completed, I gave a party at the Canal Company Residence in Ismailia. Shukri, along with everyone else who had worked with us on the picture, was there. We all made merry. After a drink or two, Shukri sidled up to me.

"Tell me", he said. "You are all British—aren't you?"

"Yes", I answered.

"You know, I began to think so when I saw that all your letters came from England".

Hearty laughter. Drinks all round. Moral—never judge a person by the shape of his nose or the colour of his skin.

Ahead of us had flown production manager Jim Petrie, and so for once I was spared the tedium of customs checks, currency exchange, negotiation for permits, and the hundred and one time-consuming chores that must be added to the schedule and budget of such a film While Petrie ran around Cairo in these pursuits, Peters and I relaxed at Mena House, testing the camera, checking the script, and enjoying the pool.

Arrived in the Canal Zone, and expecting to be housed in tents, we found ourselves quartered in luxury. Each of us had a private apartment in the Company residency. After anticipating an austere and spartan life along the canal banks, I was drinking champagne the following evening amongst a glittering company of sophistication and charm. The largely French colony of Ismailia had made it an island unto themselves: Greek, Turkish and Syrian elements adding a febrile strain to the beauty of the ladies who bid us welcome.

Passing check-points manned by British soldiers with automatic and loaded rifles, we had registered ourselves and our passports with the local police. We drove first northward to Port Said, and then south to Port Tewfik along the one hundred and seven miles of this closely guarded lifeline, drawing up a schedule of filming before embarking in a launch to try a little high-speed navigation ourselves. After a week of such reconnaissance, dalliance and preparation, the camera was set up at the end of the long breakwater which projects into the Mediterranean. Loaded with a roll of Eastman 5248, I focused on the initial scene of this, my first colour film. I used the statue of Ferdinand de Lesseps, promoter, engineer and builder of the Suez Canal—which then commanded its entrance. We little guessed that this great sea-green granite memorial was to be blown up in the retaliation which followed in the wake of the abortive Anglo-French invasion two years later.

Carved at its base were de Lesseps' visionary words: "Aperire Terram Gentibus" —'To open the World to the Nations'. From them we directed our camera on to the mechanics of their realisation—the marshalling of a convoy in the operations and control-room of the Company Headquarters here at Port Said. By radio, orders and instructions were sent to the ships waiting outside; flags and signals were run up to the top of the masthead in the forecourt. Joining the French pilot Louis Cacheux we went out to the Swedish freighter third in the line, sailing back into Lake Timsah at Ismailia as we filmed his briefing of the Captain, and his instructions to the helmsman during this navigation of the Canal's first forty-two miles.

The southern exit of Lake Timsah was dominated by two massive obelisks rising high from its western bank. At their feet two huge figures represented the two seas whose waters here became one. Along their flat base ran the inscription "1914—Défense Du Canal De Suez—1918"—a memorial to the British and Commonwealth troops who had died battling the Turks and Germans for its control during the First World War.

Two hundred miles from Alamein, and twelve years after that greatest of all battles for the possession of this narrow strip of water, I carried our camera to the heights of this imposing monument. In my composition the massive sandstone shade of the Red Sea's right hand and the azure blue of the sky were the predominant colours of a distant view of Lake Timsah, from which a freighter bound for Suez was just emerging, a tiny black speck.

At Kantara, little more than a village on the eastern bank twenty-four miles from Port Said, the railway crossed into Sinai. Here I had been ferried over on my way

Suez convoy approaching Ismailia

to Persia for my very first film. Now a Bedouin camel-train awaited such transit, and, as a great cream-coloured Italian liner steamed south, the heads of these beasts which had carried Lawrence and the original Arab Revolt to Damascus presented our camera with a lively foreground to its majestic progress. But the canal was still a passage to war. In the liner's wake came the troopship *Pasteur*, on its way to French Indo-China; but for its cargo of conscripts the last shot had been fired—Diem Bien Phu was to surrender only four days later.

Back to Port Said, and from its approaches the entry into the canal of another convoy. Dinner ashore, and a boarding of the American *Steel Advocate*. Taking up position to the stern of a British aircraft carrier on its way to the Far East, we filmed a complete transit of the length of the Canal. Affixed to the bows of every vessel a great spotlight thrust its beam ahead into the darkness of the Egyptian night. With our own photofloods rigged in the wheelhouse, we filmed a Swedish Pilot's nocturnal navigation of the first stage as far as El Tineh. Dawn came at Ismailia, as we crept past a distant and sleeping Sailing Club and War Memorial. Into the next seven mile cut at Toussoum and then, with a sudden widening of the banks at Deversoir—on to the broad waters of the Great and Little Bitter Lakes. This twenty miles of natural waterway, together with the four mile length of Lake Timsah, had always existed in the southern half of the isthmus. It only needed the imagination and vigour of the man who linked them to the Mediterranean and Red Sea.

Apart from the servants who brought our breakfasts and waited on us in the Alliance Francaise—the French Club where we relaxed of an evening—and our drivers, we saw little of the people through whose land the canal flowed. The filming and recording of a group of Arab musicians on a sailing boat, rocked to the stately rhythm of a convoy passing in the background, was little more than a gesture towards local colour. It was not until the third week of filming that we really came on the Egyptians themselves. In the village of Chalhouf, eight miles north of Suez, the life of the 'fellahin' took on the tones of a specious romanticism, thanks to our Eastman Colour film. Bullocks turned the primitive wheels drawing sweet water from fresh gullies alongside the salty banks of the great maritime canal. From biblical landscapes camels were led into the fields where, against an unconvincing background of ocean-going steamships sailing apparently through the rolling gold of growing wheat, the harvest was cut and prepared for market.

We knew that the reality of these peasants' life was a far remove from the pretty Technicolored chromatics of such a sequence. Nineteen months before, for *The March of Time*, John Peters and I had caught its truer tones in more sombre black and white.

In Ismailia on the Sunday morning of May 9th 1954, the expatriate staff of the Suez Canal Company was suffering no more than the headache which inevitably followed the revelries of a Saturday night. For Mahmoud Younes, the engineer officer who had served with him at the Egyptian Staff College, the day was still to come when Nasser would speak the two code words—'de Lesseps'—the signal for his colleague's seizure of their offices. At the Swimming Club on the sands of Lake Timsah we joined the company of some of the more attractive spirits whose marching orders were yet to be issued, basking in the sunshine of what was, after all, nationalisation or not, the final fourteen years of their own legal presence.

I began my own last week on the canal by following, and filming from its western bank, a convoy in transit between Ismailia and Suez. South of Lake Timsah its route ran through an area of low-lying sand dunes which de Lesseps was convinced had been the site of the much earlier exodus from Egypt. Here, he believed, a sudden flooding of their quicksands had accounted for the fortuitous inundation of Pharaoh's legions as they pursued Moses and the children of Israel; and here he had excavated the seventy million cubic feet which now enabled the *City of New York* to steam down its lane of deep water as we kept pace with it on land. Coloured buoys and red and black chequered markers signposted its progress past Deversoir into the Bitter Lakes. A line of concrete posts sunk into the green-blue water indicated the channel at the approaches to the smaller lake at Kabret. Entering the final fifteen mile cut at Ganeffe, and framed between outcrops of sandstone intervening between motor and waterway, the profiles of great ships passed before us like ironclad monsters adrift in the desert.

From the top of the transit control tower at Suez we filmed a convoy's clearance of the canal, its separate ships sailing away into a Red Sea overlooked by the cliffs of the Jebel Attaka. Here I had had my first glimpse of Egypt from a troopship

Filming the Suez Canal 1954

twelve years before. Spending the night at the company's rest house, and seeking a stimulation greater than that offered by ancient copies of *Punch* and *The Tatler*, Peters and I fled to a local tavern, finishing our evening seated on the edge of the parapet lining the last few yards of the subject of our film, and wondering what changes in our lives this sojourn in Egypt would bring. A few feet away there crouched the stone figure of a panther, a memorial to those of the Indian Army who had died in Egypt during the First World War; a silent witness to the ships rounding this point, and one hundred and seventy-three kilometres from Port Said, journey's end for the pilots who had guided them safely from the Mediterranean.

These pilots were a corps d'élite of the Compagnie Universelle du Canal Maritime de Suez. Their specialised knowledge of every shifting sandbank and current was taken for granted as the vital factor in the safe passage of every vessel. Sandstorms and fogs could in a moment blanket the eyes and senses of all but these supermen. Along with a sixth sense developed from years of experience, they brought to their task a skill based on a long apprenticeship which demanded an internationally recognised Master's ticket as the very least qualification for their employment. Of the more than two hundred of these highly paid experts only a handful were Egyptian—such men as El Shisty whom we had filmed guiding the *Steel Advocate* through the approaches to Suez, and now followed by launch as he was taken out to a tanker on Lake Timsah. The sudden withdrawal of their services, when Nasser announced the nationalisation of what it considered its own right of way, was thought, by the Company, to have trumped his ace.

There was a joker in the pack. Mahmoud Younes and Egyptian determination were equal to the challenge. Working sometimes seventy-two hours without a break the twenty-six trained Egyptian pilots and the thirty others still under instruction kept the canal functioning without accident or delay until the Anglo-French assault of Port Said blocked its passage eight weeks later. "I didn't know anything about ships, but I did know a lot about movement control from the army. Keeping the ships shuttling back and forth was a simple matter compared with organizing a battle", declared this fifty year old officer seven years later, when Egypt announced payment of the final instalment of the eighty million dollars compensation to the shareholders of the former 'Compagnie Universelle'.

A great hemisphere of red merging into the deepest of blues was the afterglow of sunset along the canal on the evening of May 12th. Past the silhouette of a channel buoy crept the pitchblack outline of a ship. Its navigation lights were the only pinpoints of brightness as I pushed the range of our early Eastman Colour film to its limits, filming traffic every bit as active and unrelenting by night as by day. Only a lighter touch of mauve distinguished the sky from the steely-blue cold of the water nearly twenty minutes after sundown the following night as, turning the camera at only half speed in order to increase the exposure, I caught the silhouette of a tanker laden with oil, gliding towards Europe through the moonless Egyptian night.

Little remained to be filmed. Only the streets of Ismailia, which had been our home for a month—a wayside convoy control station calling instructions to a passing ship—the roadside kilometre stone marking progress from Port Said, and south of Kantara the 'lay-by' for northbound convoys. When these final scenes were in the can, our task was over.

Still up to his neck in his *Cinerama Holiday*, our producer had all this time left us alone—a dispensation for which I for one was profoundly grateful—and, hearing that he was about to leave Paris for New York, Jim Petrie suggested that I now fly back before his departure in order to discuss the editing of the completed film of the Suez Canal.

To open the World to the Nations—Suez was awarded a Diploma of Merit at the Edinburgh Film Festival the following year. It is a film which shows the Suez Canal at the height of its historic glory and significance. Twice since my filming it has been blocked by war between Egypt and Israel. Past my camera, in 1954, it was carrying 80% of Britain's imports of oil. By 1967, when the Israelis occupied its east bank, this figure had fallen to below 60%. New sources of oil elsewhere in the world, and huge 200,000 ton tankers, were already rendering its use superfluous. By 1968—the year when the Company's original charter was due to expire, and the Canal become Egypt's property legally and forever—it seemed the world could get along alright without it.

The Atom is Neutral

The power unleashed by the atom has changed everything, except our way of thinking.
Albert Einstein

When I first went to the United States in 1951, barely more than one family in ten owned a television set. Four years later this figure was well on the way to being reversed, and in Britain it was the same story. Everywhere, cinemas were being converted into bowling alleys, bingo parlours, super-markets. Television had triumphed.

The pursuit of my Russian film had led me to the United States—and into television. *The March of Time* had been the only documentary film to be consistently shown in movie theatres. Now it had itself moved into television. Despite the failures of the TV series with which I had been hitherto associated, I was more than ever determined to conquer that little screen. The only one which could now command—and influence—worthwhile audiences of millions.

Ed Murrow's *See It Now* continued to be the outstanding programme of the Columbia Broadcasting System—and American TV. Attempting something similar of its own, the rival network of the National Broadcasting Company came up with *Background*. Its first programme was a profile of French Prime Minister Pierre Mendès-France. I was impressed, and joined N.B.C.

For *Background* I returned once more to Germany, and then to Italy. I took a look at a country where one out of three voted communist, with Frank Bourgholtzer as N.B.C.'s on-screen reporter. With Edwin Newman I covered a British General Election.

I went to Geneva to prepare a *Background* to the 1955 Summit Conference.

A couple of minutes walk from my hotel, in the lake round which the city lay clustered, a little island shaded a monument to a famous native son—Jean Jacques Rousseau, whose controversial writings had fathered both French and American Revolutions, and whose *Contrat Social* opens with the rousing declaration that "Man is born free and everywhere he is found in chains".

Such a man, and such a background, have made Geneva unique as a centre for the settlement of international disputes. From such incarnations of the conscience of the past, I turned my camera towards the final preparations being made for the reception of the architects of the political present. At the 'Maison de la Presse'— itself as large and well appointed as any theatre—arrangements were complete for the briefings and conferences to be given to an army of multilingual correspondents converging upon the city from every corner of the globe. The main telephone and cable exchange was prepared for the instantaneous transmission of an anticipated deluge of diplomatic and journalistic messages. At the airport landing lights flashed far into the night as plane after plane landed bearing the hopes of the entire world.

Reporting to the House of Commons on his return from Geneva, British Prime Minister Anthony Eden talked in terms of a solution at the summit. The Conference, he said, had "given this simple message to the whole world: it has reduced the dangers of war".

The 1955 Geneva Conference failed, however, to reach a solution of the German problem. This lay at the heart of its deliberations. Its basic agreement—unwritten and even unspoken—was however implicit in everything that was said and done: the leaders of the United States and the Soviet Union met, shook hands, and resolved not to go to war. Coming into the conference chamber for the first time President Eisenhower found the Russians standing apart, somewhat awkwardly awaiting his arrival. He cordially drew them to the table. On his return to the United States this simple and sincere man—who had spent a lifetime in the profession of arms and who had led the greatest military assault in history—reported to the American people that there were great difficulties ahead, but that "our own pessimism and lack of faith" must not be allowed to defeat the noblest purposes that we can pursue. The world wanted peace. Every other individual at Geneva had felt this longing of mankind. There was therefore "great pressure to advance constructively, not merely to re-enact the dreary performances—the negative performances—of the past". All of us, he insisted, "individuals and as a people, now have possibly the most difficult assignment of our nation's history. Likewise we have the most shining opportunity ever possessed by Americans. May these truths inspire, never dismay us".

For a brief, brief moment, it seemed as if there was to be respite for the world. But there was soon to be a swift descent from this summit of good intention. Collision courses lay ahead in the Caribbean and the South China Sea. Within a decade Eden's patchwork of peace in Indo-China lay in shreds. American troops were once again to be in combat on the Asian mainland.

Twelve days later I was back in Geneva once again: present at man's first major attempt to control the atom whose forces he had liberated and which now threatened his survival. This was the most forceful gesture yet made to end the sterility of the Cold War, and it owed much to the faith and vision of Eisenhower.

In Resolution 810 (IX) the General Assembly of the United Nations had decided by unanimous vote "that an international technical conference of Governments should be held, under the auspices of the United Nations, to explore means of developing the peaceful uses of atomic energy through international co-operation, and in particular, to study the development of atomic power and to consider other technical areas—such as biology, medicine, radiation protection, and fundamental science—in which international co-operation might most effectively be accomplished".

More than twelve hundred scientists from seventy-three countries flocked to Geneva. Academician D. V. Skobeltzin led a Russian delegation of over seventy. Four American senators accompanied an even larger contingent from the United States. From Great Britain, where the world's first nuclear power station was already in action, came Sir John Cockcroft. From Byelorussia Dr. Kuprevich. From Kiev's Academy of Sciences A. V. Palladin. From Denmark Niels Bohr. From Germany Otto Hahn.

Never since the days of UNRRA had the world witnessed a gathering more international and less political. In both promise and threat the atom was neutral. But the Chinese delegate, although a former Dean of Nanking University's College of Science, came from Formosa. Recognised by many of the United Nations, the government in Peking was still barred from membership. Thus a great world power which, within a decade, was herself to build the Bomb was, in 1955, excluded from association and responsibility in any attempts to limit and control the multiplication of nuclear weapons.

India's delegate was Dr. Homi Jehangir Bhabha. A Parsi who had been an Isaac Newton scholar at Cambridge, and a Fellow of the Royal Society at the age of thirty, Dr. Bhabha came from an India that was poor in everything but natural resources. Along the seashore of the Malabar coast seven years before, I had filmed the mining of the monazite sands from which he was now extracting both thorium and plutonium. One year after he formally closed this first conference on the peaceful uses of atomic energy, Dr. Bhabha's first reactor came into commission near Bombay. In the face of China's invasion of India's North East Frontier—and a stalemated war with a Pakistan now that enemy's ally—could the land of Gandhi long postpone the building of a Bomb of her own?

Once again I enlisted the cameras and services of Fernand Raymond of Geneva's Actua Film, and began to produce two half-hour television programmes on this momentous occasion for the National Broadcasting Company. The delegates were welcomed by the President of Switzerland who, in his address, reminded them—and all of us—of the words of Albert Einstein:

> Our world is threatened by a crisis the magnitude of which is apparently not grasped by those who have the power to take great decisions for good or ill. The power unleashed from the atom has changed everything, except our manner of thinking, and as a result we are slipping toward an unprecedented catastrophe. A new way of thinking must be found if mankind is to survive. Averting this threat has become the most urgent task of our time.

For the United Nations Dag Hammarskjöld urged his audience not to "fail to recall on this occasion that it is to the initiative taken by the President of the United States . . . that we owe the origins of this Conference. He gave expression to the deepest hope of all humanity when he rejected the prospect that 'atomic colossi are doomed malevolently to eye each other indefinitely across a trembling world'."

The Nature of reality

The penalty of realism is that it is about reality and has to bother for ever not about being 'beautiful' but about being right.　　　　　　　　　John Grierson

At Geneva, in 1955, the world was presented with a great opportunity; and at Geneva, that same year, I was offered the chance of a lifetime.

During the last week of preparations for the Summit Conference, a cable from N.B.C. in New York had been delivered to me at the Hotel du Rhone: 'Wheeler suggests Salomon have circuit talk you re Austrian project which we setting 1700 Tuesday confirm please'.

Henry Salomon, the originator and producer of *Victory at Sea:* twenty-six consecutive half hours of screen time which, drawing upon every foot of film shot anywhere and everywhere throughout the world since the Japanese invasion of China, and brilliantly edited by Isaac Kleinerman, encompassed in one great work of compilation a vivid and compelling narrative of the greatest war in history. From this chronicle, a forerunner of television's many retellings of history, Salomon and his N.B.C. Special Film Unit had turned their attention to the entire Twentieth Century.

Here was a concept that the cinema could now never hope to emulate. Only the financial resources of something as huge as the Radio Corporation of America—which owned N.B.C.—could afford it. For documentary films—films of fact—have never been commercial propositions. Despite its acceptance as an integral part of the programme, on the screens of cinemas all over the world, *The March of Time* had always lost money. Great money-makers themselves, *Time* and *Life* had been able to afford this luxury of a motion picture offspring. From its inception, enlightened government and industry had sponsored the documentary film as a public service or as a sophisticated showpiece for their policies. As far back as 1920 a fur company had financed Robert Flaherty's *Nanook of the North.* A British Empire Marketing Board had paid for Grierson's earliest experiments. Agencies of the United States Government—and Roosevelt's New Deal—had provided the money for *The Plough That Broke The Plains* and *The River.* During the war millions had been made available by national propaganda machines in documentary's finest hour.

But now the picture was different. The British and American governments had long ago disbanded their film production units. With very rare exception, industry demanded a more explicit reference to its own involvement in the films it sponsored. Where a state owned quite literally all "the means of production", an individual film maker fared no better. Eisenstein had suffered for years, at the mercy of bureaucrats who denied him opportunity to use his camera. The stream of books and drawings that poured from his pen are poor compensation for the films that he was never allowed to make.

But instead of bemoaning their lot, and looking down their noses at that monster in the living-room, some film makers had realised that in television lay their greatest opportunity. Only television, commanding audiences of more than thirty million with a single programme—a single screening—could now afford to sponsor documentary films merely for the sake of making them. Only television could afford to film a subject just because it was there—explore a situation merely because it existed.

N.B.C.'s 'Project 20' now planned a special programme on Austria. 1955's high summer of hope was to be crowned by the signing of an Austrian Peace Treaty. The occupying forces of the United States, Russia, France and Britain were to pack up and go. Austria was to be free. And the climax of this great victory for peace was to be the re-opening of Vienna's beloved Opera House.

Three years previously, for a *March of Time* TV essay on Vienna, I had filmed the patient rebuilding of what was, to the Viennese, the heart of their city and culture. In flames as the Russians drove the Germans from Austria's capital in 1945, every stone of the 'Staatsoper' had been lovingly restored to its original Habsburg elegance. Inside was now a new opera house, incorporating all the latest and most modern mechanics of acoustics and illusion. Assigned to direct the filming for 'Project 20' "An hour long study of Austria, her people, her music, her history, her spirit, centering around the opening of the Vienna State Opera", I stood now, alone, in the vast and empty auditorium, and pondered my task.

The vast empty shell had yet to echo a single note; but to me its walls resounded already with the promise of the weeks to come. I heard already the songs of Wagner's apprentices, the music of Richard Strauss, the grand choruses of *Aida*. The deserted and cavernous stage was soon to be the setting for the flirtations of Don Giovanni, the execution of Wozzeck—and the faith of Leonora. The 'Staatsoper' was to reopen with *Fidelio*—Beethoven's sublime music drama—

Author discusses filming of Fidelio *with Henry Salomon and Herbert Graf*

and it was to that masterwork of music's greatest genius that I now addressed my every thought and moment.

From the models which Clemens Holzmeister had already made of his sets for the opera I drew plans for the movement and manoeuvre of my cameras. In meetings with Ernst Marboe I worked out the actual detail and the whole schedule of my filming. I drew up contracts with Wien Film, and arranged for recording studios, technicians, equipment and processing laboratories. Costs were broken down and budgeted. Back in Geneva, on the eve of Dr. Bhabha's opening of the conference devoted to the peaceful uses of atomic energy, I sat down in my hotel room and drafted a report to New York of my findings and proposals:

"Rehearsals for *Fidelio* commence in rehearsal rooms of the Opera House October 10th. Every day following, these first set of rehearsals continue, until October 14th, but all these are without costumes, orchestra or settings. October 26th sees the first rehearsal on the actual stage of the Opera House, but still without orchestra: this rehearsal is to piano accompaniment only. The next day, October 27th sees the first full dress rehearsal against the actual sets, on the actual stage and with full orchestral accompaniment. This rehearsal will be constantly interrupted, as they see fit, by Heinz Tietjen, the producer and Karl Böhm, the conductor. The only complete, uninterrupted full dress rehearsal takes place November 3rd. There are no other rehearsals scheduled. *Fidelio* will be of course only one of seven new opera productions all being rehearsed simultaneously at this same period and opening in the first two weeks of the opera season.

"To set up cameras and merely film a rehearsal as it takes place on the stage will result in dull undramatic newsreel-like coverage. At the same time the only satisfactory way to get a clean and worthwhile sound track is to pre-record the sections of the opera that are selected for filming, and then film to this playback. Otherwise we will get different sound levels, jumps in quality and a very major editing problem.

"Dr. Marboe has agreed in principle to give us one complete day of the entire company, principals, chorus and full orchestra to do with what we will. It is suggested that we record the playback October 27th. Some day between that date and November 3rd we will be given the entire 'Fidelio' company, orchestra, opera house and stage to ourselves. During this day we will shoot the sections of the opera we desire on the stage itself, directing and lighting everything as we see fit. Complete dramatic and creative photography of the scenes will then be possible; a truly cinematic interpretation of *Fidelio* can thus be achieved. To supplement this day of our own special filming we would then film the same sections of the opera again during the final dress rehearsal November 3rd. On this second day our cameras would not be in the stage but in the theatre, and would get establishing angles and more distant shots of the same scenes already covered in close-up during our own day's filming. To our original standard playback editing and synchronisation of these two days shooting would not be difficult. Every camera angle and movement will be most thoroughly worked out and pre-planned on actual models of the sets before we get to our first day of intensive filming. By the most complete pre-planning we will be able to get everything needed in the minimum of time during this very intensive one day's special filming. The longer (more distant) shots made at the later rehearsal will round off the coverage satisfactorily."

Fidelio—*The Chorus await Author's instructions on the stage of the rebuilt State Opera House*

This was the beginning of my answer to a question asked by music critic Ernest Newman: "Have the people who talk so optimistically of a new opera genre in the television medium done any serious thinking about the matter? Do they realise all they are up against? They seem to take it for granted that a transference of opera to the television screen is an a-priori possibility. But is it? Opera is an exceedingly complex amalgam of practically all the arts, which it has taken three centuries and a half of hard thinking and unceasing experiment to bring to its present state. What earthly right have we to take it for granted that all this, or even the essence of it, can be transferred, by a little manipulation here and there, to the cramped dimensions of the television screen?"

"It was not taken for granted that such a transference could be effected with only a little manipulation", I went on to write later—after quoting these strictures and doubts delivered by that doyen of music critics—"and the following is an account of how this problem is being faced, interpreted, and executed:

"The human eye is selective, that of the motion picture camera is not, unless it is controlled and led by its director. Once the eye at a performance of opera has taken in the entire mise-en-scène at the rise of the curtain, the interest in the spectator narrows down to the actual protagonists, and in effect provides its own mental close-up. We subconsciously feel and relate the singers to the mise-en-scène, but in effect we concentrate on them, except at such times in the development of the opera when action itself on the stage again brings the mise-en-scène, the setting, into the foreground of our interest. We therefore have first to divorce our singers from the irrelevance of the artificial scenery in our filming, as otherwise the eye would be distracted by various aspects and angles of the setting in their background, which in no way relate to the mood and spirit of what is being sung and acted in front of them."

The two Wagner brothers had effected a revolution in the staging of their grandfather's works, a revolution which aimed at discarding everything of irrelevance except the suggested impression, visually, of the mood and spirit of the music and the action of the drama. To achieve this they had gone back to the origins of German expressionist art, and thrown out completely all scenery of a literal nature. No painted castles: a dungeon became a few bold shadows cast by one spotlight across a darkened stage. The music itself was to create the visual impression in the spectator's mind; the stage being used only as a symbolic setting of darkness and light for the action of the opera.

It was a happy coincidence that Wieland Wagner had recently staged *Fidelio* in this new style, and I had been able to attend every London performance of his production. Of his revolutionary interpretation, another English critic, Peter Heyworth, wrote as follows:

> "Stylistically *Fidelio* is a jumble. We start in the homespun atmosphere of Singspiel . . . in the later scenes we come close to music drama, and in the final rejoicing we emerge into the elysian fields of oratorio . . . Wieland Wagner's production . . . is in essence an attempt to unify these disparate elements and by drastic stylisation *to present* Fidelio *as a timeless parable of man's political existence.*"

Paul Schöffler—Pizarro—sings 'Ha! Welch' ein Augenblick!'

Paul Schöffler as Pizarro

Fidelio is set in Spain. Florestan, for a political offence never disclosed, is being starved to death in the lowest dungeon of a fortress governed by his implacable enemy, Pizarro. Leonora, his wife, disguises herself as a boy, takes the name Fidelio, and enters the fortress as an assistant to Rocco, the gaoler. Rocco's daughter, Marcellina, tired of the attentions of Jaquino, the porter, falls in love with Fidelio. Meanwhile Pizarro orders Rocco to kill Florestan before Fernando, the minister, can arrive to inspect the prison. Rocco refuses, but consents to dig the grave if Pizarro will commit the murder. Leonora, overhearing these plans, persuades Rocco to take her as his assistant. Meanwhile Rocco has allowed the other prisoners to come out into the courtyard for exercise. As they file out of the cells and dungeons, haggard and weak, Leonora searches each face to see if her husband is amongst them. Pizarro is furious at finding the prisoners in the court-yard and rebukes Rocco. Meanwhile Florestan, in the last stages of exhaustion, dreams of Leonora. Presently Rocco enters with Leonora and they commence to dig the grave. Pizarro enters, tells Florestan he will kill him, attempts to stab him, and is stopped by Leonora—who reveals her identity. Again Pizarro attempts to kill them, Leonora draws a pistol, and, at this moment, a distant trumpet sounds, announcing the arrival of Fernando, the minister. Florestan is saved, and is united with his wife. A scene of great rejoicing follows, as all the prisoners are freed and sing together with Leonora, Florestan, and the minister, of the freedom and liberty which all now enjoy.

The unknown political prisoner—what greater individual symbol of our times.

"This," I wrote to N.B.C. in New York, "is the synopsis of a story that is for us first and foremost the narrative outline of a motion picture, and it must be told in the terms of the cinema, using the special methods of film to make the drama come to life, and to shared experience, by means of the film's own dramatic devices of story-telling technique.

"Most powerful weapon in the film's arsenal of technique is the close-up, when correctly used in the editing pattern. In this simple and bold story of a few clearly delineated characters, close-ups will carry the main burden of its narrative."

I had declared war on all the old, lazy, unimaginative non-techniques hitherto used for the filming of opera. My plan was worked out in the utmost detail. In twenty-four closely-typed pages, which were airmailed to New York, I analysed and described my interpretation and method of filming. To quote but three sequences —the first appearance of Fidelio:

"We have established the mise-en-scène of the prison in the previous sequence; in this one we establish our heroine, and the key personality of the opera. For the first time we employ the moving camera The camera will move seldom and then only for maximum dramatic effect. For this reason when it does move, the effect will be all the greater. With this sequence our film 'Fidelio' really commences.

"Four small figures are standing in front of what we now know to be the entrance to the prison. They sing the incomparable quartet. As the most distant figure of the four, Fidelio, starts to sing, the camera slowly moves towards the group, closer and closer, past Jaquino, Marcellina and Rocco, and comes to rest on a medium close-up of Fidelio; letting our audience get a really close and long look at our heroine. For the remainder of the quartet the two medium shots of the two pairs should be intercut with the music: Fidelio and Rocco, Jaquino and Marcellina. These two medium shots are angled and composed to facilitate this complementary cross cutting. The scene should come to its end back on the close-up of Fidelio.

"Here then we have established Fidelio, in the service of Rocco, beside the latter's daughter and the prison porter. Lighting key is a little below that of the previous sequence, in harmony with the Tietjen production and again to concentrate attention on the singers, and to facilitate transition from the preceding sequence and to the one following.

'Ha! Welch' ein Augenblick!', the first big dramatic moment of the filmed opera:

"Having established Fidelio, and the gaolers of the prison, this scene introduces their master and the villain of the story, Pizarro. Lighting is bold and dramatic to emphasize the change of pace and the character of Pizarro.

"The gate of the prison is open, daylight is coming in, relieving the gloom of the previous two sequences. Soldiers are drawn up on either side of the screen. Through the portcullis, and in long shot, strides Pizarro. Down into close-up he marches, hurling defiance and hatred. Should open on the full long shot with the soldiers, and hold until Pizarro comes down the ramp on to the stage proper. Remainder of the sequence can be played entirely in the close-up into which he has walked in the other angle.

"The stage is now set: we have established the heroine, and now we know the

Cameraman/Director/Author takes light reading of Anton Dermota's Florestan and Martha Mödl's Fidelio

villain, whose plans she must somehow defeat.

The Prisoners' Chorus, the major dramatic scene of the Vienna production: "Here we see the reason for everything that has gone before—the captive prisoners, victims of Pizarro's evil ambition. Interest for us should centre, as it does for Leonora——(Fidelio)—in the search for her imprisoned husband.

"Should open on the medium long shot of the prisoners coming up towards camera out of the darkness, the old man falling to the ground, and Leonora helping him to his feet. This way we open still on Leonora and her search. Continue with closer shot of the prisoners coming forward, and then pull back to the extreme long shot, showing once again the complete stage mise-en-scène of the massive and huge prison set, against which the prisoners are filing out from the dungeons either side. They come forward, and, against this background, fill the bottom of the screen. As the lone prisoner climbs up on to the tower behind, cut to the close-up of his singing, then to the medium long shot as all the prisoners run towards him and the bottom of the screen is filled with their hands raised in an impotent appeal to freedom. Follow in medium long shot, then pan as they file back to the foreground, centering the second solo prisoner as he sings of caution. Back to the extreme long shot once again as they turn and commence their slow progress back to the dungeons, emphasizing the huge power that is overwhelming them. As they file slowly back towards their underground martyrdom, follow with the medium and close shots of the prisoners passing the camera. End on the medium long shot of the last prisoners disappearing from the courtyard, and on its con-. clusion: the lonely Leonora looking after them, and still searching in vain for her imprisoned husband Florestan, who was not amongst these momentarily freed prisoners."

I followed every rehearsal of *Fidelio* now under way, plotting the position of the principals in the stage setting, together with the relationship of each to the particular bar of the score: reducing both to diagrams of camera-placing and movement drawn up and designed in my hotel room at night. For I only had two days in which to translate this opera into the different dynamics of another medium. But first we had to record the music and song of the ten key sections selected for filming. The evening before this session in the sound studios of Wien Film, I promoted a party for cast, conductor, producer, orchestra leader, cameramen and ourselves. In one of the Bristol's reception rooms Fidelio munched a sandwich.

Martha Mödl had sung Gutrune in the Wieland Wagner production of *Götterdämmerung* which had held me spellbound in Bayreuth three years before. At that time I had been filming my way along the Iron Curtain which had split that land of the Niebelungs apart. This climacteric of Wagner's tremendous *Twilight of the Gods* had been the last work to be staged in Vienna's State Opera House before that too had perished in fire. Now a new Fidelio sipped a fruit juice with her Florestan, Anton Dermota. The Rocco of Ludwig Weber and the Marcellina of Irmgard Seefried were introduced to us by Heinz Tietjen, their producer. Only absent was the sinister Pizarro of Paul Schöffler. Their conductor, Karl Böhm, discussed technical details with Wien Film's Janetza. In front of the microphones the following evening this patient perfectionist put them all through their paces. All was set for a marathon day's filming to the playback of the sound and fury imprisoned in cans of magnetised film.

We reached the climax of twelve weeks of preparation in a frenzied but con-

Fidelio, *Martha Mödl, Vienna 1955*

trolled ten hours of filming. Despite the momentary jamming of film in one of the cameras manoeuvred and operated to split seconds of timing, and the sudden and unexpected disappearance of Fidelio from my second direction of the Prisoners' Chorus, every move that I had planned, every scene that I had envisaged, every pattern of light and shade that I had designed fell into place with complete success. Walking back to the hotel that night I had a sense of complete fulfilment. The challenge of such a responsibility, the almost insuperable difficulties of filming so much in so short a time, the pressure of a pride which could not envisage even the possibility of defeat had inspired me, I was convinced, to a work worthy of the masterpiece it sought to interpret.

Two days later the filming of the actual première and the glittering re-opening of the Opera House itself was, by comparison, a simple affair. With five cameramen positioned at various levels of the auditorium, at strategic points on the great staircase and in the packed and floodlit Ringstrasse outside, I was able to sit back in our box and enjoy myself.

Directly opposite, United States Ambassador Llewellyn Thompson was host to John Foster Dulles and Mrs. Henry Luce. As her country's Ambassador to Italy, Mrs. Luce had recently been responsible for settling the tangled frontiers of Trieste—Austria's port on the Adriatic in the days of Franz Joseph: an Emperor who had crowned his imperial capital with the original opulence of this great opera house. Nearer the stage, in this scintillating horse-shoe of the world's great and famous, with the Moscow Bolshoi's Mikhail Chulaki, shyly withdrawn sat Dmitri Shostakovich. The bitter sweet beauty and feverish melancholy of a violin concerto constituted his own personal contribution to this gala year of co-existence. Peering pixie-like at the patterns on the walls of Ceno Kosak's tapestry room I glimpsed Oscar Kokoschka. From the Paris Opera had come Jacques Ibert. From the ruthless rhythms of Detroit Mr. and Mrs. Henry Ford II. From the *Maskerade* of Viennese cinema, Paula Wessely. From an earlier *Rosenkavalier*, Lotte Lehmann, that greatest of all Marschallins.

At last, it was all over. *Fidelio* was in the can, my assignment was completed, my camera had done its utmost. And then it struck me that it could do infinitely more.

Already I had exceeded the terms of my task. N.B.C. had envisaged nothing more, in effect, than mere news-reel coverage of an opera-house re-opening, with a few scenes from the opening performances. Already I had turned a routine requirement into a labour of love. But I found that with my version of *Fidelio* as it existed, in spite of the long and meticulous planning and movement of every shot, every synchronisation of sound, every degree of lighting from the lowest practicable intensity to harmonise with the inner darkness of despair to the bold and dramatic brightness that was to heighten the glorious opening of the prison gates—with the *Fidelio* I had made up to this point, the task I had been set, the task which had already possessed me like a dream, had only begun. One more, still greater, awaited me.

I accepted its challenge, absorbed. I avoided my friends. I alienated my associates. I enraged my employers. I spent twice my allotted time and more than twice the money budgeted. I was probably burning my boats. Whatever the outcome, abysmal or apocalyptic, I did not care. Never had I felt with such certainty that in this year of 1955 I stood at a turning point of my own career.

I had learnt how to make movies the hard way: hit or miss with a hand held camera. I knew how to get the maximum on a piece of film with the minimum expenditure of footage—the need to get five or six good, usable shots on the single hundred feet rolls of negative which were the most that those clockwork cameras could load had taught me that. For years I had been filming the surface of events— the face of man in this mid-twentieth century. But I wanted to delve deeper, to portray his heart—and the forces that moved him. The camera had to do more than record, however brilliantly. It had to penetrate the glittering surface of our world, and reveal the greater truth of the total interdependence of each and every one of us, at this and every other moment of history. Griffith had done this with *Intolerance*, on a huge symphonic scale.

A film is made by a camera—and it should be made *in* a camera. Not on a type-writer producing words for it to record—passively—on the lips of those who, apart from the background, could as easily be in a theatre. Film is a visual medium, or it is nothing. But unlike the other visual arts, it does not exist only in space—but also in time. Music exists only in time. Opera attempts a synthesis between the two, between the temporal and the visual, but it is a very uneasy partnership, and by its very nature the sound must prevail. (One can enormously enjoy opera on the radio.) But by its very essence, film is itself visual music: the harmonising, in varying tempo, of all those separate little time-lengths of picture, into one complete orchestration.

So—I ought to be able to do more with *Fidelio*. To attempt, no less, another dimension.

The Prisoners sing of Freedom

Fidelio was more than an opera. It was a parable of Austria liberated; and now I began to devise moments at which my camera could leave the action taking place on what was merely a stage, for the wider horizons of the city, and the country beyond it. I would tell the story beyond the story, the one that lay right outside the opera house itself.

Sometimes the parallelism was loud and clear. The liberation of the prisoners could be a clarion call to a sequence showing both Austria's freedom from her Nazi overlords, as well as from more recent control by her liberators. At other times, the placing, the interweaving, of these interpolated sequences of actuality—these deliberate splits of focus—became more oblique and esoteric. They not only fulfilled the strikingly prophetic implications of the story but were also subtly

213

in key with its musical progression on the sound track. Making this jig-saw, juxtaposing this uncannily modern-flavoured fable—first performed in this same Vienna in 1805—became a passion.

Obsessed, I matched the final rising notes of Marcellina's opening aria, 'Jetzt, Schätzchen, jetzt sind wir allein' with the phoenix-like emergence of the new opera house—by directing the camera to tilt higher and higher, up and off the stage, until,.in the very heights, it closed on a spotlight and the figure directing its beam —the Staatsoper's chief electrician. (The spoken thoughts and reminiscence of this oldest of all employees of the Opera House—whose service went back to the days of Franz Josef himself—could serve to illuminate and link all the separate elements in the story). To the music of the Leonora overture, I took my camera into Vienna's famous fairground, the Prater. At first it was deserted and abandoned, its machinery of pleasure and amusement in decay and desolation. It awoke slowly —with the music—to a crescendo of sound and a bedlam of rejoicing people. And during the overture to *Fidelio* itself, I took my lenses out into the night. They photographed the great banner flags of the newly freed Austria dissolving into cloud and trees against the night sky; then dropped slowly to a deserted cemetery where, ranging among the tombs, they paused at a stone bearing just a single word—Beethoven.

I went further. My opera house was not only the pride of a city. Was it not the very heart and centre of a country? Was it just that this first production should enfold no more than the vicissitudes of Austria's present? Austria had an ancient dynasty and an immemorial past. This story, it seemed to me, should also be incorporated within *Fidelio's* framework; and moving beyond my second horizon my second dimension, I went back into the centuries. At the point in the opera where Pizarro marched into the prison with his soldiers, I planned that an ancient battle should be refought symbolically. I therefore brought to the screen the armoured knights of the Kunsthistorisches Museum; to recreate the clash of conflict by creative editing and the dynamics of film technique, and make a page of Austrian history live again. Elsewhere, I passed through the centuries with the portraits of succeeding Habsburgs. Interpolated into this interpretation of an opera breathing the spirit of an Austria that lived on still were scenes of Franz Josef's bedroom—where his towels still hung—of his study where the clock still ticked— of the long corridors and the ballroom of Schönbrunn, of the priceless heirlooms that were the state jewels; of the coaches, with life-size model horses in the shafts; of Mayerling; of the Danube, where it enters Austria, wreathed in mist; of the Danube as it flows through Vienna and out into the great Hungarian plain, to the east. The random element was never once allowed to intrude into these scenes. They were strictly patterned, carefully filmed. They were the raw material of Austria's history, matched to the music of the greatest artist who has ever lived. Who himself had lived, worked, and died in this same Vienna; where now I felt that I was at last achieving something really worthwhile myself.

In the Vienna of fifty years before, as a young student, the Austrian writer Hermann Broch had become aware of twentieth century man's loss of faith in an Absolute. He had been confronted by:

> "The problem of that relativism for which there is no absolute
> truth, no absolute value and hence no absolute ethic, in short, the
> problem and the phenomenon of that gigantic Machiavellianism

which has been intellectually developing for some fifty years and whose apocalyptic consequences we are experiencing today in reality".

The art of modern man has been conditioned by his consequent theories and perception of relativity. In the painting of Picasso an attempt to reconcile visually both space and time. In the writings of Joyce, every fact of the life of one city, one day, related to all the thoughts, actions, hopes, fears and dreams of one of its least important citizens in that one isolated moment of time. Never was man so fascinated by time as now—when his insatiable curiosity had released the destructive power of the atom which could end the hours and the days of his calendar for ever. In California, only ten years after Broch first faced this basic problem and dilemma of our age, in the middle of the first world war that was destroying the Austrian Empire, the son of a Confederate colonel was making the film whose conception, range and spectacle has never been approached, let alone equalled, in the following half a century of a Hollywood finally capitulating to television.

In this film wrote Paul Rotha, David Wark Griffith sought "to convey the idea that intolerance pervades the minds of all peoples, from past to present, dragging with it despair, murder, and ruin."

In the then revolutionary period of more than three hours, *Intolerance* integrated more than two thousand years of time.

The pagan pageantry of Belshazzar's feast, the hatred of the Pharisees towards the Christ born in Bethlehem five hundred years later, the bigotry between Catholic and Protestant in the France of the sixteenth century, and the savage struggle between capital and labour in an industrialized city of the contemporary

Fidelio. *The Finale of the opera*

world were all welded together by this creator of the cinema's syntax into its most staggering form. In a final crescendo of counterpoint the chariots of Xerxes rushed headlong towards the destruction of Babylon, nails were driven into a cross upon Calvary, Huguenots were butchered in the streets of Paris, and the noose was prepared for the execution of an innocent man in the United States of the present.

> "In the pursuit of journalism, perhaps more than any other profession, one comes closer to and lives more intimately and imaginatively with the world he loves. This is especially true of photojournalism; for here one joins mind and hand, and here the reporter must always come in closest contact with his subject".

Thus Carl Mydans, musing on his years as a photographer for *Life*.

For fourteen years my own inquisitive camera had led me into such similarly direct experience of the world and those that fashion and suffer its delusions and destinies. But I had become increasingly dissatisfied with its relegation to the passive role of what *The March of Time* had originally hailed as "a new form of pictorial journalism". The film could do a great deal more than merely report. In twenty short years Griffith had transformed the bioscope with which the Lumières had first recorded the 'arrival of a train at the station' into the most representational art of his century: a unique means of expression which, by its own very nature, exists both in space and in time.

> "You get no documentary by joining together documentary stills. You get no history by joining together historical events. It is ORDER, the showing up of RELATIONS which turns chronology into history. And thus it is the WILL, the IDEA behind the film which turns dead celluloid into a living documentary. To do this the film director must be a poet".

Another quotation. From the battered pages of a Nazi brochure on the Germans' film of their *Victory in the West*—found amongst the debris of a desert battlefield.

In that autumn of 1955—in the twentieth year since I first entered the soundproof door of Ealing Studios Stage 3B, and surrendered myself to the strange enclosed world of the cinema—I was determined to put these years, these theories, and myself to the test. And it would be idle to deny that during the making of this film of *Fidelio* and the rebirth of Austria I became possessed of a demon.

My filming was in fact in the nature of a personal testament. For the horizons in which I had encompassed it, wide as they were, now became far wider for me. I had worked in two dimensions. But for me *Fidelio* existed in one more. At every turn, apt and poignant, it brought not only the vicissitudes of one country before me: in microcosm it stood for country after country I had seen and filmed in two decades. There was a parallelism everywhere, for the story in which Beethoven had dreamed so strangely forward to the themes, the conflicts, the peculiar *Angsts* of a century he had the good fortune to be spared living in himself. The political prisoner, gaoled no one knew why, was not just an Austrian figure or even a European one. He was universal. I had seen him in Russia, in Egypt, in Japan. I had met him in the United States of the McCarthy era, locked away from life and work by prejudice and fear, and sometimes even his parents' origin. Those crowds that filled the dungeons had known the same darkness all over the world. I had filmed the moment when they were liberated, in Italy, in Germany, in Poland, in India. When Florestan and Leonora sang 'Oh, Gott, welch' ein Augenblick!' I saw a

Filming Fidelio

Polish family reunited in Germany at the end of the war, and setting out for their homeland, years of slave labour over at last. And as the prisoners lifted their arms and voices to the chorus of 'O Freiheit! O Freiheit!' I saw a group of people in an Athens street at midnight, and felt again the touch of their hands on my face. The background for 'Der Kerker eine Gruft' was not an agony limited to Vienna. It was a fusion of all the displaced and the dispossessed whom I had ever filmed. I saw them uprooted from Prussia and East Germany, pouring from Red China into Hong Kong, filling the packed-mud roads of India with blood and dust. The city of ruins against which Leonora sang 'Abscheulicher' was not the capital of Austria, it was Berlin, Warsaw, Minsk, Kiev, Cassino, Dachau, Auschwitz, Hiroshima—a composite city, an amalgam of all the filth and ruin which my own century's violence had let loose, and which it had been my sombre privilege to film. But the picture was not all shades of grey, and if it had for me no happy ending, at least it had hope—not limited to Vienna in this brief hour of joy, but the hope I had portrayed in Delhi and Karachi; and as for the unquenchable spirit of Man with which *Fidelio* is saturated, this was something I had seen everywhere, among the partisans of Jugoslavia and the diehards of Formosa, among the students that shivered in a library in Byelorussia; and even among the British, phlegmatically casting their votes and electing their spokesmen to the nuclear debates.

For years I had travelled the world, my camera a passport to the hopes and fears of humanity, pondering my own identity. Born a Briton, my camera had led me to the Soviet Union, the United States, and an India poised uneasily between the two and threatened by an ambitious China to the north. For much of the time the focus of that camera had been American. Speaking the same language, I felt a natural affinity with the enthusiasm, drive, and optimism of the United States. Was that land, in Jean Renoir's phrase, "a club for discontented Europeans" such as myself? Was a Briton even a European? My countrymen were shortly to be faced with this challenge when blackballed from admittance to a Common Market in danger of becoming a club for self-satisfied Europeans.

But now I was no more an American than I was an Englishman, or a European. I was a film maker.

INDEX

A.F.P.U. see Army Film and Photographic Unit
Abdullah, Sheikh 121, 122, 151
Abdullah the Great 191
Actua Film 201
Admiral Nakhimov 96
Agee, James 49, 181
Ahwaz 26-7
Alamein 36, 40, 44, 46, 49, 194
Alami, Seyyid Musa 177
Albania 51-3, 58-62, 74
Alexander, Field-Marshal 46, 73
Alexander Korda Productions 17
Alexander Nevsky 96
Ali, Mohammed 159
Ali, Rashid 24, 25
Amananachamal 143-4
Ambedkar, Bhimrao Ramji 105
American Broadcasting Company 176
Amery, Leopold 99
Ammar, Dr Abbas 177
Amritsar 109, 110, 111
Anders, General 29
Anderson, Mrs. Eugenie 175
Anglo-Iranian Oil Company 178
Anna and the King of Siam 96
Anstey, Edgar 97, 155
Anthony, Frank 146
Arliss, George 11
Army Film and Photographic Unit 18, 19-21, 22, 37, 43, 50, 78, 79
Arnim, Von 47
Asia's New Voice 152, 153, 155
Asquith, Anthony 10
Athens 64, 68, 76
Auriol, Vincent 175
Azad, Maulana Abdul Kalam 105, 124

B.B.C. 88
Background 199
Baghdad 22-4, 25, 29, 134
Bandar Shah 31-2
Banks, Leslie 11
Baptism of Fire 18
Baria, Yuvraj of 137
Baria, Yuvrani of 137
Bari Behen 147
Batchelor, Joy 189
Battle for Bread 134, 166
Battleship Potemkin, The 17-8, 94
Belletty, Ruby 145

Belletty, Terence 144-5
Bengal Lancer 157
Benoit-Lévy, Jean 127
Bernstein, Sidney 47
Bevan, Aneurin 176
Bhabha, Homi Jehangir 201, 204
Bhutto, Zulfikar Ali 158
Big Parade, The 14
Billings, John Shaw 179
Billy the Kid 15
Birla, C. D. 106
Birth of a Nation, The 16
Black, Eugene 178
Black Pirate, The 10
Bliss, Arthur 12
Blossom Time 186
Böhm, Karl 204, 210
Bohr, Niels 200
Bombay 102, 115, 146, 147
Bône 47-8
Boomerang 181
Bose, Subhas Chandra 113, 125
Botchersky, Vera Borisovna 86
Boulting, Roy 36, 45
Bourgholtzer, Frank 199
Boxall, Harold 15
Broch, Hermann 214-5
Bryan, Julien 81, 94
Bryant, Sam 161
Bundy, Commander 169
Burma Victory 49, 78
Byelorussia 81-92
Bylinsky, Ivan Semenovitch 83, 88, 91

Cacheux, Louis 194
Cairo 37, 45, 176, 190
Calcutta 127, 144, 149
Capra, Frank 49
Cassino 29, 50
Central Office of Information 154, 155
Chamberlain, Neville 154
Chang Fa-kuei, General 161
Chaplin, Charles 9, 184
Chaplin, Sidney 9-10
Chaplin, Syd 191
Chase, William Curtis 168
Chatterjee, Satyabrata 151
Chembareve, Julia 34
Chen Cheng 173
Ch'en Yi, Commander 129
Chen Yi, General 168

Chiang Ching-kuo 173
Chiang Kai-min, General 170
Chiang Kai-shek 128, 130, 133, 153, 161, 163, 164, 168, 172-3, 190
Chiang Kai-shek, Madame 172, 173, 176
China 127-134
Chulaki, Mikhail 212
Churchill, Randolph 53
Churchill, Winston S. 36, 46, 48, 70, 72, 76, 163, 190
Cinerama 186-8
Cinerama Corporation 186
Cinerama Holiday 186, 187, 198
Circus, The 9
Citadel, The 14, 15, 16
Cockcroft, Sir John 200
Columbia Broadcasting System 199
Columbia Pictures 134
Cripps, Sir Stafford 100
Cronin, A. J. 14
Crowd, The 14, 15
Crown Film Unit 45, 78, 154, 155, 160
Crowther, Bosley 173
Cudo, Joseph 34
Cunningham, Admiral 47

Dacca 124-6
Dalrymple, Ian 45
Davidson, Lieutenant-Commander 172
Davy, Brigadier-General G. M. O. 59, 60, 62
Dawn Patrol, The 192
Day, Frances 13
Day in a New World, A 45
Delhi 113, 114, 115, 126, 135
DeMille, Cecil B. 21, 96, 192
Dermota, Anton 210
Desert Victory 45-6, 49
Dewey, Thomas E. 173
Dhillon, 'Colonel' 113, 114
Dietrich, Marlene 15
Discovery of India, The 105
Dix, Richard 10, 11
Donat, Robert 15
Dorsky, Semeon 88
Doughty, Jack 128, 130-1
Dovshenko 18, 96
Drifters 99, 155
Dulles, John Foster 212

E.C.A. see United States Economic Co-operation Administration
Earth 18
Eden, Anthony 176, 199, 200
Edinburgh Film Festival 198
Egypt 176, 177, 190, 192-8
8th Army 37, 39, 41, 42, 46, 72, 77
Eisenhower, Dwight D. 200

Eisenstein, Sergei Mikhailovich 17, 94, 95, 96, 136, 202
El Shisty 197
Eldridge, Roy 34
Elliot, Walter 19, 99
Elton, Arthur 155
Empire Marketing Board 99, 155, 202
Enos, Brandt 176
Exodus 192

F.A.O. see U.N.F.A.O.
Fabian, Si 186
Fairbanks, Douglas 9
Farouk 190
Faulkner, William 192
Feisal II, King of Iraq 24
Festing, General Sir Francis 164
Feyder, Jacques 15
Fidelio 204-218
Fields, Gracie 12, 13
'Filmeries' 11
1st Army Film Unit 46, 50
Flaherty, Robert 136, 187, 202
Foolish Wives 32
Ford, Henry II 212
Ford, Mrs Henry 212
Ford, John 187
Ford, Wallace 21
Formby, George 12, 13
Formosa 160, 162, 166-173
Four Feathers, The 15
Fox, Denis 59, 60, 61, 62, 74
Frase, Robert 82
Freeman, Frank 176
Frehner, Oscar 188
Frehner, Ruth 188
Friendly, Fred 185

G.P.O. Film Unit 155
Gandhi, Devadas 106
Gandhi, Mahatma 101, 102, 105, 107, 114, 117, 124-5, 126
Gaumont-British 21
Geneva Conference, 1955 199-200
George, King of the Hellenes 71, 76
Ghosh, Sudhir 102
Gill, Niranjan Singh 112
Gish, Lillian 16
Godard, Jean-Luc 135
Godse, Nathuram Vinayak 126
Goebbels, Joseph Paul 19, 21, 113
Gold Rush, The 9
Golden Twenties, The 135
Gorki, Maxim 45
Gracey, Sir Douglas 123
Greece 63-72
Grey, Lita 191
Grierson, John 99, 100, 154, 155, 202

Griffith, David Wark 15, 16, 17, 212, 215, 216
Gupta, Karuna 150

Hadden, Briton 99
Hahn, Otto 200
Halas, John 189
Hallelujah 14
Hamamsy, Galal E. 189-190
Hammerskjöld, Dag 201
Hammett, Dashiell 21
Harcourt, Sir Cecil 163-4
Hathaway, Henry 187
Hawks, Howard 192
Henderson, Arthur 102
Henry V 96
Heyworth, Peter 206
Hitler, Adolph 17, 29, 47
Hitz, Emil 188
Hitz, Rosemarie 188
Ho Ying-chin, General 129
Holzmeister, Clemens 204
Hong-Kong 163-166
Hotz, Miss 147
House on 92nd Street, The 181
How the West was Won 187
Hoxha, Enver 74
Hser Chen-hsing, Admiral 169
Husain, Azim 103, 104, 105, 137
Huston, Walter 11

I.N.A. see Indian National Army
Ibert, Jacques 212
Ibrahim, Rakia 190
Ibrahim, Sardar Mohammed 121-2, 123
Ikramullah, Mohammed 156
India 100-6, 107-115, 135, 137-152
  see also Kashmir
           Pakistan
           Punjab
Indian National Army 111-3
Inside Nazi Germany 154
International Film Foundation 81
International Newsreel 181
Intolerance 15, 16, 212
Israel 177, 193, 198

Jaipur, Maharajah of 137-140
Jaipur, Maharani of 137
Janetza 210
Jatin 148-9
Jellicoe, Major George 63-4, 67, 68, 69
Jinnah, Fatima 117
Jinnah, Mohammed Ali 107, 116-7, 119, 122, 156
Jodhpur, Dewan of 137
Johnson, Dave 55, 59, 60-1, 62, 63, 66, 67, 74, 76
Joseph and his Brethren 186

Jugoslavia see Yugosalvia

Kanin, Garson 49
Karachi 117, 124
Kashmir 117-124
Kaur, Rajkumari Amrit 105, 150
Keating, Geoffrey 37, 38, 39, 42, 43
Keaton, Buster 9
Kendall, Kay 191
Kern, Jerome 10
Khan, Brigadier-General Akbar (General Tariq) 121, 123
Khan, Liaquat Ali 117, 156, 159
Khan, Reza 28
Khomyak, Vassily Vladimirovitch, 92-3, 94, 95-6
Khyber Pass 157-9
Kiev 92, 95
Kimmins, Anthony 47
King and I, The 176
Kleinerman, Isaac 202
Klipstein, Kurt and Margrit 188
Knight Without Armour, 15
Koenig, General 40
Kokoschka, Oscar 212
Korchits, Professor 88
Korda, Alexander 11, 12, 15, 17
Krushchev, Nikita S. 98
Kuprevich, Dr 200

La Guardia, Fiorello 86
La Plante, Laura 10
Lahore 108, 109, 117
Land of the Pharaohs 192
Lapham, Roger 131
Larsen, Roy 99, 172, 179, 180, 181
Laski, Harold 137
Lastovsky, Konstantin Lavrantievitch 83, 84, 85, 86, 88, 89
Lawrence, Gertrude 176
Lawrence of Arabia 80
Lee, Jack 181, 182
Legg, Stuart 154, 155
Lehmann, Lotte 212
Lesseps, Ferdinand de 194, 196
Li Mi, General 170-1
Life (magazine) 99, 153, 180, 202, 216
Limelight 184
Liu Po-cheng 129
Lloyd, Harold 9
London Film Institute Society 15
London Film Productions 17
Lost Boundaries 182
Lost Weekend, The 96
Loughlin, Geoffrey 76, 78
Louisiana Story 136
Loy, Myrna 21
Luce, Mrs Henry 212

Luce, Henry Robinson 99, 153, 162, 169, 175, 179
Lumière Brothers 9, 216
Lutyens, Sir Edward 102

MacArthur, Douglas 39, 176
MacArthur's Japan 152
McBride, Mary Margaret 176
McCarthy, Senator Joseph R. 180, 184
Macdonald, David 21, 22, 27, 29, 36, 37, 41-2, 44, 45, 78, 79
McEntire, Davis 82
MacLean, Fitzroy 55, 76
McLean, Grant 132
Man of Aran 136
Mao Tse-tung 129, 132, 133, 162, 163, 164, 166
Marboe, Ernst 204
March of Time, The 97-9, 100, 101, 102, 123, 124, 153, 154, 155, 160, 172, 174, 179, 180, 203
Marienbad 32
Marsh, Betty and John 188
Marshall, George 187
Martin, Harold H. 169
Mathews, T. S. 162
Matthai, John 105
May, Ralph 155
Mayer, Louis B. 186
Melnik, General 34
Men of the Lightship 21
Mendès-France, Pierre 199
Menon, Vengalil Krishna 101, 103, 153
Message Received 40
Mestrovitch, Neda 56-7
Metro-Goldwyn-Mayer 14, 21, 186, 192
Metropolis 9, 11, 15
Ministry of Information 36, 47
Minsk 81, 82, 84-8, 91
Moana 136
Modern Arms and Free Men 135
Mödl, Martha 210
Mody, Keki 146
Montgomery, Field-Marshal 39, 40, 42, 44, 45, 50, 72
Morning, Noon and Night 45
Morse, Sir Arthur 165
Mossedegh, Mohammed 178
Mother 18
Mountbatten, Lord Louis 78, 104, 105, 106, 116, 118, 119
Mountbatten, Lady 104, 105
Movietone 181
Murrow, Ed 185, 199
Mussolini 155
My Trip Abroad 176
Mydans, Carl 216

Naguib, Mohammed 176, 190, 192
Naidu, Sarojini 150
Nanking 130, 131, 133
Nanook of the North 136, 202
Narayan, Jaya Prakash 105
Nasser, Gamal Abdul 192, 195, 197
National Broadcasting Company 199, 201, 202, 203, 212
National Film Board of Canada 154
Nayar, Unni 152
Nazimuddin, Khwaja 125
Nehru, Jawaharlal 78, 101, 102-4, 105, 106, 107, 113, 114, 151, 153, 159
New Masses 99
Newman, Edwin 199
Newman, Ernest 205
Niven, David 14

O.H.M.S. 21
One Day of War 45
Only Angels Have Wings 192
Operation Fairfax 74, 76
Operation Manna 64-5, 67, 69, 76
Our Daily Bread 15
Our Times 183, 186, 187

Pagès, Jean 155
Paint your Wagon 186
Pakistan 105, 106, 107, 109, 115, 116-126, 155-9
Palestine 22, 45
Palladin, A. V. 200
Pandit, Mrs Vijaya Lakshmi 105
Papandreou, George 70, 71, 76
Patel, Maniben 105
Patel, Sardar Vallabbhai 101, 103, 105, 106, 107, 114, 121, 124, 126, 137, 140
Pathé News 181
Patiàla, Maharajah of 121
Patras 63-4
Persia, Shah of 28, 156
Pessac, Nancy 160
Peters, John 192-8
Petrie, Jim 193, 198
Pilai, Tana 26
Pirgoff, Boris Ivanovitch 34, 35
Pius XIII, Pope 155
Plough That Broke The Plains, The 202
Poland 29
Powell, William 21
Power, Tyrone 189
Preminger, Otto 192
Private Life of Henry VIII, The 11
Promise of Pakistan, The 159
Ptushko, Alexander 94
Pudovkin 34, 96
Punjab, The 103, 104, 106, 107-110, 113, 116, 117

R.A.F. Film Unit 70, 78
Ramparts We Watch, The 135
Rangaswami 26
Rank, J. Arthur 17, 97
Ratoff, Gregory 191
Rau, Lady Rama 150
Rau, Santha Rama 150
Rawalpindi 119, 120, 122
Ray, Satayjit 146
Raymond, Fernand 201
Reading, Lady 175
Reed, Carol 49
Renoir, Jean 218
Resnais, Alain 32
River, The 202
Road to Rome 49
Roberts, Dudley 186
Rochemont, Louis de 181-2, 183, 184, 185, 186-8, 189, 192
Rochemont, Richard de 160, 161, 181, 183
Rodwell, Ken 76
Rohner, Adrian and Catharine 188
Rommel, Erwin 37, 38, 39, 41, 44, 46
Roosevelt, Eleanor 174-6
Roosevelt, Elliott 174, 175
Roosevelt, Franklin D. 36, 41, 47, 73, 163, 190
Roosevelt, Theodore 187
Rostand, Jean 98
Rotha, Paul 97, 155, 215
Rousseau, Jane Jacques 199
Russians Nobody Knows, The 98, 100, 103, 155

Salomon, Henry 202
Samotya, Andrei Antonovitch 89-91
Samy, Captain Riad 192
Sassoon, Sir Victor 134
Saud, Abu al 190, 192
Scarface 192
Schaeberle, Edward 34
Schildkraut, Joseph 10
Schöffler, Paul 210
Schumacher, Kurt 176
Scobie, General Ronald, 65, 76
See It Now 185, 199
Seefried, Irmgard 210
Sen, Brigadier 119
Shanghai 128
Shantaram 146-7
Shastri, Rama 141, 142, 144, 145
Shostakovich, Dmitri 45, 212
Show Boat 10
Shukri 193
Singh, Sir Hari 117-8, 121
Singh, Mohan 111, 112, 113, 114, 125
Singh, Ranjit 111
Singh, Sardar Baldev 105, 111
Singh, Tara 111, 114
Sitwell, Osbert 84, 86

Skobeltzin, D. V. 200
Slim, General William J. 113
Slutsky, Mikhail, 45
Smith, Bill 22, 26
Smith, Kenneth 34
Sofoulis, Themistocles 76
Squire, Harry 187
Staempfli, Jacques and Lucile 188
Stalin, Joseph 29, 70, 73, 163
Stanley Warner Theater Corporation 186
State of the Nation, The 179
Steiger, Andrew 81, 82, 83, 89
Steinbeck, John 15
Stewart, Hugh 46, 48-9
Stewart, Malcolm 192-8
Stone Flower, The 94
Stradling, Harry 15
Street Scene 15
Stroheim, Eric von 32
Submarine Pirate, The 10
Suez Canal 37, 190, 194, 195-7, 198
Sun Yat-sen 133
Svolos, Alexander 71
Swiss National Tourist Office 188

Tabriz 34-5
Tagore, Rabindranath 150
Tallents, Sir Stephen 99
Tarauchi, Field Marshal 111
Taylor, Robert 14, 192
Teheran 28-9, 30-1, 33, 35
Tell England 10
Ten Commandments, The 192
Thagadore 143-4
Thief of Baghdad, The 9, 17
Thimayya, General 119
Thin Man (series) 21
Things to Come 11, 15, 17
13 Rue Madeleine 181
This is Cinerama 186
This Man in Paris 21
This Man is News 21
This Modern Age 97
Thomas, Lowell 153, 186
Thompson, Llewellyn 212
Thompson, Malvina 175
Thompson, Walter 186
Tietjen, Heinz 204, 210
Time (magazine) 99, 153, 186, 202
Time-Incorporated 161, 179, 181
Ting Fu-tsiang 127
Tito, Marshal 53-4, 55, 58, 76, 80
To open the World to the Nations—Suez 198
Trans-Iranian Railway 28, 36
Trauner, Alexander 192
Troller, Beatrice and Fred 188
True Glory, The 49
Truman, Harry S. 160, 170